ARCHITECTURES OF JUSTICE

Architectures of Justice
Legal Theory and the Idea of Institutional Design

HENRIK PALMER OLSEN
University of Copenhagen, Denmark
and
STUART TODDINGTON
University of Westminster, UK

Routledge
Taylor & Francis Group
LONDON AND NEW YORK

First published 2007 by Ashgate Publishing

2 Park Square, Milton Park, Abingdon, Oxon OX14 4RN
711 Third Avenue, New York, NY 10017, USA

Routledge is an imprint of the Taylor & Francis Group, an informa business

British Library Cataloguing in Publication Data
Olsen, Henrik Palmer
Architectures of justice : legal theory and the idea of institutional design. - (Applied legal philosophy)
1. Justice, Administration of 2. Law - Philosophy
I. Title II. Toddington, Stuart
340.1'1

Library of Congress Cataloging-in-Publication Data
Olsen, Henrik Palmer.
Architectures of justice : legal theory and the idea of institutional design / by Henrik Olsen and Stuart Toddington.
p. cm. -- (Applied legal philosophy)
Includes index.
ISBN: 978-0-7546-7234-0
1. Law--Philosophy. 2. Sociological jurisprudence. 3. Law and the social sciences.
I. Toddington, Stuart. II. Title.
K235.0437 2007
340' .1--dc22

2007020571

ISBN 978-0-7546-7234-0 (hbk)
ISBN 978-1-138-26624-7 (pbk)

Contents

Series Editor's Preface *viii*
Acknowledgments *ix*

Introduction: Fuller, Gewirth and the Idea of Eunomics 1
The Architecture of Justice 1
The Story So Far 3
Gewirth's Argument to the PGC 4
The Integration of Ethical and Legal Theory 8
Objectivity and Perfectionism 10
Idealism or Pragmatism? Objections to the 'Foundational' Argument 11

1 The Methodology of Eunomics 15
Part 1: Explanation, Critique and Human Interests 15
Social Norms and Legal Norms 18
Incommensurabilism, Pragmatism and Proceduralism 24
Selznick, Fuller and Pragmatism 25
'Variability' 27
'Normative Theory' 28
'Baseline and Flourishing' Criteria 28
'Weak Definitions/Strong Theories' 29
Why Does Pragmatism Reject Foundationalism? 33
Part 2: Pragmatism and the 'Incommensurability of Values' 35
Incommensurability and Natural Law? 36
Goods, Rights, Values and Principles 38
Incommensurability and Moral 'Dilemmas' 49
Shaun Pattinson: Extrapolating From Basic Principles 52
Principle, Procedure and Authority 57
On the Incommensurability of Systemic Rules 58
Part 3: Fuller's Proceduralism and the Morality of Law 59

2 Means, Ends and the Idea of Freedom 67
Negative and Affirmative Freedom 68
Institutional Design: Means, Ends and the Concept of Freedom 71
The Metaphor of Architecture 74
Means, Ends and Sociological Method 78
Freedom and the Source of the Legal Impulse 80
Fuller, Gewirth and the Idea of Effective Agency 81

3 The Politics of Affirmative Freedom 87
Hume and Mill on the Social Contract 88
'Of the Original Contract' 89
J.S. Mill's 'Critique' of the Social Contract 92
Liberalism: Individual Freedom and Public Authority 93
(i) The Abstracted Self 95
(ii) Arbitrariness of Ends 96
Thinking About Institutional Design 98
Affirmative Freedom and Human Nature 99
Towards a Synthesis 103
The Complexity of Eunomic Freedom 104

4 Natural Law, Sovereignty and Institutional Design 107
Constitutionalism and the Locus of Sovereignty 108
The Persistence of the Hobbesian Objection 109
The Power to Interpret the Laws 110
The Prudential, the Moral and the Legal 111
A Continuum of Practical Reason 119
The Discontinuity Thesis 121
Kant's Concept of Obligation 123
Eunomics and Civil Society 131
Civil Society or 'Civil Society Talk' 132
Civil Association and the PGC 135

5 Why 'Pluralism' Fails a Pluralist Society 139
From Universalism to Multiculturalism 139
Equality and Inclusiveness 140
A Brief History of Pluralism 144
Carl Schmitt's Analysis of Pluralism 149
Beyond Schmitt and the Pluralists 152
From Pluralism to Multiculturalism 153
'Descriptive' and 'Critical' Conceptions of the Pluralist Condition 156
Multiculturalism and the Case of the *Hijab* 161
The Wider Lesson of the *Hijab* 167
The Reflexive Fallacy in Multicultural Critique 173
Pluralism and Eunomic Design 176

6 Obsolescent Freedoms 177
Religion and Human Rights
Origins of the Freedom of Religion 178
The Character of Religion 179
The Right to Freedom of Religion and its Absorption into Other Rights 180
Freedom of Religion and Freedom of Association and Assembly 182

Freedom of Religion and the Prohibition Against Discrimination on the Ground of Religion 184
Rituals and Rites 186
The Right to Observe Religious Rituals 188
Freedom of Religion: Conviction and Action 193
Arguing Against the Special Status of Religious Belief 195
Evans:Toleration and Peace 197
Ahdar and Leigh: Liberal Justifications for Special Protection 200
Ahdar and Leigh : The 'Duty vs. Preference' Argument 201
Stephen D. Smith: 'Democratic Civic Virtue' 203

Epilogue: Equality, Diversity and Limits to Social Freedom 205

Author Index *211*
Subject Index *213*

Series Editor's Preface

The objective of the Applied Legal Philosophy series is to publish work which adopts a theoretical approach to the study of particular areas or aspects of law or deals with general theories of law in a way which focused on issues of practical moral and political concern in specific legal contexts.

In recent years there has been an encouraging tendency for legal philosophers to utilize detailed knowledge of the substance and practicalities of law and a noteworthy development in the theoretical sophistication of much legal research. The series seeks to encourage these trends and to make available studies in law which are both genuinely philosophical in approach and at the same time based on appropriate legal knowledge and directed towards issues in the criticism and reform of actual laws and legal systems.

The series will include studies of all the main areas of law, presented in a manner which relates to the concerns of specialist legal academics and practitioners. Each book makes an original contribution to an area of legal study while being comprehensible to those engaged in a wide variety of disciplines. Their legal content is principally Anglo-American, but a wide-ranging comparative approach is encouraged and authors are drawn from a variety of jurisdictions.

Tom D. Campbell
Centre for Applied Philosophy and Public Ethics,
Charles Sturt University, Australia

Acknowledgments

We would like to thank colleagues and students old and new for their inspiration and support over the years. Christiane, Rikki and Jens, Carol, Anna and Elizabeth must, as always, receive our gratitude for their enduring forbearance. Special thanks must go to Tom Campbell who first suggested that we might contribute to the series, and who has throughout provided us with invaluable advice and encouragement.

Henrik Palmer Olsen and Stuart W. Toddington
Copenhagen and London
March 2007

Introduction: Fuller, Gewirth and the Idea of Eunomics

The Architecture of Justice

It is not unreasonable or uncommon to think of justice as being the body of principle behind the authoritative rules and judgments applied to the way we live, organize our affairs and treat each other. Law is often thought of as consisting of these rules and judgments: rules of law and legal decisions. The relationship between law and justice, therefore, can be straightforwardly described as a relationship between, on the one hand, rules and decisions, and on the other, the principles of rightness that are assumed to underlie them. Thinking about law and justice in these relational terms raises some obvious questions. We might, for example, ask what qualities or attributes, if any, a rule must possess to qualify as a *legal* rule, or what considerations are the appropriate concern of judges when making difficult decisions about the application and interpretation of legal rules.

Law, however, consists not only of rules and decisions, but also of a framework of institutions providing a structure that forms the conditions of its workable existence and acceptance. This book is about these conditions: what they are and how they shape our understanding of what constitutes a legal system and the role of justice within it. The *architecture of justice* therefore, refers to the art and technique of a form of institutional design. And in the same way that architecture aspires aesthetically and ethically to achieve more than the purely functional demands of the mechanics of building engineering, using the ideas of law and justice to design a system of social order should aspire, as Lon L. Fuller reminded us, to achieving '*Good* order and workable social arrangements'. This is a project to which Fuller gave the name, *Eunomics*, and this book will be a theoretical study of what might constitute the *Eunomic* principles of institutional design.

In embarking on such a study there is no map or manifesto to follow or apply from scratch, for we inherit legal systems and with them the complex and powerful institutional frameworks in which they operate. Because of their organic nature it would be naïve to suggest that these arrangements and practices are unproblematically susceptible to renewal and modification. What we can try to do, however, is explain something about the nature and function of *Eunomic* principles in relation to human interests and, importantly, attempt to determine the level of abstraction at which they might usefully be discussed if we are to grasp any opportunities to contribute to the rational revision of the existing socio-legal order.

In the process of writing the book we have been confronted by the question of which building blocks (in the form of concepts and institutions) are the most fundamental to contemporary legal systems. 'Fundamental' here must mean 'constitutive of', but our starting point is not a particular constitutional document as might be found in Europe or in the US, nor is it a specific constitutional practice like the English parliamentary process. It is instead an attempt to identify and bring together some of the ethically central concerns of constitutional theory understood as a product of political philosophy and social critique.

Alienation from the constituent disciplines is often, however, the fate of inter-disciplinary research. Constitutional lawyers might find our discussions too speculative; political scientists might find the book uninteresting because it targets basic legal concepts rather than engaging in studies of power-structures, and social scientists might mourn the lack of an empirical basis for the account of social relations. But unearthing a common core of assumptions shared by ostensibly different disciplines is in itself of great practical utility. Our work is 'applied philosophy' in that the *application of philosophy* is properly directed at *theory*. Theory thus scrutinized and made aware of its own presuppositions and interrelations becomes optimally effective in its empirical and practical application. *Theory* – in the sense of a body of explanatory principle – is thus the *mediator* between philosophy and action, and rather than drawing a distinction between 'philosophy' and 'applied philosophy', it might be more instructive to concern ourselves with the degrees of generality and specificity a philosophical inquiry exhibits in its attempt to construct or *develop* an aspect of theory.

More concretely, the central questions we will pursue and revisit in the chapters of this book through our analysis of the relationship between constitutional law, political philosophy and social theory, are as follows:

1) What is meant by *pragmatism* as a theoretical strategy for social and legal science?
2) What is the relationship between individual freedom and collective order?
3) Can practical reason guide us from prudence, to a theory of moral judgment and beyond to law and an understanding of political institutions?
4) What is meant by the 'dialectical' nature of the relationship between 'the state' and 'civil society' and can legal institutions reconcile the two?
5) Does the concept of sovereignty still function as the core notion of legitimacy in contemporary legal systems, and if so what are the are the sociological and ethical implications for its continuance in the condition of social diversity we call 'pluralism' or 'multiculturalism'?
6) If a genuine depth of pluralism is acknowledged and accepted, does religious belief constitute a form of cultural 'sovereignty' that overpowers other freedoms? Or is time to recognize that commitment to a genuine pluralism renders some former 'freedoms' obsolete?

In respect of these concerns we might note that there is a widely subscribed view that these familiar or 'traditional' categories of constitutional, jurisprudential and political inquiry have been superseded by the dramatic geopolitical changes we see in train today. We address some of these objections in Chapter 5 of the book, but we defend our selection of subject matter by pointing out that, as noted, determining the appropriate level of abstraction for critical discussion is of central importance and, at the level of *Eunomic* analysis, the ethical content and relevance of principles of institutional design can transcend even the most severe economic, demographic and geographical reorientations of the problems of legal and social order.

The Story So Far

In *Law In Its Own Right*[1] published some years ago, we tried to give expression to a non-positivistic conception of law that suggested that legal reason is situated upon a *continuum* of practical reason. This continuum might be imagined to move linearly along an axis of practical rationality from the instrumentality of self-interested action employing appropriate means to given or self-selected ends, through to the logic of 'other-regarding' (or moral) duties[2] and beyond to the idea of the reorientation of morality in civil society by means of the 'artifice' of Law. From the proposition that an agent must, as a matter of the logic of practical reason, acknowledge natural rights and duties, the idea (found explicitly in Kant and broadly in the traditions of Social Contract theory, although rendered 'prudentially' in Hobbes)[3] is that a moral agent must then acknowledge as indispensable, arrangements for the authoritative supervision of issues of right. In Kant's terms, an *omnilateral* authority must replace the *unilateral* affirmation of moral right if moral reason is not to undermine itself through the inevitable fomentation of conflict of assertion, interpretation and applications of right arising in the context of action and association. Rationally constituted, the expression of an omnilateral will can be seen as the paradigm case of Sovereign Right. The idea of *the legal*, therefore, is, as expansive as the idea of the institutional expression of morally legitimate power.

The moral law that gives rise to the rational necessity of an *omnilateral* sovereign right makes both formal and substantive demands in respect of the validity of its promulgation and application. In order to assume a genuinely

---

1 Henrik P. Olsen and Stuart Toddington *Law In Its Own Right* (Oxford: Hart Publishing, 1999).

2 Prudential logic suggests instrumental 'duties' in that one 'must', to be rational, employ appropriate means to achieve self-defined or self-selected ends or interests; 'other-regarding' duties refer to rational obligations to act in accordance with the interest of others regardless of what one considers to be one's own prudential concerns and even, perhaps, contrary to one's inclinations. Demonstrating the existence of such duties is, in our view, the primary task of moral philosophy. See also Alan Gewirth *Reason and Morality* (Chicago: Chicago University Press 1978) Chapter 1.

3 See, for example, Immanuel Kant *The Metaphysics of Morals* (Cambridge: Cambridge University Press [Mary Gregor Trans.] 1996); Jean Jaques Rousseau *The Social Contract and Discourses* (London: Dent [G.D.H. Cole Trans] 1983; Peter Laslett (ed.) *John Locke's Second Treatise on Government An Essay Concerning the True Original, Extent and End of Civil Government* [1690] (Cambridge: Cambridge University Press, 1960); Thomas Hobbes *Leviathan* [1651] C.B. Macpherson (ed.) (Harmondsworth: Penguin, 1968).

authoritative character, *omnilateral* right is not to be seen merely as a privileged or arbitrarily aggrandized *unilateral* will, nor can it be adequately subsumed under the notion of a majority of unilateral wills. Rather, it leads us to reflect upon the complex mechanism of transforming the notion of a *public* and *represented* power into a *General Will* under an egalitarian principle of civil association. The conditioning principle is that 'the freedom of each is conditional upon the freedom of all'. This is the substance – not just the procedural form – of Rousseau's account of freedom and citizenship in *The Social Contract*;[4] of Kant's 'categorical imperative', and perhaps the insight that forms the ethical basis of Habermas's 'Communicative Ethics'[5] and John Rawls' notion of 'Justice as Fairness'.[6] There is much to be said about the status and derivation of this egalitarian principle, and to hasten over the detail of it in relation to legal authority runs the risk of conflating a simplistic sociological argument for the necessity of 'order' with an ethical question of great complexity. Because we intend to show throughout this work the empowering compatibility of Gewirth's Ethical Rationalism with Fuller's architectural and genuinely Eunomic method of sociological jurisprudence, it is perhaps appropriate at this point to explain fully what we mean by the Gewirthian derivation and defence of such a principle.

Gewirth's Argument to the PGC

In *Reason and Morality* Gewirth maintains that he can show that there is an objectively defensible and universally valid basis for moral rights and duties arising out of the dialectical analysis of uncontentious prudential reasoning.[7] He calls this a 'supreme principle of morality' and has labelled it the 'Principle of Generic Consistency', or, henceforth, the PGC. This principle states that an agent must respect the generic rights of the recipients of his or her actions, and these generic rights relate to the basic wherewithal for action: the 'non-subtractive', 'maintenance', and 'additive' dimensions of practical well-being, that is, those capacities that are the instrumental precondition of contemplating successful purposive activity in any form.

An agent, that is, one who *voluntarily* employs means in the pursuit of ends, is dialectically committed to acknowledging the indispensability of the basic bodily and cerebral wherewithal for action. This viable minimum of bodily and mental integrity might be variously conceptualized, and the actual content of what might constitute this wherewithal is undoubtedly context dependent. On the

4 Jean-Jacques Rousseau *The Social Contract and Discourses* (London and Toronto: J.M. Dent and Sons, 1913) translated with an Introduction by G.D.H. Cole.

5 Jurgen Habermas *The Theory of Communicative Action* Vol. 1: *Reason and the Rationalization of Society* (London, Heinemann, 1984) and Vol. 2: *A Critique of Functionalist Reason* (Cambridge, Polity Press 1987).

6 John Rawls *A Theory of Justice* (Bellknap, Harvard University Press, 1971).

7 Alan Gewirth *Reason and Morality* (Chicago: Chicago University Press, 1978) Chapter 1.

surface of the moon this might entail special thermal and respiratory equipment; in routine and mundane social circumstances it requires life, consciousness, an orientation to surroundings, and a degree of freedom from psychological and communicative restraint such that one might realistically contemplate a range of present and prospective purposes.

From the perspective of the agent, this wherewithal for purposive action – or what we shall call the 'generic features' (GF) of agency – does not appear at the surface of practical consciousness in the form of subjective decisions to engage in means/ends activity. But neither are they buried in the fathomless depths of a philosophy of practical consciousness; they are revealed by reflection on what constitute the immediate exigencies of practical action in a particular situation, and from this point can be gleaned more generally by imagining the requirements of a fairly wide range of not completely specific, but plausibly anticipated, *prospective* practical activity. Gewirth's argument starts from this model of the *prospective, purposive agent*, or, in the jargon, from the viewpoint of the 'PPA'.

Logically, the PPA must acknowledge the indispensability of his or her (we should say 'its' because agency is not co-extensive with, nor a synonym for, humanity – we'll use personal pronouns for convenience) generic features of action, or GF. This is 'Stage 1' of the argument. Gewirth wants to say that this entails the counter-intuitive consequence that he or she must, *therefore*, claim *rights* to GF. This is stage 2 of the argument. It is perhaps more illuminating to present this inferential move by saying that a PPA who logically desires to remain a *prospective, purposive agent* must positively value and thus, if necessary, defend his/her generic wherewithal (or GF) for purposive activity against any attempt to destroy or even diminish it. An indifference in this regard entails, again ideal-typically from the perspective of the agent, an indifference to sustaining one's status as a PPA. To wish to sustain one's status as a PPA and simultaneously display an indifference to the security and integrity of one's GF, is a contradiction. To defend one's GF entails adopting a position which might be articulated in a prescription to others to refrain from any activity that might imperil it. It is, then, logically accurate to note that if one values the end of defending one's GF, one must be prepared to countenance the means by which to achieve it, and this entails a practical resolve far removed from the state of indifference mentioned immediately above. This now *focused* state of practical resolve consists in the understanding (and might, for our expository purposes here, also be expressed in the form of an issued warning to others) that force might be used proportionately against those who ignored or defied this prescription. Can we say that this prescription (and the implicit sanction that attends it) is justified? If we can, then we can say that not only must a PPA *claim* rights to GF or face contradiction, but, at least from the perspective of the particular PPA making such claims, must consider that he or she *has* these rights.

Stage 3 of the argument consists in the logical universalization of the dialectical results of stages 1 and 2. The validity of the PGC rests upon first, demonstrating that this rights claim arises necessarily and *sufficiently* from the possession of the attribute of agency and *not for any less general attribute* pertaining to the identity of the PPA. So, to move from the third person description of agent reasoning to the dialectical viewpoint in the first person, that is, to 'my' point of view as a PPA, I must acknowledge that I have these rights to the integrity of my generic features of action – my agent freedom and well-being – *simply because I am an agent*. Secondly, it must be shown that I must necessarily acknowledge the *universality* of this claim in respect of others agents *qua* agents. In acknowledging that another PPA validly claims rights to her 'freedom and well being' (or GF) in this regard, Gewirth suggests that on the basis of the reciprocity of rights and duties, I must therefore acknowledge certain duties to other agents. This would amount to an acceptance of the Principle of Generic Consistency, that is, the principle that all agents must act in accordance with the generic rights of the recipients of their actions as well as themselves. A practically reasonable agent would accept that they ought not to pursue ends that will, or plausibly might, occasion harm to the freedom and well-being (the GF) of other agents. The merely *prudential* logic of agency (were this universalization step to be valid) would thus turn out to have *other-regarding* or, to put it simply, *moral*, implications. The 'authoritative', 'distributive' and 'substantive' questions of ethical inquiry – respectively (i)'Why should I be moral?' (that is, accept the existence of duties to value the interests of others) (ii) 'Whose interests should I consider?', and (iii)'What interests in particular should I respect?' are thus answered in a general, yet clear and logically impeccable way:

1) I have moral duties because logically as an agent I must pro-actively value my purposes and thus validly claim rights to the wherewithal to pursue them – regardless of whether I anticipate co-operation and acceptance in response to this claim from others. I claim these rights to GF on the sufficient basis that I am an agent; *this entails that other agents can and must claim the same sort of rights to their GF.* Note that this inference is not the product of an auxiliary *moral* principle to the effect that, 'one *ought* to extend to others the same privileges or rights that one claims for oneself'. This *petitio principii* would, of course, invalidate the entire argument to the PGC. Thus I recognize valid rights claims on the part of other agents (PPAOs) and correlatively, duties to them. In short I have *other-regarding* duties which, in answer to the authoritative question, is why I must incorporate a moral dimension to my practical deliberations.
2) The answer to the authoritative question contains the answer to the distributive question: I must, when I act, consider the interest of other agents as well as myself.
3) The answer to the substantive question is also contained in the answer to the authoritative question: specifically, I must respect *the generic features of action* of other *agents* as well as myself.

The argument can be stated in more scrupulously formal terms,[8] but we are of the view that unless it works at this fairly informal level of articulation, no great

8 See, for example, Deryck Beyleveld *The Dialectical Necessity of Morality* (Chicago: Chicago University Press, 1991).

improvements will be made, or no rhetorical progress achieved, that will serve us any better. But first, in extraneous support of it, let us say a few words about why we place this confidence in Gewirth's analysis, when the tenor of the times is antithetical to objective demonstrations of moral rationality.

The first is that the argument has considerable resonance with Natural Law arguments from Aquinas to Locke, and with enlightenment accounts of autonomy and responsibility. In this sense it is not a novel, isolated and idiosyncratic strategy among many, implausibly chosen as *the* right answer; but rather, it can be seen as a particularly insightful articulation of a broad and long-standing intuition about the latent content of self-conscious practical reason. We could list in support a host of connected themes from philosophical accounts of freedom and morality, to the most commonsensical understandings of, for example, what it, means to have a right to self-defence. It is also contingently presupposed by any acceptance and endorsement of the existence of human rights, for example, those stated in documents like the ECHR:[9] most ironically, we find simultaneously in our universities, our positive law, and in the most articulate and dominant mainstream political movements, an implacable commitment to the recognition and protection of human rights, yet precisely the same amount of fervour dedicated to the denunciation of the possibility of objective, rationally grounded, and universally valid maxims of morality. But to say that a person X has a specific right R, by virtue of X's membership of the species *homo sapiens*, is to announce simultaneously by presupposition that X also has the more general rights to the goods required to make possible any feasible and reasonably anticipated exercise of human right R. If a regime is to announce that all humans are to be regarded as having the right to reproduce, express themselves religiously, or politically, or move freely within a certain region, then that regime acts irrationally, immorally and, in constitutional terms, illegitimately, if it actively or negligently undermines access to, or provision of, the instrumental, social and physical wherewithal required for individuals to utilize these rights in the process of fulfilling their legitimate purposes. In short, a document like the ECHR presupposes the validity of the PGC even if its originators and signatories dispute the methodology of *arriving at* the PGC, or are entirely unaware of the PGC. They could not, however, charitably be assumed to be unaware of the general instrumental relationship between means and ends, and thus must be assumed to endorse the practical-logical point in question. Whilst supporters of the dialectically necessary articulation of the validity of the PGC might be counted, if not on the fingers of one hand, then on the pedimentia of a moderately-sized weevil, the dialectically *contingent* endorsement of the vast army of human rights supporters – even if latent – provides some comfort for the committed Gewirthian.

The second is that, if successful, it very directly demonstrates that moral reasoning (by which we mean categorical and other-regarding practical reason) is logically *continuous* with prudential reasoning. In other words, if we can acknowledge the logic of agent-prudence as being captured by the idea that: 'I

9 See Deryck Beyleveld 'Legal Theory and Dialectically Contingent Justifications for the Principle of Generic Consistency' *Ratio Juris* (Vol. 9, 1996) pp. 15–41.

voluntarily do *m* for end *E*, and, no matter what *E* might be, I *must value* the generic capacities of action which are a precondition of the possibility of the successful pursuit of *E*', then Gewirth makes a powerful case for saying that this very admission dialectically and necessarily entails the valuing of generic capacities; a rights claim to these capacities, and, given the universal interface of the entirely general idea of agency, the plausible prospect of a logical universalization of this claim leading to a range of 'other-regarding' duties correlate to these claims and affirmations of prudential rights.

The Integration of Ethical and Legal Theory

In Kant's argument, the Principle of Freedom in the form of the Categorical Imperative or, in the Gewirthian terms we employ here and in *Law In Its Own Right* does not become disconnected from the notion of *institutionalized* authority. Nor is this personal *and* 'other-regarding'[10] maxim over-ridden by it. Rather, the logic of basic right gives *moral* and not merely 'prudential', 'organizational' or 'functional' coherence to the idea of legal validity, and moral rationality must inform and infuse legal authority if the idea of an *omilateral* will is to remain consistent and integral with the continuum of practical reason. In other words, the touchstone of our understanding of 'Natural Law' or, more precisely, Legal Idealism (as opposed to Legal Positivism) is that the idea of individual or agent rights is to be integrally, consensually and authoritatively contained within the idea of the Institutionalization of Right that takes shape as Law in Civil Society.

The argument for the much discussed *autonomy* of law is not, then, simply the *prima facie* plausible one arising from the generally sound observation that, if confrontation and disagreement are to be avoided an authoritative and effective terminus of argument must be established; this demand for 'an allocation of the say' could be made and defended common-sensically from a multiplicity of interest orientations. In its most rudimentary form this 'argument' for order is but a tautology that amounts to the proposition that the need for a final say is justified simply on the grounds that there is a need for a final say. The Legal Idealist argument must provide an epistemological defence of the logical and moral priority of objective and universal precepts inherent in what we have described as the continuum of practical reason.

In Kant, and in Gewirth, this is located in a model of individual agency. The individualist point of departure has not found favour with our most influential theorists. Habermasians have pejoratively labelled this approach a 'monological' model of analysis. This designation is set negatively in opposition to a 'dialogical' approach that is claimed to provide a more socially egalitarian, and communally responsible account of the ethics of *generalisable* interests. We have responded jointly and severally to this objection elsewhere,[11] but let us here simply reiterate

10 See Alan Gewirth *Reason and Morality* (op. cit.) Chapter 1.

11 See, for example, Stuart Toddington 'The Moral Truth About Discourse Theory' *Ratio Juris* (Vol. 19, No. 2, June 2006) pp. 217–230.

that the Kantian or Gewirthian model of the rational individual agent is a *point of departure* from which we might coherently explore the very possibility of grounding *other-regarding* obligations, not the ethical terminus and endorsement of a one-sidedly 'individualist' position. Neither should it be assumed that Kantian or Gewirthian ethics are antithetical to a 'pragmatic', 'dialogical' or context-sensitive account. This requires some considerable explanation of the scope and implications of the contemporary and Enlightenment accounts of the Ethical Rationalist position and, correspondingly, a fairly detailed critique of others, but let us for the moment simply note that the moral-practical precepts we have in mind are prudential not in a 'game-theoretic', 'selfish-gene' or 'contractarian' sense, but in a generically *consistent* sense in relation to the agent's own viewpoint of practical reason. Gewirth's Principle of Generic Consistency (PGC) is a precept of practical reason that relates to the rationality of one's self-interest *whatever* those interests might be. In this sense it is both *prudential* and *categorical*; but this categorical-prudential precept emerges from the logic of agency in general (not from personal, biographical or indexical reasons) and its *consistency* depends on its *logical* (not its morally charitable) universalization. When universalization occurs, the precept not only governs the prudential concerns of 'oneself' or any particular agent in question, but oneself, any and all agents. Thus the Gewirthian logic of what constitutes rational action in support of prudential interests has *other-regarding* implications that amount to moral duties. Ironically, and to reiterate the importance of the epistemological issues involved, it is only through an analysis of *individual* agency that we can mount a *non-question-begging* critique of amoral selfishness or simplistically 'prudential' individualism.

It is the *other-regarding* scope of the logic of agency that both defines and serves our cognitive interest in morality and ethical rationality. These other-regarding dimensions of agent rationality in relation to a concept of law provide the basic prescriptions or guidelines for legitimacy in the way legal reason might operate in regulation, dispute resolution and social co-ordination. The Legal Idealist position would be that law broadly conceived would strive to cohere as transparently as possible with the nature of moral right. This expansive conception does not deny law's 'autonomy' nor (as do some sociological approaches past and present in their eagerness to expand the writ of 'jurisprudence' or 'legal science') does it subsume *all* normative phenomena under the concept of law. On the contrary, one of the jobs of a serviceable legal theory is to show that the *autonomy* of law in the sense of autonomy *from* political morality is a pre-condition of an authoritatively *effective* approach to social regulation and that the transparency of its special forms of reasoning is the key to its legitimacy. Genuine legal reasoning thus acknowledges its roots in moral reason and its provenance as an *artifice* intended to overcome not the relativity and chaos of value concerns, but the problem of the *unilateral* assertion of moral right arising from what Kant called the objective moral law. Law, then, transcends the political whilst remaining forever open to scrutiny in the institutionalized form of public practical reasoning.

Objectivity and Perfectionism

The claim that there are objective moral principles and that these principles should inform legal reasoning does not entail that there are, or that we should expect to find, objectively perfect answers to every moral question arising in our experience. It means, rather, that there exists, as Kant pointed out, a moral compass in human affairs as opposed to an endless and relativistic disorientation. And although we might face a plurality of reasonable decisions in response to a given conflict or interpretation of a rule, this is very different from surrendering to the convenient dogma of 'the incommensurability of values', where 'incommensurable' means, because of the alleged 'intransitvity' of values,[12] that no substantive question of any complexity can be settled, because no value judgment is to be preferred over another. Neither does it mean that all that law requires of us is that we do our own idiosyncratic best. Rather, we may lay claim to an *authority* of law on the basis of the existence of objective basic right and the concomitant need for the institutionalization of right; but only on condition that we strive to incorporate and combine what is constant in the *substance* of basic right with what is constant in the *formal* precepts of its institutionalization. *Constancy* might be the virtue required in the interminable process of weighing, balancing and interpreting principle in the application of public norms in complex and changing circumstances. But, as Gustav Radbruch pointed out with as yet unequalled brevity, this constancy should not be confused with the qualitatively different demands of a positivistic plea for the priority of 'predictability' or 'certainty' in legal judgment, particularly where the benefits of certainty or uniformity are held to override moral rationality in the process of reaching a decision.[13]

Gewirthian ethics provides a universalisable logic of a *natural hierarchy of goods* that enables the *content* of basic right to function in legal reasoning. We elaborated upon this point in relation to the analysis of legal substance and form that we put forward in the final chapter of *Law In Its Own Right*.[14] If we apprise ourselves of what *formally and organizationally* is required to manage our affairs in accordance with the *substance* of basic right, we discover first and foremost that the institution of authoritative reasoning in respect of issues concerning basic right must be removed from the theatre of conflict and discourse where determinations of its scope are called into question. This, as noted, explains what might be meant by the *autonomy* of law and the institution of a framework of legal reasoning. It is the need for an autonomous sphere that gives rise simultaneously

---

12 See John Finnis 'The Authority of Law in the Predicament of Contemporary Social Theory' *Journal of Law, Ethics and Public Policy* (Vol. 1, 1984) pp. 115–137 at 123–127.

13 See Gustav Radbruch *Rechtsphilosophie* also '*Five Minutes of Legal Philosophy' (1945)* [Bonnie Litschewski Paulson and Stanley L. Paulson Trans.] *Oxford Journal of Legal Studies* (Vol. 26, No. 1, 2006) pp. 13–15, first published as *Fünf Minuten Rechtsphilosophie*' in the *Rhein-Neckar-Zeitung* (Heidelberg), 12 September 1945; also Thomas Mertens 'Nazism, Legal Positivism and Radbruch's Thesis on Statutory Injustice' *Law and Critique* (Vol. 14, No. 3, 2003) pp. 277–295.

14 Op. cit. Chapter 6.

to the need and the demand for *transparency* in legal reasoning. But autonomy and authoritative competence notwithstanding, it is basic right that must furnish the criteria appropriate to a continuous and parallel social and political critique of the legal process in relation to other civil institutions.

Idealism or Pragmatism? Objections to the 'Foundational' Argument

The specific concerns of this present work were given shape and impetus by the special IVR session devoted to arguments in *Law In Its Own Right* in Lund, 2003.[15] The invaluable attention and discussion that our efforts attracted there have largely shaped the first half of this book. The main objection that emerged in these sessions was that whilst our analysis of the autonomy of law and the account of transparency and critique presented in *Law In Its Own Right* was not without merit and appeal, the 'moral fundamentalism' (that is, Gewirth's Ethical Rationalism) upon which it was established was at once 'dogmatic' and unnecessary. Criticism led by Sanne Taekema[16] suggested that foundationalism should be abandoned and replaced by a 'pragmatism' gleaned from a mixture of the insights of John Dewey and Philip Selznick. Following the IVR sessions we were thus forced to explore a challenging range of arguments that led us into an area of inquiry that has seen the enthusiastic revival of Fullerian Scholarship. In particular, Fullerian methodology has been re-examined and re-interpreted in the language of the now widely subscribed notions of value-incommensurabilism and recent refinements in the methodology of pragmatism.[17]

---

15 *The International Association for Philosophy of Law and Social Philosophy.*

16 Sanne Taekema 'What Should Be Transparent in Law? A Pragmatist Strategy to Justify Legal Decisions' (IVR 2003, Draft 2, 30 July 2003) p. 1 She says:

> The important claim [in *Law In Its Own Right*] is that the substantive moral reasons for law as an autonomous system can never be made completely invisible, because law's authority relies on its promise to solve or prevent moral conflicts. In my view, this connection between legal validity and moral reasons is well argued, but I disagree with the way they further develop their view on the moral background of law …
>
> First, I disagree with the need to use an objectivist, rationalistic, moral epistemology as a basis to weigh the reasons for a legal decision…it is not a necessary step to appeal to sound foundational principles. If we focus on the justification of a particular legal decision, it is enough to appeal to reasons for a solution which are acceptable within the legal practice. This can be defended on the basis of a pragmatist epistemology.
>
> Second, I disagree with the claim that it is possible to arrive at a hierarchy or commensurability of values. In my view, it is possible to distinguish the *a priori* incommensurability of values from the need for a reasoned choice between values in a particular situation.

17 An invaluable introduction to these writings is to be found in Willem J. Witteveen, and Wibren van der Burg (eds) *Rediscovering Fuller: Essays on Implicit Law and Institutional Design* (Amsterdam: Amsterdam University Press, 1999).

These understandings of Fuller seem to hold out the possibility of articulating a sociologically and ethically sensitive alternative to the poles of Legal Positivism and traditional conceptions of Natural Law. The insights that have spurred this new phase of sociological jurisprudence are, of course, to be found throughout Fuller's many works, but we find good examples of them in his use of the metaphor of *architecture* allied to his guiding precept that we should seek the key to understanding the *evolution* of legal form and principle from the *informal* practices of human association. The use of this promising analogy demands that we think more carefully about the relationship between means and ends in the context of practical activity. In developing and defending the ideas we advanced in *Law In Its Own Right* we intend to work outwards from the reception and interpretation of Fuller's core ideas and determine the extent to which, if at all, they require us to espouse incommensurabilism and pragmatism in jurisprudential method.

We begin by examining the epistemology of pragmatism stemming from Dewey and developed in the work of Philp Selznick[18] argue that it makes moral claims identical to, or in excess of, those made by the allegedly 'dogmatic' and 'foundationalist' analyses of ethical rationalism. We then go on to examine the alleged 'pragmatic' function of the incommensurability thesis and show how this latter provides an impoverished concept of legal authority and validity.

In Chapter 2, and in the light of our critique of incommensurabilism, we explain why Fuller's recently discovered paper, 'The Case Against Freedom' forces us to reconsider the distinction between 'negative' and 'affirmative' conceptions of human freedom, and why the former is deficient whilst the latter demands legitimate and rational institutional expression. This fundamental orientation to institutional design is, as Fuller says, basic and evolutionary; and in it we find the key to Fuller's understanding of how formal legal processes grow out of the informality of social practices, and why the demands and intrinsic worth of an *affirmative and responsible* freedom lead us to rational understanding of the 'inner morality of law'. Chapter 3 explores the complexity of the notion of affirmative freedom and its contentious expression in political philosophy. We show that valuing freedom ('negatively' or 'affirmatively') necessarily implies the adoption of a social contract model of the individual and society. The sociological imagination developed thus far shows us that what we understand to be' law in society' or 'civil society' is a critique of 'natural' institutions from the perspective of a self-conscious affirmation of freedom, and that Legal Order reveals itself essentially as sovereignty guaranteeing institutional development. It is perhaps at this point that the Fullerian idea of an architecture of justice becomes, for sociological jurisprudence, literal rather than metaphorical.

---

18 In Chapter 1 we concentrate on Selznick's method as developed in, for example (with Phillipe Nonet) *Law and Society in Transition: Toward Responsive Law* (New Brunswick: University of Columbia Press) 1 978; *Law Society and Industrial Justice* (New York: Russell Sage,1969) *The Moral Commonwealth: Social Theory and the Promise of Community* (Berkeley: University of California Press, 1992); 'Natural Law and Sociology' in John Cogley. *Natural Law and Modern Society* (Cleveland: World Publishing Co., 1966) pp. 158, 170.

In Chapter 4 we return to epistemological concerns. Here we give a detailed explanation of the logical structure of what we have referred to as *the continuum of practical reason*. If prudential reasoning can be shown to imply moral or other-regarding duties, then we arrive at a model of genuinely natural rights – that is rights which do not appeal to positive law for their justification or provenance, The problematic generality of the normative content of principles of natural right, whether expressed in Kantian terms as *the* categorical imperative or in terms of *a* categorical imperative in the form of Gewirth's PGC, is what leads us to develop a response to the potential conflict of unilateral affirmations of right. This, as we have explained, is the point on the axis of the continuum of practical reason where we find the necessary link between *natural* morality and the *artifice* of legality. Legality is, in effect, the general solution to the existence and potential expression of natural right.

Given this general and highly abstract account of the institutionalization of right we re-focus in the closing passages of the chapter on some of the sociological, political and legal issues arising from an attempt to come to terms with the concept of civil society in the diversity and complexity of present circumstances. In noting the fashionable nostalgia of the tendency to conceive of civil society as 'community' and 'association' untouched and unsullied by law, state and corporate capital, we explain and endorse Jean Cohen's[19] conception of it as a sphere of contested values and identities. This contestation is inevitable and perhaps, as pluralists and multiculturalists have suggested, desirable. But far from sounding the death knell of the idea of sovereignty, this condition of diversity in contemporary civil society brings its role into dramatic relief. We try to show that there is still much to learn from the classical (Enlightenment) accounts of the relationship between individual freedom and public authority in civil society: theoretically, contemporary legal theory must acknowledge a politically integrated conception of law and legal obligation that looks to the wider responsibilities of critical institutional design, not merely to the insular processes of legislation and adjudication; practically and politically, we remind ourselves that, in a highly diverse society, sovereignty still functions, as Martin Loughlin suggests, as the guarantor of 'the autonomy of the political'.[20]

In the constraints of the present work we cannot hope do justice to the complexity and scope of the now vital and fascinating interface between the political and legal-theoretical dimensions of legitimacy in late modernity. We choose, however, to focus in Chapter 5 on some of the most pressing moral and legal issues arising in the context of multicultural society. Here we defend the Enlightenment orthodoxy by attempting to show that pluralism or

---

19 See J. Cohen 'American Civil Society Talk' Report From The Institute for Philosophy and Public Policy; later published as: 'Trust, Voluntary Association and Workable Democracy: The Contemporary American Discourse of Civil Society' in Mark E. Warren (ed.) *Democracy and Trust* (Cambridge, 1999), pp. 208–248. See also (with Andrew Arato) *Civil Society and Political Theory* (Cambridge, MA: MIT Press, 1992).

20 Martin Loughlin *The Idea of Public Law* (Oxford: Oxford University Press 2004) p. 72.

multiculturalism requires not a normatively *neutral* perspective, but one that affirms as supreme, and is prepared to enforce, an egalitarianism based not on the prospect of the 'parallel governance' of autonomous subcultures, but on the natural rights constitutive of expressive and affirmative individual freedom. To this end, in Chapter 6, we argue further that the residual special-pleadings of religious subcultures is an obsolescent form of freedom in a genuinely open and diverse society.

Chapter 1

The Methodology of Eunomics

Part 1: Explanation, Critique and Human Interests

Lon L. Fuller used the term *Eunomics* to refer to his understanding of the type of sociological jurisprudence most appropriate to the systematic development of a theory of 'Good order and workable social arrangements'. 'Good' order suggests a type of inquiry distinct from, if not a cut above, a concern with 'mere' social order, but implicit in this distinction is a methodological idea that requires some careful explanation.

At the core of the understanding of social science and of law, and of the relationship between the two, is the difficult idea that to understand a social institution, or even to be in a position to identify its existence, one must adopt an evaluative or judgmental perspective on the practical rationality of the activity in question. In *Law In Its Own Right* we devoted some time to a discussion of this controversial methodological point. Let us try to restate the position here with the benefit of some reflection and by way of a defence of Fuller's suggestion that we should seek to incorporate the aims of *Eunomics* as the methodological basis of Legal Theory.

In, *Law In Its Own Right* in a section entitled 'Conceptualising Society'[1] we noted that the classical structuralist accounts of the subject matter of sociological investigation asked us to imagine the entire set of social relations as a system, and more precisely, a system of norms embedded in various types of institutions such as roles, practices, beliefs or authoritative conventions. Large scale institutional aspects of social action appear as vital and ubiquitous elements of the social system and hence form the central concerns of the structuralist analysis. Not all schools of sociology are happy with the label of 'structuralist', and even among those who might be, some would resist the broadly 'hermeneutic' or 'interpretive' account of normative structures that follows. Nevertheless, we have argued at length elsewhere that (a), some conception of a social structure is either explicit or implicit in all sociological analysis (even that which emphasizes the importance of symbolic and individual interaction),[2] and (b), that 'describing' a normative system entails more than technical or instrumental judgments about practical rationality.

---

1 Henrik P. Olsen and Stuart Toddington *Law In Its Own Right* (Oxford: Hart Publishing, 1999) Chapter 2, p. 57.

2 See *Law In Its Own Right* (op. cit.) Chapter 2.

We are familiar in sociological texts and texts books[3] with a traditional classification of method that separates 'actionist' from 'structuralist' schools of thought; and of the latter we might point to accounts of large-scale institutional phenomena (for example, the family, gender, education, work, power and politics) variously labelled as Functionalist, Marxist, and Feminist perspectives. Let us, then, take the phenomenon of gender purely as an illustration of the problem of constructing a genuinely *sociological* account of it. Gender undoubtedly has a biological dimension, but the extent to which biology determines gender consciousness, behaviour and inter-personal expectations, and the relationship between both gender and the technical division of labour, and gender and social power and authority, is highly contentious. By way of illustration, let us consider a simple but plausible account of the phenomenon of gender in the social structure. We might characterize *the social organization* of, for example, reproduction and childbirth, and the weaning of infants as a set of unproblematic empirical phenomena arising from the facts of physiology and biology. But this would overlook the complexities of historically and culturally conditioned forms of *institutionalization* of the role of females in the division of labour, and instead swiftly assume them to be *natural* facts explained by basic biological differences. But the energy or, as Durkheim says, the 'external and coercive' force of the social structure in maintaining and strengthening the accretions of normative expectations of gender roles in the division of labour is not a 'natural' or biological energy; it is a *normative* energy that resides in the individual and collective social consciousness.[4] This is not to say that social consciousness about gender is not related to, or to some extent determined by, 'natural' or biological facts. Rather, *despite* the biology, the *social system* in general, and the organization of gender in particular, is a system of norms, and norms, broadly speaking, are made manifest in attitudes about what is right, good, useful, proper, decent, fair, and, ironically, 'natural' in relation to other attitudes, assumptions and speculations about what human beings *are* and what best serves their individual and collective *interests*. We do not have to accept wholesale a theory as uncompromising as, for example, Marx's account of ideology and *false* consciousness to realize that sociological *explanation* must inevitably take the form of, or imply, a critique of the practical rationality of social institutions; we have merely to consider the possibility that normative consciousness might be susceptible to changes, alterations, – perhaps improvements – of orientation. This critical aspect remains, however, even if we wish simply to endorse the normative rationale of *existing* institutions. Let us pursue this line of thought a littler further.

Sociology – intentionally or otherwise – must dissolve the solidity of what appears to be 'natural' in the cultural, sexual, economic and political world. Gender roles (and all other institutionalized aspects of social organization)

---

3 A straightforward overview of the main approaches is to be found in the now classic M. Haralambos and M. Holborn *Sociology Themes and Perspectives* (London: Unwin and Hyman, 1990) pp. 1–20.

4 This notion is developed in Emile Durkheim *The Division of Labour in Society* (New York: The Free Press, 1947).

are exposed as ephemeral and mutable in the process of critique. We come to realize that institutions, taken as the focus of our *cognitive interests* as social theorists, exist not naturally and immutably as solid fact, but ideal-typically in the form of *contestable* normative assumptions. This does not mean, of course, that sociology has always automatically adopted, or must in future adopt, a revolutionary stance on the subject matter. Its impulse might be apolitical insofar as it expresses a concern merely to inquire and explain. But whatever the intentions of the sociologist, there are some inevitable critical commitments to be faced. Let us try and explain this by assuming that *if* sociological critique *does* takes the form of straightforward *revolutionary* contestation, it must in so doing explain first, the reason for the appearance of the solidity or naturalness of the existing configuration of institutionalized social relations. It must then offer a *reinterpretation* of these relations. This process of reinterpretation through the prism of a normative rationality (though historically unpalatable to 'system theory' in general and especially to some Marxist structuralists) is what is properly meant by an 'interpretive' or *hermeneutic* approach to sociological method. Despite the impressive etymology, in broad terms, an interpretive or structurally hermeneutic analysis will first show how and why, over and above the *genuinely* natural, physical, physiological and biological constraints of the situation, one set of norms has structured and perpetuated a particular set of social relations and expectations over another possible form of organization. Continuing our illustration, a simple (and perhaps accurate) example would be the analysis that concludes that women always end up looking after the kids because it serves the interest of men; and that men have the physical and economic power to safeguard and protect their interests at the expense of the interests of women or children. The analysis will then explain how we might bring alternative concepts of normative rationality to bear on the way we understand the phenomena: Perhaps, for example, men ought to re-evaluate their responsibilities in this regard enabling women to have a wider experience of economic participation. Critique has thus two phases: the first *describes* the existing normative phenomena, the second *prescribes* an alternative set of institutional relations. A great deal has been made of the distinction between *prescription* and *description* in social science, and the suggestion has been that, methodologically speaking, we might remain on the straight and narrow path by avoiding the former and sticking to the latter. It is fairly obvious however, that the even the so-called 'descriptive' phase is evaluative: it presupposes an insight into the *real* – or what are presented as implicitly *more rational*, more progressive, more egalitarian – interests of men and women. In short, imposing templates of normative rationality on unprocessed social phenomena boils down to making explicit or implicit claims about human interests and these claims are unavoidably 'value-laden' Some of these claims, such as, for example, that some individuals and groups ought to take into account and safeguard the interests of other individuals and groups, are straightforward moral judgments.

Methodological discussions about the disjunction between description and evaluation, or 'description and prescription', are euphemisms for the sceptical question of whether social science is or can be 'objective' about its subject matter. The idea seems to be that we might describe a situation (for example, our selection for illustration of the role of women in the economy) impartially and disinterestedly, or we might make all manner of subjective, 'value-laden' or 'political' judgments about it. The former attitude is, of course the one most routinely associated with a 'scientific' approach. But the question is not whether we ought to confine ourselves to description and avoid at all costs judgmental comment, the question is whether or not we accept or reject the claim that sociological analysis relies indispensably upon conceptions of human interests in the normative modelling of the phenomena it takes to be its subject matter. There may be many ways to *do* sociology, but if the broadly hermeneutic account is accepted, then the issue is not whether sociologists should be 'descriptive' or prescriptive', it is, as we have seen, whether or not there is any point in taking a scientific approach to the discussion of human interests.

Eunomics, as Fuller understood it, aspires to differentiate Good Order from, presumably bad or defective forms of order, and, on anyone's view of the social or natural world, there is nothing incoherent or illogical about this. There are forms of social order that through a structure of norms, create and perpetuate particular forms of economic, sexual and cultural relations. If one can accept that there are, in principle, alternative normative possibilities of the forms of social organization, then there might be more or less rational ways of *describing* our predicament and *prescribing* our options. This approach to the problem offers the prospect of coming to terms with what might usefully be understood as *objectivity* as opposed to *subjectivity* in social and legal science and we might thereby overcome the sterility of the so-called 'fact/value distinction' or the ill-conceived opposition of 'description and evaluation' in social science.

Social Norms and Legal Norms

Let us say a little more in this vein about the relationship between 'social' norms and 'legal' norms, and the implications of this distinction for understanding the similarities and differences between social theory and legal theory – especially Fuller's conception of legal theory. Pursuing the illustration of gender, we can imagine a situation where it might empirically be the case that child care in a particular society is held to be the sole responsibility of females. Empirical accounts of social practices might confirm this, and empirical accounts of attitudes and beliefs might discover widespread acceptance of the naturalness or rightness or normality of this state of affairs. Assuming the complete absence of any formal legislation relating to the issue of the propriety of female child care duties, the *social* norms governing this aspect of the division of labour are, let us also assume, effective, accepted, and observed by all members of the society or the great majority. Let us also imagine plausibly that justifications for these arrangements are to be found in the common understanding of individual men and women, in religious teaching, in socialization strategies within the family or in wider educational institutions, and perhaps even in what passes in this hypothetical society for the 'scientific' practices of psychology, biology and perhaps, 'sociology'. Where social norms are in operation, says Durkheim, transgressions attract a tangible response: negative sanctions in some form will accrue to the offender. Effective and operative 'social' normativity in this sense is not, therefore, 'optional', other than in the disingenuous sense that, if one discounts punishment, harm or loss accruing to oneself, any physically possible behaviour appears as 'an option'. The interesting point is that this generic description of *social* normativity does most of the work required to describe *legal* normativity. In an attempt to differentiate the latter as a species of the former, the issue of codification, perhaps, could be raised; so too could the issue of recognized formal authority to promulgate the norms. But that fact that a norm is widely if not universally understood and observed seems to make the fact that it is not written down appear quite trivial, especially if codification is to be presented as a key criterion of *the legal*. And it would be a mistake to assume that 'recognized authority' to promulgate and endorse norms cannot be found to lie behind social norms: parental instruction, elders, the church, common sense, tradition, and so on undoubtedly have been and perhaps still are regarded as 'authoritative' sources. Furthermore, if we turn this inquiry into norms towards the language of obligation, we find an even greater blurring of the social and the legal: the bodies that we routinely *do* recognize as *formal* sources of legal 'authority' are often accused of a variety of inadequacies in this regard. The message is often that the norms promulgated as law, and thus attracting legal sanctions and penalties for transgression, often lack the moral, commonsensical, or utilitarian *substance* to command genuine compliance and support. This 'lay' or popular criticism of law, we must note, arises from a body of informal normative attitudes or 'social' *mores* that operate behind, alongside or despite the intrusion into social life of 'legality'. Here is a good example, then, of a common situation where it is not *form* that seems to make the difference in the quality of normativity, but the practically relevant *substance.*

The importance of the preoccupation with fathoming the essence of law, or with explicating through scrupulous philosophical inquiry *the* concept of law, seems to recede. But whilst this appears to relieve us of the burden of demarcating the legal from the social, our progress to a critical understanding of sociology, and thence to a sociologically informed 'hands-on' jurisprudence is not without its difficulties. The discovery that the understanding of social institutions involves an appraisal of the *substance* of norms in relation to a conception of human interests, and that social norms exhibit in ways materially analogous to legality a 'coercive' dimension of non-optional *obligation and compliance*, brings us to the realization that a *rational* account of social order containing *within* it *legal order* presumes a comprehensively *general* understanding of the *legitimacy* of norms – whether these norms are held to be 'social' or 'informal' or 'legal'.

Thus, theoretically, we now face double trouble. The entire social system is a normative system, but legality appears within it as a normative subsystem; and so do the organizational relations of gender, family, education and so on. We must now, therefore, differentiate legal norms from other social norms, but we can't do it conveniently on the back of criteria that appeal to 'recognized' authority, non-optionality of obligation, or legitimacy; for in a critical conception of social theory, these criteria apply quite validly and relevantly to all institutional aspects of social phenomena. What advice does Fuller's project of Eunomics have for us in this predicament?

In his introduction to a revised collection of Fuller's essays published under the title of *The Principles of Social Order*,[5] Kenneth I. Winston takes the opportunity to restate what he takes to be the essential elements of Fuller's philosophy of law. There are two: first, the unswerving commitment to the fundamentally moral nature of legality that must be assumed to distinguish its strictures from mere coercive threats, and secondly, the acknowledgment of the pragmatic and continuously transformative efforts of social collectivities to sustain an institutional framework in some way faithful to the demands of legitimacy – demands that, according to Fuller, lie at the very heart of the concept of law. To these axioms, and because of Winston's discovery of a previously unpublished paper, 'The Case Against Freedom' we might add a third, namely, the indispensable task that falls to social and political theory to articulate and defend an affirmative and engaged conception of individual freedom as opposed to a negative conception of liberty understood as mere freedom from constraint. These are indeed the three pillars of Fuller's legal and social philosophy and the foundations of his aspiration to develop a science of Eunomics. These elements, in our view, serve as a general guide to any such aspirations in this regard. In *Law In Its Own Right*, we concentrated on the first issue, that of the relationship between law and morality; in what follows we will focus on the second and third elements, namely, the dynamics of the institutional framework of social order, and the place of human freedom and autonomy within it.

Ironically, and given Fuller's critical *milieu*, his expansive approach to legal theory can be seen as genuinely *realistic*, as opposed to the then hegemonic 'Realist' analyses of what has since been famously categorized as 'American Realism'.[6] This focus on real social processes, according to Winston, allows Fuller to avoid a philosophically unpleasant engagement with the 'abstract moral principles … characteristic of traditional natural law' and hence, to avoid 'top-down methods of reasoning'.[7]

Fuller's jurisprudential orientation does take institutional processes seriously, and gives life to a concept of law within the dialectic of historical and social activity. This approach has been swiftly characterized by influential Fullerian scholars as a form of Pragmatism, and this is, perhaps, a suitable label for the activity. But labelling, however apt, solves no methodological problems. It might even give rise to a few, especially if we were inclined to assume that we might conveniently substitute the apparent tangibilities and commonsensicalities of

5 Kenneth I. Winston (ed.) *The Principles of Social Order: Selected Essays of Lon L. Fuller* (Oxford: Hart Publishing, 2001).

6 Oliver Wendell Holmes, John Chipman Grey, Karl Llewellyn, Jerome Frank et al. For an introduction see H. McCoubrey and N. White *Jurisprudence* (London: Blackstone Press) Chapter 10.

7 Kenneth I. Winston (ed.) (op. cit.) p. 4.

'pragmatic' social activity for ontological concepts in general, and moral ontology in particular. Winston seems to lean to this view of Fuller's thinking:[8]

> The sociological insight on which Fuller depends is that the authoritative principles necessary for a critical assessment of conventional practices are not derived from an external source *but from a deeper understanding of the practices themselves*. In particular, the resources for moral criticism and justification emerge ineluctably in any society, because moral conformity is itself a reflective practice, generating criteria for its own assessment. [Our emphasis]

This is perhaps a fair assessment of the Fullerian approach. But, as Winston points out,[9] it could also be said of Herbert Hart's views in *Law, Liberty and Morality*,[10] or of Dworkin in *Taking Rights Seriously*.[11] We might add that it is also applicable to perhaps the majority of anthropologically and sociologically informed texts in that it is almost universally regarded as axiomatic that the *essence* or the focus of *critique* of authoritative institutions is to be found in 'deeper understandings' of real institutional processes. In specifically jurisprudential texts, law, in its most fundamental sense, is to be distinguished from mere habit or naked coercion by '*criteria*' that, again, let us admit, emerge 'ineluctably' from the practice of moral reflection. This is, conceptually and sociologically, 'getting real' about the place and primacy of theory and moral judgment in legal philosophy But a 'deeper understanding' of social practices suggests a host of theoretical candidates for what might count as 'deep', and, in substantial terms, we can expect to encounter a wide range of moral criteria emerging from these avenues of reflection.

Let us consider, by way of example, the general orientations of what until very recently were widely influential approaches to critique: variants of Marxist and of Feminist analysis. Both strategies offer to expose the 'genuine' or deep motivation behind our most powerful and enduring normative routines and economic institutions. These approaches, unlike Fuller's, begin with an assumption that hegemonic sectional interests (that is, in these examples respectively, capital and patriarchy) condition and sustain (Marx would have said 'reproduce') the character of normative institutions by presenting the sectional view of rational and proper societal organization as a universal view. Here are a couple of orthodox examples of this way of thinking about concept formation and critique: Saul Newman gives an impressive account of the Marxist view:[12]

> Arguing against the Hegelian idea that the state embodies the general good, Marx saw it always as a particular state, one which paints itself as universal. Its universality and independence from civil society are only a mask for the particular economic interests

8 Ibid. p. 5.

9 Ibid.

10 H.L.A. Hart *Law Liberty and Morality* (London: Oxford University Press, 1963).

11 Ronald Dworkin *Taking Rights Seriously* (London: Duckworth,1977).

12 Saul Newman 'Anarchism, Marxism and the Bonapartist State' *Anarchist Studies* (Vol. 12, No.1, 2004).

– such as private property – that it serves.... Marx was later to develop from this the position that the state represented the interests of the most economically dominant class: the bourgeoisie. For Marx, it was the economic forces of society that determined all historical, political, cultural and social phenomena: 'the economic structure of society is the real basis on which the juridical and political superstructure is raised, and to which definite social forms of thought correspond ...

Winston's remarks earlier about striving for a 'deeper understanding' become especially relevant when we read the following account of the idea of a 'standpoint theory in general', and of Feminist Standpoint Theory in particular, offered by Elizabeth Anderson:[13]

> Standpoint theories [in general] become controversial when they claim epistemic privilege over socially and politically contested topics on behalf of the perspectives of systematically disadvantaged social groups, relative to the perspectives of the groups that dominate them. The scope of the claimed privilege includes the character, causes, and consequences of the social inequalities that define the groups in question. This type of standpoint theory *classically* claims three types of epistemic privilege over the standpoint of dominant groups: First, *it claims to offer deep over surface knowledge of society*: the standpoint of the disadvantaged reveals the fundamental regularities that drive the phenomena in question, whereas the standpoint of the privileged captures only surface regularities. Second, in virtue of this, *it claims to offer superior knowledge of the modality of surface regularities, and thus superior knowledge of human potentialities.* Where the standpoint of the privileged tends to represent existing social inequalities as natural and necessary, the standpoint of the disadvantaged *correctly* [our emphasis] represents them as socially contingent, and shows how they could be overcome. Third, it claims to offer a representation of the social world in relation to universal human interests. By contrast, the standpoint of the privileged represents social phenomena only in relation to the interests of the privileged class, *but ideologically misrepresents these interests as coinciding with universal human interests.* [Our emphasis]

These two accounts of method are penetrating. They show clearly that the approaches to critique in question do not so much avoid 'top down' or 'abstract' moralizing, as refuse to engage with the issue of moral evaluation on its own philosophical terms; preferring instead merely to assert the historical or existential authenticity and inevitability of the interest perspective that informs the standpoint critique adopted. But what is theoretically assumed to be the *real* standpoint or interest perspective of the constituency in question ('the proletariat' or 'women'), that is, what is to serve as the normative blueprint of practical rationality that provides the template of critique against which present institutional practices are compared and condemned, must necessarily be an idealized conception. One might want to argue that the ethical assumptions at the heart of these examples of institutional critique are not 'top down' in the very plausible sense that they are somehow 'democratic' or 'underdog'

---

13 Elizabeth Anderson 'Feminist Epistemology and Philosophy of Science' *The Stanford Encyclopedia of Philosophy* (Summer 2004 edition) Edward N. Zalta (ed.), http://plato.stanford.edu/archives/sum2004/entries/feminism-epistemology.

perspectives. This might plausibly be argued to be the case, but they are most certainly abstract and moral, and in this regard they must face the same tribunal of epistemological scrutiny that awaits all normative-practical assumptions embedded in interpretive schemes of sociological critique. In other words, any claim to represent a 'deeper understanding' of social practices must be supplied with epistemological justifications as to why, in relation to the mode of analysis and understanding of a particular set of phenomena (p), conceptual framework (x) ought to be preferred to conceptual framework (y). Our point is simply that any *non-arbitrary* justification adduced in support of one framework over another will involve a moral judgment.

Fuller's striving for a 'deeper understanding' does not, of course, bluntly and obviously appeal to a particular 'standpoint' constituency of interest to provide his 'reflective moral criteria', nor does he opt for a proprietary 'top-down' conception already on offer: perhaps, for example, versions of the doctrine of the Virtuous Mean, the Categorical Imperative, Utilitarianism, Reflective Equilibrium or a calculus of Rational Choice or Game Theory. But we can say that he operates with a universalist notion of just and civilized humanity revealed in the phenomenon of legality, and he famously points us towards an 'internal' procedural morality of law and an 'external' aspirational context – 'the morality that makes law possible'.[14]

This is insightful and attractive in that it makes us think expansively about not only the regulatory and co-ordinatory techniques required to sustain a practical striving for Good Order, but more specifically and technically, about just what conception of the Good is pre-supposed in our acceptance of the good sense of transparent legal procedures.[15] But the question of just how far the humanist imagination of Fuller's immanent critique of law might get us without some independent and substantive moral commitment has been the focus of some of the most accomplished Fullerian scholarship of recent years.[16] In the following chapters, we will suggest that the considered answer to this question is, perhaps, 'not far enough'; but this is hardly to detract from Fuller's contribution. For the genuinely interesting dimensions of the naturalist/positivist debate, in our view, start precisely here with Fuller's invitation to engage with the central and unresolved moral-philosophical problems of concept formation relating to normative organization in general: an engagement postponed and perhaps unintentionally diverted into a different direction by Herbert Hart and assiduously followed by the increasingly technical discourses of contemporary legal positivism.[17] Our reservations are merely that Fuller's clarity and comprehensive appreciation of the essentially sociological subject matter of legal science, and the

---

14 Lon L. Fuller *The Morality of Law* (New Haven, CT: Yale University Press, 1969) Chapter 1.

15 See *Law In its Own Right* (op. cit.) Chapter 6.

16 This is examined in detail in William Witteween and Wibren van der Burg *Rediscovering Fuller* (Amsterdam: Amsterdam University Press, 2000).

17 See, for an overview, David Dyzenhaus 'The Genealogy of Legal Positivism' *Oxford Journal of Legal Studies* (Vol. 24, No. 1, 2004).

role of 'pragmatism' or *praxis* in understanding it, should not be received as an epistemological miracle that might absolve us from the *a priori* labours demanded by legal-theoretical issues.

Incommensurabilism, Pragmatism and Proceduralism

In relation to the above it should be noted that there is a threefold combination of methodological assumptions and predilections at work in much of the literature surrounding the Fuller revival. Principally, we can point to: (i) the appeal of a (Selznickian)[18] pragmatic approach to legal analysis and concept formation; (ii) allied to this, the acceptance of the thesis of the incommensurability of underlying values; and (iii), in respect of rule application and interpretation (and especially in the light of the comparatively recent legal theory of Habermas and Alexy) a heavy investment in *proceduralism* as opposed to a substantive, value-based objectivism. This latter, of course, is inevitably supported by a reading of Fuller's eight tenets of legal rationality alleged to constitute the 'inner' or 'internal' morality of law. The central methodological arguments we want to make by way of response are, correlatively, threefold.

First, more in clarification than opposition we will argue that 'pragmatism' is indeed an inevitable aspect of a social scientific (and thus a legal-scientific) approach to the problems of regulation and institutional design, but a pragmatic approach to analysis or to action requires, nevertheless, a substantive ethical base and thus does not of itself replace the need for 'moral foundations'.

Secondly, although it is beyond doubt that, in some sense, to some extent and at a certain level of discussion, the ' incommensurability of values' characterizes our ethical experience, we must clarify to what extent this observation affects the methodology of the social sciences. One can accept that one might never discover whether a night at the opera is a loftier experience in the scale of human values than an afternoon spent watching football, but is this mystery so thoroughgoing that it rules out the possibility of establishing a general framework for constructing a hierarchy of practical goods? More perniciously, does acceptance of the thesis of the incommensurability of values entail the debilitating idea that even if we *can* establish some basic and uncontentious principles of right, these principles remain utterly basic and incapable of expansion, elaboration and hence application to ethical experience of any significant contextual complexity? The prospect of moral paralysis brought about by flirtations with the apparently innocuous claims of incommensurabilism should not be underestimated.

Thirdly, the antipathy to substantive ('foundationalist' or 'objective') ethics has given an impetus to proceduralism in several forms, not only Fullerian

18 Philip Selznick's important works include (with Phillipe Nonet) *Law and Society in Transition: Toward Responsive Law* (New Brunswick, NJ: University of Columbia Press), 1978; *Law Society and Industrial Justice* (New York: Russell Sage, 1969) *The Moral Commonwealth: Social Theory and the Promise of Community* (Berkeley, CA: University of California Press, 1992); 'Natural Law and Sociology' in John Cogley *Natural Law and Modern Society* (Cleveland, MD: World Publishing Co., 1966), pp. 158, 170.

proceduralism based upon the tenets of 'the inner morality of law', but in developments stemming from Habermasian social theory and critique. Most notably for legal theory, these have been given expression in Robert Alexy's elaboration of the relationship between a theory of legal argumentation and Discourse Ethics.[19] There is an extremely close relationship between, on the one hand, the Habermasian conception of Universal Pragmatics arising from the normative presuppositions unearthed in the analysis of the concept of Communicative Action, and, on the other, Fuller's analysis of the Principles of Human Association and especially the basic interests he identifies in his classic paper, 'The Forms and Limits of Adjudication'.[20] The Habermas-Fuller nexus is forged in the striking formal and substantive similarity of argument that locates the legitimacy of regulatory institutions and the validity of norms in general in the mutual desire to create institutional conditions that operate as a guarantee of the opportunity for individuals to present and defend, with a view to general acceptance, reasons for their action and choices.

For our present concerns, however, we will examine the general status of procedural morality alleged to inhere in Fuller's account of the 'inner' or 'internal' morality of law. Whilst the design of rational procedure is an essential element of the legal enterprise, we will argue, as with pragmatism, that it is not, in and of itself, a substitute for substantive value analysis, but rather, the seemingly formal imperatives of procedure hold the key to the notion of *authority* and arise necessarily and validly *because* of the existence of substantive foundations.[21] There is an unavoidable overlap between these three issues but we will attempt to deal with them as far as possible in the order we have introduced them above.

Selznick, Fuller and Pragmatism

Selznick is centrally important to our understanding of Fuller and to the ethos of the revival in Fullerian scholarship. One might say that his sociological work in general and his sociology of law in particular has been taken by many as a continuation and refinement of Fuller's project of establishing the sociology of law in the form of a critical Eunomics. We turn in this regard to the work of Sanne Taekema. In *The Concept of Ideals in Legal Theory*.[22] Taekema offers a

---

19 See Robert Alexy *The Argument From Injustice: A Reply to Legal Positivism* (op. cit.).

20 See for example, Jurgen Habermas *The Theory of Communicative Action* (Cambridge, MA: Polity, 1998) *Between Facts and Norms*; also Robert Alexy *The Argument From Injustice: A Reply to Legal Positivism* (Oxford: Clarendon, 2002); Lon L. Fuller 'The Forms and Limits of Adjudication' *Harvard Law Review* (92, 1978) 353–409.

21 See Stuart Toddington 'The Moral Truth About Discourse Theory, *Ratio Juris* (Vol. 19, No. 2, June 2006) pp. 217–230; and also, Dereyck Beyleveld and Roger Brownsword 'Principle, Proceduralism and Precaution in a Community of Rights' *Ratio Juris* (Vol. 19, No. 2, June 2006) pp. 141–169.

22 Sanne Taekema *The Concept of Ideals in Legal Theory* (The Hague: Kluwer Law International, 2003). (See also an endorsement of Selznickian method in Vibren van der Burg 'The Importance of Ideals' *The Journal of Value Inquiry* (Vol. 31, No. 1, March, 1997).

clear and not uncritical account of Selznickian method in her exposition of the importance of pragmatism in contemporary legal theory. This should allow us to see what, if anything, distinguishes Selznickian 'modified pragmatism' from an open commitment to what in our previous works, and in this present contribution, we are content to acknowledge as a substantive 'ethical rationalism'.

Selznick's work has for over thirty years had a close connection with Fuller's thinking. In 1970 in reviewing Fuller's *The Anatomy of Law* Selznick coined the term 'legal naturalism' broadly to describe Fuller's approach and his own understanding of the combination of, on the one hand, pragmatist method and on the other, its relationship to the secular and sociologically informed impulses of contemporary developments in the theory of Natural Law. The modern epistemology (or anti-epistemology) of pragmatism (although suggested in David Hume) stems, of course, from C.S. Pierce and John Dewey, and the broad thrust of the principles established by these figures remain in the modified version Taekema's detects and largely endorses in the work of Selznick. The basic principle of Pragmatism, primarily relating to the method of the natural sciences, is that a fixation with 'essentialism' and acceptance of a 'correspondence theory of truth' formerly prevented us from arriving at the insight that theory does not aim at truth, but at usefulness in problem solving. It was Dewey in particular who urged us to acknowledge the lesson for ethics and social theory here. In his view the historical explosion of progress in the technological application of the natural sciences could be attributed to the pragmatic rationale behind its experimental method. If ethical thinking would abandon its assumptions about universal natural truths and instead accept the role of a theoretically reflective aid to problem solving in the contextuality and dynamic provisionality of social relations, it too might experience progress in the manner of the natural sciences. A further step would be to integrate, rather than compartmentalize, ethical (Natural Law) thinking with the idea of inquiry in the social sciences, and it is this conception of an integrated form of sociological critique that has occupied Selznick for several decades. The core of Selznickian pragmatism is contained in four tenets that comprise a general theory of concept formation offered as distinctively 'pragmatist' as opposed to what is seen as the 'dogmatic' stance of an explicit 'foundationalism' or substantive ethical rationalism. They are those of acknowledging the methodological importance of the specific Selznickian notions of 'variability', 'normative theory', 'baseline' as opposed to 'flourishing' aspects of an enterprise (such as law or democracy), and the idea of 'weak definitions' allied to 'strong theories'. These aspects of method are integrated and given critical substance by Selznick's notion of a 'Master Ideal'. In speaking of a Master Ideal (we could say a concept or rational model) of *law* this critical device, he suggests, can bring together the most fruitful aspects of the traditions of Legal Positivism and Natural Law. These are respectively, the positivistic allegiance to certainty and the 'autonomy' of law, and the idealist concern with the primacy of justice. More generally, we might at last envisage a sociological synthesis of Natural Law's defence of universal values with Pragmatism's emphasis on context and provisionality. Let us look at the anatomy of the Selznickian method in more detail.

'Variability

In relation to empirical phenomena Selznick offers the observation that sociological concepts do not and can not 'cover' or 'correspond' uniformly to the phenomena to which they attempt to refer. There are several ways we might receive this proposition. In speaking in defence of the epistemology and method of pragmatism and against 'dogmas', Quine famously pointed out the error of assuming that the *meaning* of a proposition (its *intensional* aspect) could be equated with its *extensional or denotational* aspect. The denotational 'meaning' of a term is supposedly an empirical correspondence assumed to be achievable by reducing its elements to states of affairs in the world. The problem, however, is that meaning and denotational reference can differ. The example offered by Quine was that of attempting to refer to 'the morning star' and 'the evening star'. We are reliably informed by astronomers that these two different phrases refer to the *same* object, namely, Venus. Thus the *denotation* of both phrases, that is, the object or class of objects named by them, is exactly the same, whereas their 'meaning' or *intension*, differs in an obvious sense. But the direction of this critique is perhaps a little too abstruse for our purposes here. Quine's 'pragmatic' critique is aimed at even low level empirical propositions such as, 'Water boils at 100C'; (not the obviously contentious, qualitative judgments of social and political critique), and the core of Quine's objection is that theoretical concepts do not *refer* or *correspond* – other than in arbitrary ways – to empirical phenomena. This obstacle to truth and correspondence was and is the main impulse for the shift to developing a pragmatic understanding of epistemology. References to 'the world' – or even to logical principles – according to Quine, operate and cross-refer only in a network or web of claims constantly subject to revision in the light of problematic experience, and the predictive or explanatory *usefulness,* as opposed to *the truth,* of theoretical claims is, as noted, the key to epistemology. We shall see below, however, that a simpler and more intuitive objection to the uses of extension and correspondence in the theory of meaning is raised in explication of the four Selznickian precepts noted above. The 'variability' that interests Selznick and his expositors is found in the fidelity of *actual* institutions to their ideal or theoretical conceptualizations. This is easy enough to understand in respect of qualitative phenomena: 'democracy', for example, can, in practice, and for the sake of argument, be more or less developed; more or less deficient. We can ask of a particular system of political, social, legal and economic relations, 'To what degree is it democratic?' This presupposes in the asking, and requires in the answering, criteria for full and developed democracy prior to an empirical inquiry. It requires at least, as Selznick says, a 'master ideal' in the sense that we must fix some reference points of success or failure of the enterprise if only for the purposes of distinguishing it as *the enterprise in question* and not something else. This observation, of course, is going to spill out into issues of 'normativity' and 'weak definition' as we pursue the other tenets of method. If this notion of 'variability', therefore, is what a 'pragmatist' conception of social science advocates, then we are in full agreement, for the logical implication of it is that, scientifically speaking, we must urgently begin the task of constructing ethically defensible and non-arbitrary criteria in the form of Master Ideals of social action. Pragmatism's dispute with ethical rationalism or foundationalism, therefore, does not lie here. Rather, the point of rupture is the pragmatist claim that not only is rationalism unable to secure such criteria *a priori*, but also that it hampers theoretical progress in the attempt. The pragmatic alternative holds that some experiential encounter with, and understanding of, practical action can overcome this obstacle. It seems, therefore, that Selznickian pragmatism would have us do our conceptual groundwork on the basis of empirical information. But how are we to accomplish this data collection if, as Seznick maintains, we must proceed from the perspective of a Master Ideal? Let us move to Selznick's second and related methodological precept, 'Normative Theory'.

Normative Theory

The idea of 'normative theory' springs quite clearly from the discussion of conceptual 'variability' above. Put simply, a 'normative' theory is an explanatory account that purports to understand the nature of the phenomena it takes as its subject matter in order to make value judgments about it. This should come as no surprise for 'normative' simply means 'relating to a standard of correctness or rightness'. The standards of correctness or rightness in operation need not necessarily be standards of moral correctness or 'value-laden' criteria; we can have a normative view of welding or plumbing. But normative judgment must relate to *some* set of criteria for correctness or rightness. Where a set of phenomena is conceptualized as an aspect of social action embodying or aspiring to a set of ethical, moral or aesthetic *values* (as, from the point of view of our *critical* cognitive interests, are all social phenomena) normative theory thus makes what social theorists habitually refer to as *value judgments*. Application of the 'variability' principle, therefore, necessarily amounts to the espousal of a normative theory because it recognizes that some institutional phenomena (for example, parenthood, friendship, legality, democracy, and so on) inevitably vary in relation to the extent to which they realize, or fail to attain, the stated or implicit standards inherent in their theoretical conceptualization. This again, in our view, is perfectly unobjectionable and illustrates precisely the very meaning of the much abused word 'critical' in references to critical social or legal science.

'Baseline and 'Flourishing' Criteria

The normative criteria of which we speak above can be regarded, says Selznick, as either 'baseline' or 'flourishing'. The gist of this is intuitively obvious. Logically, at one extreme, 'baseline' denotes minimum criteria for inclusion in, as we shall discuss presently, the 'weak definition' of a conception of a social practice and thus the minimum practical conditions for scraping into the penumbral fields of the definition. At the other end of the scale, 'flourishing' refers to instantiations of ideals approaching optimal requirements and excelling in relation to the evaluative criteria supplied by the variable-normative concept. This, of course, resonates powerfully with Fuller's conception of the morality of *duty* (baseline) and the morality of *aspiration* (flourishing, excellence, virtue, *areté*) famously presented in the first chapter of *The Morality of Law.*[23]

Weak Definitions/Strong Theories

This aspect of method is, curiously, indistinguishable from explicitly and notoriously idealist and essentialist approaches to concept formation.[24] It is the idea that we must employ *weak definitions*, yet place them within the context of *strong theories*. Selznick is right to insist upon this. It is the idea that, logically, we must circumscribe a field of phenomena before we can argue about its precise nature; this is true of vegetation and of insects as much as it is true of law and democracy or culture and education, but the problem, of course, exhibits acutely contentious normative-moral and political dimensions in the critical conception of social, as opposed to natural, phenomena. The general methodological point is that prior to a scientific investigation, a field of phenomena must be identified as constituting the appropriate subject matter of investigation. This preliminary characterization, indispensable as it is, opens the opportunity for the investigator to impose severe *a priori* limitations on what is to qualify as the subject matter. In legal science, because the concept of law comes packaged with powerful associations of normative authority, legitimacy, non-optionality and thus obligation, and, of course, an implied apparatus for coercion, the problem is particularly acute. The term 'law' has plausible associations of usage and reference that allow the investigator to exploit commonsensical, popular or professional self-understandings of the phenomenon. Thus, and what provides, for Fullerians, a superb example of the problem; it might be *stipulated* that law is 'what courts do about disputes'; or alternatively, 'law is the body of rules that issue from officially recognized and codified sources', and so on. Unless we are to accept the inevitability of a vast plurality of conceptions of the phenomenon of law, and thus accept, in effect, the failure of the project of establishing a critical legal science, we must see the initial conceptualization stage as crucial. For it is at this point in the methodological proceedings that we might, on the basis of a parochial or deferential failure of the imagination, an institutional prejudice or a predilection to discount all activity not possessing the self-ascriptions of 'lawyer', 'legislator' or 'judge', rule out *a priori* a host of other phenomena vital and relevant to our understanding of law.

In saying this, of course, we bump into an uncomfortably large chunk of essentialism. We can say that one is more a 'pragmatist' than an 'essentialist' to the extent that one finds this experience in concept formation unpleasant. By this we mean that for rationalists, there is a confidence that reason can provide a solid semantic core of understanding behind language, whereas, for pragmatists, this assumption is abhorrent. Pragmatists, above all other things, hold that the

---

23 Lon L. Fuller *The Morality of Law* (New Haven, CT: Yale University Press, 1969).

24 See for example, Deryck Beyleveld and Roger Brownsword *Law as a Moral Judgment* (London: Sweet and Maxwell, 1986) Chapter 2.

practice itself constitutes the reality of a phenomenon, and that improvement in *practical effectiveness* is the rationale for critique. But *whose understanding* of the practice, *what selection* of features of the practice, and *what criteria* for improvement or effectiveness are we to accept as our *datum*? There is, of course, no need to remind the reader that *datum* means, 'that which is *given*'.

There is good reason to be troubled by this problem and not only Fuller, but Unger in *Law in Modern Society* and Beyleveld and Brownsword in *Law as a Moral Judgment*, have explained why: The history of sociology shows us that insight into to the human situation is to be found in the study of the way in which forms of normativity have developed and changed, and particularly how formal structures of regulation and channelling have grown out informal interaction. There is, therefore, a double lesson in the importance of concept formation here and a curious twist in the attraction of a 'pragmatic' approach. It is, after all, Fuller who points out that that there is at least as much to be learned from the informal demands of justice than from the official declaration of it. A concept of law admitting exclusively into its ambit, for example, only appellate decision-making would ignore entirely this vital ontological link with wider social practices. The consequences for a critical sociology of law or a sociological jurisprudence of a lack of methodological rigour in this regard are thus obvious. But so is the fact that there is much philosophical work to be done to glean what are, *essentially*, the *informal* demands of justice.

Selznick rightly says, therefore, that before an investigation into a phenomenon takes place it must be identified as such. In other words, we must know from the outset when we correctly speak of law, or famously in Selznick's work, of 'management' or of 'culture'. Not all rule-guided behaviour, for example, is law; but when is the transition made from a loose form of social organization to a legal system? *Definitions* mark the boundary of the field to which a theory is applied, but must be 'weak' in that they must not *normatively load* the phenomena to be investigated. They must, however, be 'strong' enough to illuminate and encompass a class of potentially interesting objects of research. Ironically, this first Selznickian step of 'weak definition' is what foundationalists *par excellence*, Beyleveld and Brownsword, in *Law as a Moral Judgment* refer to as settling upon an 'agreed referent'. Ironically, the weak definition Beyleveld and Brownsword adopt is Fuller's formulation of the legal enterprise as that of 'subjecting human conduct to the governance of rules' – yet the Fullerian Selznick opts for Hart's famous conception of 'the union of primary and secondary rules'. In explaining Finnis's version of the weak defininition/strong theory approach, Beyleveld and Brownsword say:[25]

> Theorists setting out to develop a concept of law, identify (in an essentially stipulative manner) the field which they are attempting to understand in their analysis. This may take the form of a declaration to the effect that 'When I talk about law I am talking about X.' If different theorists identify the same X, analysis may then proceed.

25 *Law as a Moral Judgment* (op. cit.) p. 105.

This is the 'weak definition' stage alluded to by Selznick which, in practice, say Beyleveld and Brownsword, 'is identifiable quite neutrally between many theorists' and 'certainly between Hart, Fuller, Raz and Finnis' as 'the enterprise of subjecting human conduct to the governance of rules'.[26] But this is not the end of the inquiry, inasmuch as the 'weak definition' serves as an initially identifying 'concept' of law, genuinely 'strong theory' – conceptual analysis – 'consists of the formation of a *conception* of this ... identification'.[27]

We know how important this first step is because we are by now familiar with the far reaching and, for the past fifty years, highly contentious, results held to be necessary implications of this weak definition or initial referent. The next step, however, is that of 'refining the agreed referent'. But where does this indisputably sensible approach to the logic of concept formation lead? It leads, we suggest, right back to the question addressed by Aristotle in the form of Focal and Central Case analysis; to the question addressed by Aquinas in the analysis of the content of objective basic goods in the account of practical reasonableness, and to the issue of the validity of the allegedly value-neutral Ideal Type in Weber. The question thus arises as to how Selznick proposes to refine this referent.

In 'Sociology and Natural Law', Selznick emphasizes the importance to sociological critique of a 'Master Ideal'. Taekema says:[28]

> Selznick argues that important social phenomena such as parenthood, love, scholarship, or citizenship cannot be understood unless they are seen as oriented towards a master ideal. All of these are 'phenomena in the social world whose very nature encompasses the realization of values' ... The distinguishing feature of such phenomena, called 'normative systems' ... is that they are governed by a *master ideal.* Friendship, for instance is an intricate mix of feeling, behaviour, thought and norms that is held together by a commitment to the ideal of friendship. This means that one can never fully understand what friendship is, unless one [understands] ... the ideal ... at which this normative system is aimed.

This is undoubtedly correct, although there is nothing new in announcing it. Aristotle enunciated this view in his analysis of this very problem (the concept of friendship), Aquinas articulated it, and John Finnis re-presented it in *Natural Law and Natural Rights*. Weber, of course, endorsed it and held that the Master Ideal or the 'Ideal Type' was indispensable to a sociological *verstehen* (that is, for the purpose of satisfying our cognitive interests in social phenomena). The lack of novelty is, of course, of no consequence to Selznickian pragmatists or Ethical Rationalists. The interesting and important point is whether this indispensable methodological tool can be constructed *without recourse to moral judgment.* If pragmatism is in any serviceable sense to be regarded as a methodological alternative to the apparently unattractive attribute of the 'foundationalism' of ethical rationalism, then it must show us how this is to be done.

---

26 Ibid.

27 Ibid. Our emphasis.

28 Sanne Taekema *The Concept of Ideals in Legal Theory* (op. cit.) p. 107.

To answer the question, then, let us for a moment reflect on what might be entailed by the claim that a parent or a police officer or a judge or a friend or a government minister might fail to attain or fully realize the requisite normative standards inherent in the 'Master Ideal' of say, parenthood, law, friendship, or democracy. Might a parent fail to be a parent by failing to chastise a child sufficiently? Might a parent fail to be a parent by resorting to corporal punishment before considering other means of correction; or failing to spend enough time playing or reading with a child? Should a person reveal secrets confided by a third party acquaintance to a close friend if those secrets affected the friend adversely? Should a police officer prioritize the value of diversity of race, culture and religion and structure their day to day discretionary powers accordingly, making allowances for minorities; or should an officer strive to treat infractions without regard to these matters? We could go on in this vein, but we pose these questions to ask first whether these and other practical failures affect *the definitional status* of the objects in question (parent/friend/police officer and so on), and if so, secondly, whether or not these 'failures' are failures of *duty* to one or another person or to a community of persons? If they are, do these duties correlate to rights? If so, do these duties and rights exist in a scale of hierarchical importance? If the scale of importance is to be action-guiding, are priorities to be decided in relation to the *content* of the duty or to the *type* of relationship in question (implying a hierarchy of types of relationship), or in relation to the status or subjective concerns of the actors involved in the relationship? These are very interesting moral questions. What would be the 'pragmatic' response?

The point is that, in constructing the 'Master Ideal' for the purposes of 'normative theory' alert to the 'variability' of phenomena we can now illustrate the importance of the question of whether or not we must first consider and account for a possible set of rights/duties relationships between individuals in general, and between individuals, groups and power holders located in particular configurations of association? The answer, of course, is 'yes': notions of rights and duties are obviously presupposed by notions of 'normative theory' and by notions of a 'Master Ideal' that purport to build on 'weak' or provisional definitions of practical phenomena. The Master Ideal suggests that it is possible to identify basic standards or failings thereof in persons or institutions in respect of obligations to respect and safeguard the interests of others. The acknowledgment of the existence of *other-regarding* as opposed to *self-regarding* or *prudential* interests is the essential and defining focus of *moral* reason; Morality *can* be defined in other ways, but only defectively and incompletely so. The Master Ideal, therefore, presupposes not just the existence of, but, insofar as it functions normatively, the objectively rational defensibility of, moral rights and duties. It is at this point that we must say something about how a Master Ideal or ideal type is to be constructed for the purpose of critical investigation. This overlaps unavoidably with our discussion and analysis of the issues of incommensurability and of proceduralism treated more fully below, but at this juncture it is vital that we consider the implications of the discussion thus far for the development and articulation – towards the point of empirical operationalization – of 'Master Ideals' or 'ideal-typical' modelling.[29]

Why Does Pragmatism Reject 'Foundationalism'?

If the acceptance of a matrix of morally indispensable norms and principles is to be received as dogmatically *un*pragmatic in the Selznickian scheme of things, then this is not, it seems because of the suggestion that this fixed matrix should serve as a frame for understanding social enterprises or large institutional forms and networks. Accepting such a matrix as a starting point for social inquiry is neither more nor less than what Selznick advocates in defence of his notion of the Master Ideal. Thus the objection to moral foundationalism must lie elsewhere. Let us recall that a recurrent observation is that a 'pragmatist' (as opposed to a 'dogmatic') acknowledgment of the unavoidably normative aspects of critique is to be distinguished and preferred in that it takes the form of a *contextual* analysis of the problematic aspects of the practices under investigation. Sanne Taekema says:[30]

> The pragmatist warning not to forget that things happen in experience, with specific conditions and consequences, has been taken to heart: Selznick continually reminds us of the limits and conditions for the realization of values. So although a normative theory strongly evaluates – it assesses empirical situations according to a theory – it does this by examining both the potential for and the obstacles to value realization.

But does one need to be a pragmatist in general or a Selznickian in particular to acknowledge the obvious sense of this pronouncement? It is difficult to imagine a philosophical position that could frame an objection to it.

The core message of pragmatism tells us that as theorists we must abandon the notion of absolute truth and of 'essences' in favour of flexible problem-solving usefulness; but does this also mean that pragmatists must make an irrational commitment to a principle of anti-foundationalism? For it is Selznick who informs us of the requirements of a Master Ideal – a device, let us reiterate, that is to serve as the basis of a contextual and pragmatically sensitive critique of institutions and normative systems. What we need to know, and what foundationless pragmatism cannot and thus will not tell us, is *which* or *whose* understandings

29 If, as Gewirthian social theorists and Legal Idealists we are to be distinguished from Selznickian theorists as dogmatically unpragmatic in our approach, it is not, it seems, because we maintain that a Master Ideal of a social enterprise or of large scale institutional forms must begin from an understanding of the status of basic social relations. Gewirthians such as Beyleveld and Brownsword construct ideal types of these relations in terms of the practical reasonableness of the PGC (Principle of Generic Consistency). It is important in the present discussion to note that because the moral content of the PGC and thus of the ideal-typical construct in question can be gleaned and demonstrated *conceptually*, this does *not* mean that they have no *contextual* basis or application in the social and biological aspects of human existence.

30 Sanne Taekema *The Concept of Ideals in Legal Theory* (op. cit.) p. 94.

of the nature and scope of values are we taking as the *substantive* components of the Master Ideals and thus of individual and social goals deemed worthy of pursuit. If the Master Ideals of structurally central social practices are merely to be assumed vaguely and commonsensically, or if they are to be set at the lowest common denominations of a selection of *vox pops*, then one can perhaps see the connection between espousing pragmatic contexualism and denouncing moral foundationalism. This approach to settling the methodological orientation would offer 'the pragmatist' the opportunity to offer guidance on 'the realization of values' on an instrumental or technical model of practical rationality in its most basic and uncritical form. But if the values or ideals posited were the product of an *a priori* analysis of ethical reason specifying the grounds and scope not only of an individual's or group's prudential interests in security and well-being, but in *other-regarding duties*, then these components of the 'variable' and 'normative' theoretical conception of the institution in question (say, law or democracy) would necessarily appear as products of a form of ethical idealism. The *contextual* sensitivity of the analysis would not rescue 'pragmatism' in general from banality. More significantly for the pragmatist intent on methodological *Apartheid*, it would not distinguish pragmatism from ethical foundationalism.

Talk of *context* does not explain the methodological distinctiveness of pragmatism, for it is obvious that any ethical perspective is absurd if it is not sensitive to the concrete conditions applicable to the employment of principles of practical reason. In fact, this sensitivity to context is one simple example of the good sense of the Kantian maxim that 'ought implies can'. The pragmatist cannot, as we have seen, have a normatively operational Master Ideal without presupposing and specifying objectively defensible rights; in conceding this, the pragmatist might want to say, however, that the notion of values (relating, of course, to the realization and respect for rights) implicated in the master ideal are taken as merely contextually and provisionally valid, whereas the ethical foundationalist holds to the universal and eternal status of their basic principles of value. Two things can be said about this.

First, and yet again unavoidably pre-empting later discussion, Selznickian pragmatism, when pushed, does admit to locating value-rationality in a functionalist mixture of traditional Natural Law conceptions of human nature and human biology. Quite apart from what might be said about the specific drawbacks of this point of departure, let us concede that *if* the rationality of values can be grounded validly in certain aspects of human nature and certain aspects of biology, and if the continuing validity of the application of the analysis is held to be contextually and provisionally dependent upon the continuing status of these aspects of human nature and biology, then we can acknowledge that the theory of value in question is indeed 'pragmatic' in this contextual and provisional sense. But the same can be said about Gewirthian ethical foundationalism in that the analysis of *agent* rights depends upon the continuing validity of the mental and physical characterization of the agent specified, for example, as a being that voluntarily employs means to ends. It would be invidious for the Selznickian to complain that the Gewirthian grounds are, 'conceptually' rather than 'pragmatically' derived and thus immune from the dynamic and ever changing flux of experience.

And this *must* be the point here: pragmatism wants to assert its superiority over rationalism by virtue of its empirical and experiential bases of conception formation as opposed to rationalism's static or 'dogmatic' conceptualism. But neither Selznick nor anyone else can enlist the unmediated 'facts' of human nature and biology in their aid. Hume's dictum that one cannot derive an 'ought from (at least an empirical) is' is still a sound observation. Could we say that Selznick, unavoidably, therefore, must make do with not only selective and empirically patchy, but *normative* conceptions of human nature and biology.[31] Accepting this charge might be the pragmatist's least damaging option.

For, secondly, if, as staunch pragmatists, we were to maintain an antipathy to foundationalism, would we want to criticize the ethical rationalism of Gewirth for selecting *enduring* aspects of human experience and existence as the basis of theory as opposed to *ephemeral* ones? If so, this would merely suggest that pragmatism, absurdly, and quite unrelated to any epistemological concerns, would seek to make a virtue of the uncertainty and provisionality of analysis. The truth, ironically, however, is that Selznick believes that human nature and biology *are* enduring aspects of the human condition.[32]

Part 2: Pragmatism and the 'Incommensurability of Values'

Pragmatists do not dispute that law ought be understood normatively, nor that there exists a conceptual relationship between law and morality. Some pragmatists, like Selznick and Taekema endorse the claim that this conceptual relationship is a necessary one in the sense that there can be no morally neutral concept of law. But what all pragmatists do oppose is the idea that the concept of law should be founded on what are held to be objective moral principles. We have discussed the pragmatist antipathy to foundationalism above in the context of the necessity of establishing a rights-based conception of the notion of a Master Ideal. Raising the issue of rights at that point was important in the sense that it forced the issue of the pragmatist understanding of the basis of the value rationality required to construct the Master Ideal and it is important here in our understanding of the role of holding to the 'incommensurability of values' in pragmatist theorizing.

It is interesting to note that some writers are more at ease talking about the incommensurability of *values* than they are about asserting the incommensurabilty of rights. In talking about the incommensurability of values, as we hinted at above and discuss below, one must be clear about the plane of analysis on which discussion takes place. It is an error to assume that we can talk coherently yet in an entirely undifferentiated way about 'values' in terms of the incommensurability of divergent or competing 'conceptions of the Good'. Some *values,* that is, some aspects of human choosing and judgment that invest importance or worth or

31 See Philip Selznick 'Sociology and Natural Law', 6 *Natural Law Forum* 84.1963, at p. 101.

32 See Philip Selznick *The Moral Commonwealth: Social Theory and the Promise of Community* (Berkeley, CA: University of California Press, 1992) p. 119.

desirability in the achievement of various ends, relate to subsistence and the very possibility of viable inter-personal relations; some to the comparative attributes of varieties of Belgian chocolate. This being said, it is the greatest irony to have to point out that the foundational premises of ethical rationalism – not 'pragmatism' – proceed from the ultimately *practical* insight that there are *goods* that are indispensable to one's very existence as a being capable of practical activity *per se*, and that *pragmatically* one has no option but to *value* and *secure* these goods above all others or *renounce* one's practical nature.

This is not a moral or an ethical claim and thus, in the context of this discussion, not a 'value-laden' or contentious assertion. It is one concerning the purely technical or instrumental aspects of the simplest conception of prudence on the part of a being that purports consciously to employ, and prospectively to continue to employ, means to various ends selected for whatever reason. This kind of being, an agent, logically speaking can but conceive of the realm of the Good as *differentiated*: broadly, this differentiation takes place first between those goods that are indispensable to his or her continuation as a practical being, and, this continuation being secured, those that appear as furthering the scope of agency in other ways optionally desirable. The realm of *the objectively indispensable*, however, in terms of fundamental subsistence as *a practical being* – an agent, or, if we wish to elevate the debate to the context of modern political philosophy in terms of the fundamental requirements of a *citizen*, is indeed the source of our understanding of *basic right*, but as we will explain, this conception of the Good is not limited to the notion of 'basic right', but capable of extremely complex substantive extrapolation. These observations form the fundamental premisses in a Gewirthian understanding of a *foundational* theory of rights and duties Such an understanding rejects the idea of incommensurabilism at this level of analysis, but is it not thoroughly pragmatic, nevertheless? A Master Ideal of any institution or social practice that claims to have normative significance must surely start here. Thus to what aspect of these observations would a pragmatist of any hue object? And if there are no objections, what is supposed to be *more* pragmatic about pragmatism and what is the significance of the thesis of 'the incommensurability of values' to it?

Incommensurability and Natural Law?

There are a number of variants of the thesis of incommensurabilism, and in *Law In Its Own Right* we dealt with one jurisprudentially influential source of it, namely, that proposed by John Finnis in several of his important works. It will be useful to explain his position again here and reiterate our objections to it because the basic themes of the incommensurabilism Finnis proposes relate closely to the 'pragmatist' versions lately discussed. This discussion also presents an opportunity to clarify, in opposition to the mysteries of Aquinas, precisely what we mean by 'basic goods' and their relationship to the accumulating debris of allusions to 'basic' interests, 'basic rights', values, norms and principles.

In *Natural Law and Natural Rights* Finnis re-works Aquinas's view that sees moral reason inherent in the very idea of practical reason. In other words, one who can think in a *practically* reasonable fashion must acknowledge the necessary connection between means-ends reasoning and moral reasoning. This argument is established by an appeal to 'self evidence' presenting the idea of practical reasonableness as an integrated and indivisible complex of 'Basic Goods'. These goods are listed as life, knowledge, aesthetic experience, sociability (friendship), religion, practical reasonableness (itself?), religion and play. A 'practically reasonable' person must presuppose these Basic Goods in all their reasoning. Aquinas held that it is not reasonable in the precise sense of the word to select, exclude or prioritize among these goods for, according to Aquinas and Finnis, all these goods are *equally basic, equally important*. They must be taken as a whole for *together* they embody practical reason and practical reasonableness.[33] The Finnisian argument for Natural Law as opposed to Legal Positivism is, then, that law is a necessary means to our achieving a synthesis of the Good through practical striving, and thus law, and the values inherent in practical reason are conceptually or necessarily connected. In other words, it would not be possible to formulate a *practically reasonable* conception of law without incorporating *essentially* the idea that law's ultimate and general end or goal is the realization of the Basic Goods.

More recently, however, the Finnisian account of Natural Law has become almost indistinguishable from a form of Legal Positivism. Finnis has suggested that although the idea that moral reason can be seen as a 'natural' feature of practical reason, the application of morality as legal authority is incoherent and impractical in that we must acknowledge the fact of 'incommensurability of values'.[34] For an expositor and a proponent of Aquinas this is not an unexpected discovery for we have seen that Aquinas believed that 'The practically reasonable life is a pursuit of the good, but the good takes many forms and no one form can be regarded as better or more worthwhile than any other'.[35] This even-handedness might often prove to be a convenience, but it cannot fail to cause logical problems.

The Basic Goods listed above appear commonsensically important to us all; but is there not an equally commonsensical 'hierarchy' (in a prudential-technical sense) amongst them. For example, 'life' is a basic good, but so is 'sociability' 'play' and 'religion'; yet we are told to receive all of them as *equally* valuable and what is logically more taxing, all as equally *fundamental*. For example, there is no doubt (as its greatest devotees have shown) that one can practise religion whilst remaining relatively if not entirely unsociable, yet it is difficult to see how it would be possible to do this if one were bereft of *life*. Can we not say then, that some of the Basic Goods are more basic than others? And further, would it be unreasonable to suggest that there is a fairly obvious *arbitrariness* in the

33 For a more comprehensive analysis see Stuart Toddington R*ationality, Social Action and Moral Judgment* (Edinburgh: Edinburgh University Press, 1993) Chapter 6.

34 See 'Natural Law and Legal Reasoning' in R.P. George, *Natural Law Theory*. Finnis's *Natural Law and Natural Rights* (Oxford: Clarendon, 1981) was pregnant with the idea of incommensurability – see Chapter IV – but it was never articulated as such.

35 John Finnis *Natural Law and Natural Rights* (op. cit.) p. 92.

selection of what are to count as Basic Goods? If we examine the practical scope of sociability, aesthetic experience, and religion, there seems to be no room at the table of practical reason for the recluse, the Epicurean, or the atheist. But we, along with the unsociable, the irreligious and perhaps the less playful members of society, would feel entitled to take issue with aspects of the Finnisian account of 'equally fundamental' 'Basic Goods' without being categorized as *practically un*reasonable *tout court*. In fact our view is that there is so much illogically in Aquinas's presentation of the Basic Goods, and consequently in Finnis's flawless repetition of it, that it cannot fail to undermine itself as a basis for an account of incommensurability and consequently, as we shall see, of legal authority. Such are the limits of a reliance on the appeal to 'self-evidence'. But first, let us re-establish a workable basis for the use of some basic normative terminology and offer some elaboration on the strategy we will employ in opposition to it.

Goods, Rights, Values and Principles

Gewirth's argument to the Principle of Generic Consistency (PGC) shows us that there are indeed certain basic or generic goods that all agents must value as conditions of their prospective agency and that these are goods that agents must value whatever else they might value. In this straightforward sense they are simultaneously *pragmatic* – in that they are necessary for action – and *categorical* in the sense that they are to be valued whatever purposes an agent might have in mind. This latter observation is an instrumental observation on *prudential* requirements, not a moral judgment. The contentious judgment that appears at stage 2 consists in showing that an agent must *claim rights* to the 'generic' goods of 'freedom and well-being' indispensable to the exercise of prospective agency, *and acknowledge the validity of similar claims in all other agents*. In other words, an agent, to be practically reasonable, must acknowledge the indispensable value of *the wherewithal* to act purposively, this wherewithal being termed in Gewirth's philosophy as we noted earlier, the Generic Features of Action or (GF) and denoting the most general category of objects and capacities required for feasible agency.

When something is conceived as an end worthy of pursuit by a practical being, that is, when it becomes an end in view, it appears as a phenomenon of *value*. Something deemed worthy of pursuit in this way is a good. The goods (objects and capacities) constituting agent 'freedom and well being' must be valued whatever else an agent values and thus might reasonably be referred to as *basic goods.* The most general formulations of *entitlements* correlate to them, derived *a priori*, constitute a notion of *natural rights*, and because of their generic nature, they are thus *basic natural rights.* When positively endorsed they might be referred to as *basic positive rights.* Nothing important turns on the nomenclature, but the term 'generic' seems more precise in relation to their derivation than 'basic', and references to 'generic' goods and 'generic' rights help us to avoid confusing these ideas with Aquinian/Finnisian accounts of 'Basic Goods' and 'basic rights'.

We suggested above (and have argued elsewhere)[36] that the Aquinian conception of 'basic goods' is not conceptually or necessarily 'intrinsic' to practical reason in that it is not the case that they create contradiction if not espoused (ideally) by agents in exercise of their practical capacities. But notwithstanding this set of issues, and even if all seven *were* necessary or intrinsic features of practical reason in the sense we would demand, let us recall that Aquinas and Finnis say that *all* the Basic Goods are 'equally fundamental'. Finnis concludes that they are thus 'incommensurable'. This implies results like: 'life is as fundamental as play', and that, in being 'practically reasonable', 'practical reasonableness' is equally as important as a religious attitude to life; or as the valuing of play; or *vice versa*, or in whatever permutation of Aquinian 'Basic Goods' one can imagine. These simple derivations from the premises of Aquinian conceptions of basic goods appear not merely arbitrary and false, but difficult to render intelligibly.

In Gewirth, the basic or generic goods are those aspects of freedom and well-being required for a realistic and feasible prospect of present and future purposive activity: subsistence, a viable minimum of physical and cerebral freedom and security, access to basic information and so on. These goods are naturally hierarchical in that they manifest themselves as 'additive', 'non-subtractive' or 'maintenance' goods. In this sense, water and food to a starving agent is more important in terms of maintaining or not reducing its present capacities for purposive activity than securing broadband access or yoga classes might be to the 'additive' dimensions of it. Thus we can say that the basic or generic *goods* are those objects, capacities or conditions comprising the freedom and well-being necessary for agency; basic or generic *rights* are natural or rationally derivable entitlements to these goods; basic or generic *interests* thus refer to the range of actions, decisions, and social relations tending to maintain or improve the conditions under which generic goods and rights to them are as far as possible guaranteed and enhanced.

Norms are action-guiding precepts, when legitimate, they arise from an acknowledgment of the nature and value of *basic goods, rights and interests* and of the proper conduct conducive to their general maintenance and enhancement. *Norms* may be more or less general, more or less specific, thus a useful distinction legally and customarily is that between *Principles* and *Rules*, yet this quantitative distinction has qualitative implications. A *principle* is a general norm requiring that, as far as is contextually possible, some more or less fundamental aspect of agents' *interests* be served *optimally*. Theoretically speaking, and from a Gewirthian point of view, when principles clash or appear to clash, they point to tensions between provision or protection of basic rights to basic goods. *Principles* derived from this understanding of rights and goods are hierarchicalised as non-subtractive, maintenance and additive dimensions of the generic features of action and weighed and balanced in context to provide an optimization of the normative content of the principle applied vis-à-vis the agent's interests. *Rules*

---

36 See Stuart Toddington *Rationality, Social Action and Moral Judgment* (op. cit.) Chapter 6; also *Law in Its Own Right* (op. cit.) pp. 135ff.

guide action in specific and concrete contexts against this background of more general principle.

Having said this, and in the hope that some progress has been made, we can proceed by noting that 'incommensurability' suggests an undifferentiated and intransitive quality to that which is held to be 'Good'. To deny, as we do, that incommensurability applies at fundamental levels of the analysis of action and agency should not be taken to mean that we deny also that incommensurability (or the appearance of it) does not exist, perhaps intractably, at more complex, moral and aesthetic-experiential levels of human action and valuing. Our point is that one can accept the existence of incommensurability at certain levels of complexity without being committed to an inversion of the logic of the situation. But it should not be assumed that our claim is that we avoid incommensurability only at 'basic' levels of theorizing the Good. Rather, the hierarchy of basic or generic goods that can be demonstrated through analysis of the necessary presuppositions of purposive action serve as a point of departure to energize and guide practical judgment over a wide and complex range of moral contention; no sensible person would, however, want to assert the rational tractability of the entirety of it. We might illustrate this presently with some procedural and substantive examples of applied Gewirthian analysis to what are widely regarded as difficult areas of moral and legal contention. But for the moment let us pursue the issue of incommensurability not at its source, but as an accepted assumption, and examine how it damages our understanding of the concept of legal *authority*.

Utilizing the ethical rationalism of Gewirth to structure our version of Legal Idealism, we take as central the claim that *prudential* reason necessarily implies *moral* reason. In short, one who, as a prospective, purposive agent understands the logical force of 'prudential duties' in pursuit of one's self-interest must also acknowledge the dialectical necessity of *other-regarding* duties. This claim runs counter to much recent influential theory in that it does not characterize morality as a form of enhanced prudence, where looking after the interest of others can be shown to be contingently beneficial to one's own interest. Gewirth shows that moral reason stands quite independently of one's contingent prudential requirements. John Finnis appears to endorse this substantive account of moral reason in his vehement criticisms of the shortcomings of contemporary analysis. He speaks of the grave deficiencies of 'emaciated' conceptions of practical reason found in 'Game Theory, 'Social Choice Theory', Benthamite Utilitarianism and Rawls's idea of the Original Position.[37] True to Aquinas, Finnis makes the point that we, on other grounds, are anxious to endorse, namely, that practical reason takes us beyond prudence conceived as mere self-interest and into the communal sphere of morality. But after this progress, Finnis finds it necessary to make centrally significant the claim that practical reason starts – and ends – in a complex matrix of moral goods in which no hierarchy of value is to be found. This, of course, is what he means by the incommensurability of values and the

37 See John Finnis 'The Authority of Law in the Predicament of Contemporary Social Theory' in *Journal of Law, Ethics and Public Policy* (Vol. 1, 1984) pp. 123–127.

alleged 'intransitivity' of Goods. This, we must note, is the precise co-ordinate at which Selznickian Pragmatism meets Finnisian Natural Law Theory.

Incommensurability and Natural Law reasoning are held to be mutually consistent because, according to Finnis, the authority of law appears as a universally valid precept of practical reason in that it is required to establish the conditions under which the complex and multi-dimensional idea of the Good might be pursued. But, says Finnis, this 'authority' 'cannot claim a moral omniscience to judge and rank the many and various forms this pursuit might take'.[38] On the other hand, according to Finnis, this authority *can* claim almost total *legal* omniscience. This is because the requirements of practical reason are so vague, that in almost every legal case, the *determinatio* (that is, the concrete rendering in particular circumstances of the requirements of practical reason – what Finnis, with Aquinas, calls *implementations* of general directives) takes the form of 'more or less free authoritative choice'[39] This looks very much like a positivistic conception of law, but Finnis pulls back at the last moment by adding that the *determinatio* although free, is:[40]

> ... not only linked with the basic principles by intelligible relationship to goals (such as traffic safety ...) which are directly related to basic human goods, but also is controlled by wide-ranging formal and other structuring principles (in both first and second-order form) which themselves are derived from the basic principles by the first mode of derivation [*conclusions* from general principles].

This is not crystal clear, but we are at least provided with the idea that the requirements of practical reasonableness and the Basic Goods, although inadequate to the task of determining every detail of the law, can provide a framework for legal reasoning. This much seems to be supported by what he says in the following paragraph:[41]

> ... the need for authority is the luxuriant variety of appropriate but competing choices of 'means' to 'end'. Now we can see how this range of choices is both increased *and* controlled by the complex interacting 'principles of law'. True, the reasoning of those in authority frequently ends without identifying any uniquely reasonable decision; so the rulers must choose and their choice (*determinatio*) determines what thereafter is uniquely just for those subject to their authority. But having stressed that it is thus authority, not simply reasoning, that settles most practical reasons in the life of a community, I now must stress the necessary rider. To be, itself, authoritative in the eyes of a reasonable man, a *determinatio* must be consistent with the basic requirements of practical reasonableness ...

He then adds:[42]

38 Ibid.

39 John Finnis *Natural Law and Natural Rights* (op. cit.) p. 289.

40 Ibid.

41 Ibid. p. 289.

42 Ibid. pp. 289–290.

> … though it need not necessarily or even usually be the *determinatio* he would himself have made had he had the opportunity; it need not even be one he regards as 'sensible'.

This dilutes the 'necessary rider' quite considerably. For if even a *reasonable* person cannot dispute the reasoning applied by the legal authorities, then what is left of the insistence that the decision should be 'consistent with the basic requirements of practical reasonableness'? The problem, it seems, is that Finnis's theory of morality (the account of Basic Goods and the idea of practical reasonableness) is developed as a now detached and ineffectual backdrop to the blunt theory of authority. The entire methodological exercise and aspiration of the Natural Law impulse to place moral rationality at the heart of the concept of legal authority and obligation is apparently abandoned. The rigours of 'focal' or 'central case' analysis advocated by Finnis, whereby the Selznickian 'weak definition' or the Beyleveldian and Brownswordian 'agreed referent' of law is through a moral epistemology conceptually developed and differentiated from arbitrary or despotic authority – however benign – is thus effectively rendered meaningless.[43] It might be worth repeating Finnis's own main methodological point in *Natural Law and Natural Rights*:[44]

> Among those who, from a practical viewpoint, treat law as an aspect of practical reasonableness, there will be some whose views about what practical reasonableness actually requires in this domain are, in detail, more reasonable than others. Thus the central case viewpoint itself is the viewpoint of those who not only appeal to practical reasonableness but also *are* practically reasonable.

However, Finnis' own analysis of the relationship between law and practical reasonableness noted above puts almost all the emphasis on *authority* as the proper source of law. This, as we have seen, arises from his reliance on a theory of morality derived from the Aquinian account of Basic Goods and Practical Reasonableness that, apparently by definition, is incapable of being operationalized in concrete contexts of regulation.

But are we, as proponents of a rival theory of practical reasonableness, being too demanding here? What, after all, are pragmatists, Natural Lawyers, Legal Positivists or 'Ethical Foundationalists' and Legal Idealists supposed to be in *significant* disagreement about? Can we not all accept first that it is the case that practical reason *eventually* 'ends in a complex matrix of moral goods in which no hierarchy of value is to be found' and that, obviously, law cannot thus 'claim a moral omniscience to judge and rank the immense complexity of the good'; and yet, secondly, that *surely* it is the case that law is 'the only promise of providing a method of relating burdens to benefit among the complexity of human relations'? It does not seem reasonable to dispute these matters; but the problem is that Finnis's matrix of practical rationality leads us to the contention that it is *the*

43 See John Finnis *Natural Law and Natural Rights* (op. cit.) Chapter 1.

44 Ibid. p. 15.

incommensurabilty of values that forms the *very basis of the justification for legal authority.* This way of thinking is so defective, yet so very nearly captures the truth, that we must pause and rewind the sequence of reasoning.

For Finnis, the idea of practical reason begins with instrumentality and prudence. The 'self evident' multi-dimensionality of the notion of practical reasonableness leads us beyond 'emaciated' conceptions of self-interest to the notion of the Good. The Good, for Finnis, embraces not just the aesthetic and spiritual dimensions of our experience of valuing and choosing, but notions of *equality* of persons ('practical reasonableness' involves 'no arbitrary preference amongst persons'[45] and thus mutually *other-regarding* duties. Let us also remember that such duties are properly called *moral* duties. Conditions establishing the practically feasible pursuit of the Good, according to Finnis, demonstrate the necessity of the institutionalization of *authoritative* practical reasoning in the form of law. We, as Gewirthians, can quite happily agree with this much. But, says Finnis, apart from 'the *most basic categories* of moral right'[46] the Good is incommensurable in regard to the direction we then must take.

We are thus left with an idea of authority which, says Finnis, creates a general obligation to obey the law *because law is a necessary means* to the pursuit of (what we now know according to Finnis) is a realm of incommensurable goods.[47] But we were also told earlier that this 'authority' '*... cannot claim a moral omniscience to judge and rank the many and various forms this pursuit might take*'. We must infer then, that law's authority relates only to '*the most basic categories of moral right*'[48] Thus we have the very convenient duality of, on the one hand, 'basic moral right' which is *not*, according to Finnis, affected by the curse of incommensurabilism, and on the other, 'the many and various forms' of valuing that, for the sake of legal analysis, are beyond ranking. But even if this rough and ready division into moral sheeps and goats is accepted, what criterion is it that turns some goods into 'basic moral rights', yet renders others as matters of incommensurable preference?

Finnis wants us to accept the idea that there exist 'basic rights' yet that these rights are confined to obvious and 'basic' moral situations beyond which incommensurability reigns. The dominion of incommensurability requires for its resolution the idea of 'authority'. This suggests a picture of practical reason and practical experience that can be rendered by visualizing some sort of scale of complexity of principle and application. Let us imagine a metre long bar with gradations in millimetres and centimetres from 0 to 100. The Aquinian, Finnisian and generally pragmatist/incommensurabilist view seems to be that practical reason allows us insight into the basic components of the good, say from 0 to 1cm, but the comparatively vast remainder of the scale, from 1–100cm is of an intractable, incommensurable complexity immune to the application of basic principles.

45 Ibid. p. 17.

46 See John Finnis 'The Truth in Legal Positivism' and George's reiteration of this point in R.P. George (ed.) *The Autonomy of Law* (Oxford: Clarendon Press, 1996).

47 Ibid. p. 137.

48 Ibid.

Persisting with this image we, in response, would say that we have the same idea that there are basic (generic) goods, rights, interests and general principles occupying the first few gradations on the scale of moral experience – the argument to the PGC occupies this relatively small 0 to 1cm space – but that the *implications* of the discovery of the basic content of morality can become the focus of reflection and conceptual elaboration with genuine practical significance leading to the secure and principled occupation of –at least – a few more centimetres of the scale. The 'first few centimetres' progress would be made by drawing out the implications of the 'basic' or generic goods and rights to them to provide some principles of social organization related to the pursuit of individual and collective interests. If this could lead us to an insight into the fundamental principles of organization in law in civil society, we might, as many have suggested, from Hobbes, Locke, Rousseau and up to and including Finnis, establish theoretical models of optimum forms of association conducive to the instituitionalization of norms conducive to yet further moral progress. But we want to characterize this as a *continuum of practical reason*, not as the incommensurabilists insist, a jump from foundational basic right into a void of value-preferences regulated by 'authority', where 'authority' is understood as 'what is needed to settle disputes arising from preferences between incommensurable values'.

What we shall discuss in more detail in later chapters is that *the continuum of practical reason* opens up before us when we realize that the discovery of the intrinsic rationality of basic or generic goods and rights (whether, for the sake of argument, Aquinian ones, Kantian, Lockean or Gerwirthian equivalents) imply, in the context of human association, acknowledgment of the problem of *unilateral* interpretations of their import. This, after all, is what Finnis argues in explaining the role of *determinatio*. This leads to a recognition of the need for *omnilateral* arrangements, and this is evident prior to the discussion of any *particular* issue of application. That this brings us to matters of the design of *rational procedures* (that is, PGC-compatible procedures)[49] is not the proof of incommensurabilism, but it is, in the elaboration of what is immanent in moral reason, further *substantive* (even in relation to procedure), if modest, progress along the metre-bar of rationality applied to our moral experience.

The fact that the indirect application of fundamental principle in increasingly *complex circumstances* – relating both to the specific, substantive nature of a moral problem at hand (for example, the use of nano-technological devices of communication and surveillance or powerful bio-technological techniques in reproduction), and to the dynamics of societal relations (for example, multicultural intensity in post-industrial nation states) poses difficult problems of analysis, but it does not demonstrate the validity of the doctrine of incommensurabilism, nor does it establish the *legitimacy of authority*. It does, of course, point to the rational *indispensability* of the latter, but the *need* to produce an authoritative solution to a moral problem is not in itself an *authoritative* solution to that moral problem.

---

49 See, importantly, Deryck Beyleveld and Roger Brownsword 'Principle, Proceduralism, and Precaution in a Community of Rights' *Ratio Juris* (Vol. 19, No. 2, June 2006) pp. 141–169.

Rather we are reminded of the fact that moral reasoning – from generic goods to the more specific prescriptive and action guiding norms of practical reason in complex association – mandates us to strive to (a) overcome the interpretative problems associated with the indirect application of principle (*determinatio*) and (b) given our predicament as social beings, to consider a solution to the regulatory and co-ordinatory problems of the conflictual potentials of unilateral affirmations of basic right. This latter, if achievable at all, cannot be achieved in human society without authoritative institutions and force. The problems of understanding the implications of moral reason seen from the perspective of authoritative institutions geared to *enforcement* constitute, as Beyleveld and Brownsword say, the essential theoretical subject matter of legal science and thus, in the theoretical apprehension of the relevant range of phenomena, a concept of law as 'morally legitimate power'. But again, let us repeat, without much qualification the *need* for authoritative institutions does not of itself *legitimate* institutions claiming authority, nor, if we are to assert that values beyond the most basic are essentially incommensurable, does it give us an indication of its content. Finnis does not tell us where basic rights end and where complex incommensurable ones begin, and if he did, then he could no longer tell us that the Basic Goods are all equally fundamental.

Finnis states the general problem very clearly:[50]

> Someone reflecting on the fact of human freedom in moral choosing, or on the basic values of authenticity and freedom in practical reasonableness, may be moved to ask how any man can have authority to require one to choose what one would not otherwise have chosen. Orders and rules may weigh with me because of accompanying threats, or because of my uncritical conformism or careerism. But can they have for me the authority of a fully critical conclusion of authentic practical reason?

This is an urgent question, and in *Law In Its Own Right* we suggested that Finnis's own analysis of the relationship between Practical Reason and Authority did not provide a satisfactory answer to it. In these passages we noted that the rationale for law, or what we referred to there as 'an autonomous normativity' rested, as Finnis has always maintained, on the idea that its authority is seen as a *necessary means* to the pursuit of the Good. 'The Good' is merely shorthand for what 'authentic practical reason' mandates us (i.e., compels us rationally) as practical beings to do. But we also observed that this impeccable formulation did not rest easily with the incommensurabilist claim that the vast majority of the regulatory uses of authority could claim no rational basis in relation to decisions involving judgments of value. We suggested that the more plausible assumption was to the contrary, that although the general notion of authority is born of the demonstration of the existence of basic goods, it can and must appeal to a derivable hierarchy of goods that provides a reliable and transparent, if not perfectly comprehensive, guide to the exercise of authority in promulgation,

---

50 See John Finnis *Natural Law and Natural Rights* (op. cit.) p. 231 and also Henrik Olsen and Stuart Toddington *Law In Its Own Right* (op. cit.) pp. 146–148.

interpretation and application of the laws. This is not, of course, an argument designed to defeat the many and varied accounts of incommensurabilism, it is simply a common sense option that at least avoids instant self-defeat for a Finnisian, and alerts us to what, logically, is at stake in making generally incommensurabilist claims. And it does pave the way for reversing the burden of proof; for it points to the shortcomings of the pragmatist/incommensurabilist strategy when it comes to real-life situations. The problem is, that if there can be no coherent and objective moral criteria that can structure our analysis of the law, then there can be no objective morality for deciding legal disputes. But if there can be no objective morality for deciding legal disputes, then what are the grounds for claiming authority for legal decisions? The incommensurabilist answer to this question is worth considering carefully: it suggests the ground for claiming authority to decide one way or the other is precisely that that there is not, was not and never will be an objectively valid reason for deciding one way or the other. At worst then, one might have to conclude that Finnis wants to base legal authority not on its necessity as a means to the pursuit of the Good, but on the impossibility of pursuing the Good *coherently* (because the Good consists of incommensurable values).

The ambiguity of the position allows Finnis to claim simultaneously that (a) moral *foundations* for law are to be discovered as inherent aspects of practical reason *and* (b) that law is rationally powerless in the face of the alleged incommensurability of values. This *elision* of the epistemological with the empirical mirrors the pragmatist confusion of the orders of analysis at the methodological level that prevents the Selznickian from differentiating, on the one hand, those substantive value judgments that constitute the *presuppositions* of a critical pragmatism in formulating a Master Ideal, from, on the other, the kind of undoubtedly substantive, yet historically and culturally contingent, value phenomena that appear at the level of social action as the subject matter of sociological investigation. Understanding Selznick and Selznickians becomes much less taxing once we realize that the Selznickian pragmatist who rightly argues for the necessity of a Master Ideal is not – logically, epistemologically or ethically – *anti-foundationalist,* he or she is just obsessively anxious to be seen as progressively open-minded (within reason) about the great variety, fluidity and potential value of *folkways.* But this anxiety, of course, is easily given a respectable scientific role when supported by a convenient and well-subscribed doctrine, that of the incommensurability of values.

Let us contrast this directly and immediately with our position as stated in *Law In Its Own Right.* There we conceded that the rational apprehension of the objective principles of basic right – even if they offer us a systematic and commensurable opportunity for weighting[51] – do not allow us to overcome the problem of the *unilateral application* of the principles of basic right, and therefore lead us to the practical-logical need to install an *omnilateral* authority. The

51 These derive from the 'additive', 'maintenance' and 'non-subtractive' dimensions of agent well-being. See Alan Gewirth *Reason and Morality* (Chicago: Chicago University Press, 1978) pp. 53–58.

indispensability of instititutionalized authority is *not* a concomitant of the claim that basic goods or complex goods derived from basic goods are *incommensurable*. Our position is that a moral authority can become genuinely autonomous from the flux of interpersonal and group conflicts only if it *simultaneously* solves the problem of the *unilateral assertion* of basic right whilst holding to the *fundamental precepts of basic right*. This is made possible, as we argued, by transforming natural morality into artificial morality – an artifice we will call law and legal reason. Legal decisions, then, should be seen as artificial transformations of natural morality, a transformation required by the need to give *unilateral* claims *omnilateral* validity. We might add that in effecting this transformation from 'natural' to 'artificial' moral reasoning, one cannot duck the *general* moral issue arising by denying that legal decisions do in fact claim authority (or impose obligations), for this would be to re-define law as *not* containing its most intuitively and empirically central feature: the characteristic of non-optionality. The central problem of legal theory – the nature of legal obligation – would simply be ignored. If it is to be confronted, however, an appeal to the incommensurability of values does not offer a satisfying account of it. Affirming the incommensurability of values is simply to announce that, normatively speaking, authority is unfounded. Why then, should anyone accept it? We might, in order to make a comprehensive case against the idea, consider a number of possible 'pragmatic' rejoinders to this criticism.[52]

A possible way out for the pragmatist at this stage would be to propose as an oncoming solution to this problem a distinction between '*a priori* incommensurability' and 'reasons for deciding a particular conflict of values'. This would amount to some form of argument that suggested that although the first principles of practical rationality (or basic goods) are incommensurable, there do exist second-order principles that might supply reasons for deciding a particular concrete conflict even though such a conflict might involve two or more incommensurable values. A solution like this would not be unfamiliar to Fuller or Finnis, but there are two problems arising. The first one is that this strategy treats the reasons for deciding a particular conflict of values as technical non-moral reasons, what Finnis calles *techne*.[53] To suppose that law can be described in these terms may be true, but only up to a point. The artificial rationality of law always comes up short when the dogmatic (technical) analyses leading to 'the right legal answer' are forced into contextualization or, in other words, when the 'source' or 'pedigree' issue is raised rather than just tacitly presupposed. The point we wish to make is that *techne* and *areté* do not flow in two separate channels, but are rather integrally linked parts of a continuum of practical reason. Thus, if values were indeed incommensurable, then the reasons for deciding a particular conflict of values, would, as Finnis points out, boil down to a question of subjective preference. If on the other hand it is possible to give genuine reasons for a decision, then these reasons must hierarchicalize the values which are at

52 The following is inspired by Sanne Taekema's paper at the IVR conference, Lund 2003.

53 See. Finnis *Natural Law and Legal Reasoning* (op. cit.) p. 150.

play in the decision – but then, of course, these values could not be said to be incommensurable.

This brings us to a second problem facing pragmatist theory: Why should we insist that goods/values are intrinsically (*a priori*) incommensurable? Pragmatists, as we have seen, generally do not reject the claim that law ought to be understood normatively, nor do they dispute the existence of a conceptual relationship between law and morality. Some pragmatists, like Taekema, endorse the necessity and insist there can be no morally neutral concept of law.[54] But what Taekema, along with other pragmatists do oppose is the idea that the concept of law should depend on *objective* moral principles. The position seems to be that a necessary connection between law and values is accepted only if the values are seen to be elusive and incommensurably dynamic. The unease behind this position for theorists like Finnis and Taekema seems to be concerned primarily with preserving a special place for moral deliberation, and of protecting a notion of human freedom and genuine moral choice rather than a concern to explain to us how they know, *a priori*, that values are *in fact* incommensurable. Finnis writes:[55]

> Indeed, morally significant choice would be unnecessary and, with one qualification, impossible if one option could be shown to be *the best* on a single scale which, as all aggregative reasoning does, ranks options in a single transitive order. If there were a reason (for doing x) which some rational method of comparison ... identifies as rationally preferable, the alternative reason (against doing x), being thus identified as rationally inferior, would cease to be rationally appealing in that situation of choice. There would remain *no choice* of the sort that moral theories seek to guide. For, the morally significant choices which moral theories seek to guide are between alternative [incommensurable?] options, which have rational appeal.

So moral deliberation has to do with choice (which can be guided), but the guidance cannot (or must not) be seen to be so informative as to result in a rational preference for one action over another. In the same vein, Taekema argues that the most important reason for believing in the incommensurability of values is the existence of genuine moral dilemmas. Like Finnis, she adheres to an assumption that morality at its core is characterized as giving rise to difficult choices which cannot be resolved rationally. She refers (as we shall discuss more fully below) to the issue of abortion where the 'right to life of a foetus' can be said to conflict with a 'woman's right to determine her own life and procreation'. Finnis refers to a wider palate of incommensurable choices:[56]

> One meets incommensurability in humble contexts, such as having to choose between going to the cinema, and talking to friends. One meets it in relation to grand social choices, such as whether to reject or renounce a nuclear deterrent

54 See Sanne Taekema *The Concept of Ideals in Legal Theory* (op. cit.) Chapter 1.

55 Finnis in R.P. George (op. cit.) pp. 146–147.

56 Ibid.

But this is to give a banal and absurdly wide definition of what incommensurability is supposed to mean. In addition, even on the best reading of Finnis's observation, it begs the entire question at issue if the argument for the incommensurability of values is premised upon the stipulation that a latent condition of *undecideability* is an inherent property *of* value choices; obviously, if true, this would justify the *conclusion* of the incommensurability of values. Quite apart from the fact that the existence of *genuine* moral dilemmas might readily be acknowledged with impunity by moral foundationalists (there might, after all, be reasons for the existence of moral dilemmas other than incommensurability) it is thus the tautological presumption of the incommensurabilists that is irksome here: In short, we must ask, 'Are values incommensurable because there can be no appeal to a transitive hierarchy of values, or can there be no appeal to a transitive hierarchy of values because we are to accept the as yet unsubstantiated assertion that values are incommensurable?'

For let us note that the *assumption* of the axiom of the incommensurability of values can be used powerfully and *rhetorically* to *create the appearance* of moral dilemmas – or at least the appearance of undecideable choices between values. But even pragmatists (one hopes) would not equate the success of rhetoric with the idea of truth, and it might turn out that, on further scrutiny, the intractability of an apparent dilemma could be dissolved. Let us consider this in more detail, for responding to this successfully would kill two troublesome pragmatist birds with one ethical rationalist stone. The first concerns, as noted, the often unwarranted presumption of the existence of 'dilemmas' to support incommensurability claims; the second refutes the scepticism of the Finnisian assertion encountered earlier that, in the main, incommensurabilty characterizes the vast majority of our ethical and thus legal experience, and that the role of moral reason is confined solely to the unserviceably general and 'self-evident' axioms of *basic* right.

Incommensurability and Moral 'Dilemmas'

In criticizing some of the claims for ethical rationalism made in *Law In Its Own Right*,[57] Sanne Taekema, commenting on our suggestion that one requirement of a serviceable moral theory is to offer 'guidance on the determination of a hierarchy of basic 'goods' or principles' says:[58]

> It is indeed important that a moral theory offers criteria to distinguish rights or genuine interests from wants or preferences, because only the first category merits legal protection. It is something else altogether to conclude that this entails establishing a hierarchy of basic principles. For example, in abortion cases the right to life of a foetus can be said to conflict with a woman's right to determine her own life and procreation. A

57 See *Law In Its Own Right* (op. cit.) p. 145.

58 Sanne Taekema 'What should be Transparent in Law? A Pragmatist Strategy to Justify Legal Decisions' *IVR Lund 2003* (definition given by Jurriaan de Haan *The Possibility of Moral Dilemmas* (unpublished dissertation, The University of Amsterdam, 2000) p. 130.

resolution of such a conflict of two basic interests is not simply justified by resorting to a hierarchy of basic principles. Moreover, the idea of a hierarchy of principles depends on the notion that values are commensurable, which I think is mistaken.

She goes on:

> An important part of Olsen and Toddington's argument is devoted to proving that incommensurability of values is not true. One of the reasons for adopting a rationalist moral theory is that its foundational principles can be used to establish a hierarchy of values. Considering their argument I cannot help thinking that their main reason for believing in value commensurability is that it is necessary for the rest of their theory ... they emphasize the necessity of reasoned choice in legal matters and they believe that value incommensurability makes reasoned choice impossible and [m]oreover, [that] the coherence of a legal system is undermined if the values it is based on are incommensurable. In my view however, incommensurability of values is highly plausible, but not fatal to theory formation. [Our interpolation]

Importantly, and citing Juurian de Haen[59] she offers an argument in support of the existence of incommensurability:

> The most important reason for believing that incommensurability of values is true is the existence of moral dilemmas. If it is possible to establish a hierarchy of values, meaning that we can determine *a priori* what the relative importance of values is, a true moral dilemma would be impossible. A moral dilemma is a situation in which there is no right thing to do, meaning that the action taken cannot be fully justified.

Her point is that the existence of moral dilemmas is evidence of the existence of value-incommensurabilty and that because dilemmas exist, we must accept the fact and adapt legal theory to it – pragmatically. She offers three (of many actual or hypothetically possible) examples of intractable dilemmas:[60] '... in abortion cases the right to life of a foetus can be said to conflict with a woman's right to determine her own life and procreation. A resolution of such a conflict of two basic interests is not simply justified by resorting to a hierarchy of basic principles'. A second illustration is that of a war-time judge in a country occupied by a murderous foreign regime facing the choice of 'resigning (and thereby making room for a judge appointed by the regime) or collaborating (in order to resist from the inside). By choosing collaboration he is able to save lives, but this completely compromises his own integrity by being an accomplice to the regime'. A third example is that of the general difficulties surrounding policy decisions involved in balancing economic and environmental concerns. The particular example she offers concerns the choice between increased noise pollution and an extra landing

---

59 Jurriaan de Haan *The Possibility of Moral Dilemmas* (op. cit.) p. 30.

60 Sanne Taekema 'What should be Transparent in Law? A Pragmatist Strategy to Justify Legal Decisions' (op. cit.).

strip at a major international airport.[61] Such moral dilemmas are best explained, she says, '... in terms of incommensurability of values: two (sets of) values are at stake that cannot be compared on a single scale'. But even though these issues are examples of the fact of incommensurability they are not, according to Taekema, beyond reasonable resolution. She says:[62]

> Moral dilemmas are a special case of the larger category of (moral) conflicts. Most conflicts, unlike dilemmas, can be solved, although this does not imply that the values that are involved in the conflict are necessarily commensurable. This is because it would be wrong to conclude from the incommensurability of the values involved that there are no good reasons for a particular solution. A distinction must be made between the *a priori* incommensurability of values and the reasons for deciding a particular conflict of values. Incommensurability means that we cannot devise a hierarchy of values in which they are ordered according to relative importance, but that does not mean that we cannot choose between particular values at stake in a conflict.

In referring to the airport capacity *versus* noise pollution issue, she says:

> ... we cannot decide in the abstract what the trade-off should be between the value of a clean environment and the value of a healthy national economy. However, in the particular case of noise pollution caused by an extra airstrip at the national airport, it is possible to argue that the extra flights are not as essential now to the airport as is the living comfort of the thousands of people who suffer from it. There are good reasons for making such a choice for the environment and against the economy in this case, while this does not imply that the relationship between these two values is now fixed: circumstances in the future may call for a different decision. A conflict of values can only be resolved in the context of a particular situation: the reasons for the solution are not valid in the abstract but make sense as a specific constellation.

We must emphasize, she says,

> ...the context of a decision and the constellation of values found there, instead of trying to establish order among values beforehand ... a hierarchy is not necessary because there is a different way to defend [the claim] that values are objectively valid ... considering a particular situation, object or action, we can pronounce a judgment that it does or does not have value, meaning a judgment that it is worthy of esteem.[63] This change of starting point is quite significant: instead of considering the validity of a value *in itself*, value is considered as *an aspect of* a particular thing. Generalizing from valuable objects by conducting an inquiry into the circumstances and consequences that make them valuable generates objective value standards. The objectivity of the value in question is the result of a critical inquiry into the consequences of adopting it.

---

61 This example was inspired by the recurring conflict regarding Schiphol Airport near Amsterdam, whose fifth airstrip causes serious nuisance to people living in the area.

62 Sanne Taekema (op. cit.).

63 See John Dewey 'Moral Judgment and Knowledge' in Larry A. Hickman and Thomas M. Alexander *The Essential Dewey, Volume II* (Bloomington: Indiana University Press, 1998) pp. 328–340 at 329.

Two responses must be made at this point: one concerns the characterization of these examples as moral dilemmas, the other relates to the proposed non-foundationalist – or pragmatic – solution to them. Thus first we must note that whilst the foregoing are genuinely profound examples of the difficulties we face privately and publicly as sexual, moral and political individuals, and whilst unguardedly, conversationally or journalistically, we might reasonably refer to these examples as 'moral dilemmas', some extravagant philosophical license is taken by Taekema in the attempt to pass off these vignettes of experience as logical demonstrations of the failure of rationalism. Secondly, the problem that pragmatists and incommensurabilists face here can be illustrated easily by asking a simple question and answering it candidly and honestly. That is, and taking the example of abortion, if someone was to spend several years researching and constructing a principled solution to an apparent collision of rights arising, and offered a commensurable solution to the mother/foetus problem illustrated above, would we have to bother reading the work, or could we conclude *a priori* that the 'dilemma' remained as intractable as ever?

If the answer is the one on offer from the pragmatist/incommensurabilist, then we need not take the trouble to read Shaun Pattinson's scrupulous inquiry into bio-ethics in his *Influencing Traits Before Birth*[64] In this work, in addition to showing how the epistemological acquisition of knowledge of the very basic or generic goods intrinsic to rational agency might be developed and expanded into theory that can guide the legal regulation of complex and contentious areas, he also re-casts our common-sense understandings of the status of rights arising and accruing to actual and potential actors in the reproductive enterprise. His work is of specific, intrinsic and substantive merit, but here, let us emphasize strongly, we present it first and foremost *as a general illustration of the failures of incommensurabilist thinking.*

Shaun Pattinson: Extrapolating from Basic Principles

What Pattinson shows us is that the idea of basic right does not lead immediately to the miserable confusions of *determinatio* we find in Aquinas and his expositors. In an attempt to apply maximally general precepts to complex concrete situations there is a philosophical *second-stage* of analysis that builds upon the logic of basic right and seeks to develop it in particular directions of potential application. The details of the concrete circumstances themselves give us clues to lines of possibly fruitful inquiry.

Before examining some of the arguments that Pattinson provides against the confusions and assumptions of incommensurability, let us first, in opposition to the intellectual defeatism encountered hitherto, note his general attitude to moral analysis. Pattinson says that in discussing any specific, contentious and complex area (here the influencing of traits before birth, embryo-testing, pre-natal diagnosis

64 Shaun Pattinson *Influencing Traits Before Birth* (Aldershot: Ashgate, 2002).

and thus, in the face of some test results, the inevitability of abortion and the destruction of embryos), there is a general point to be made:[65]

> The abstract moral principle discussed above [that is, the Gewirthian PGC] might seem far removed from the ethical and regulatory questions asked at the beginning of this chapter. Indeed it is. This starting point needs considerable expansion and supplementation before it can be applied to the subject matter of this book. The mere supposition of a moral principle granting rights to the generic features of agency to all agents does not, by itself, tell us much about the morality of the techniques of prenatal influence or how to regulate their use. ... This criterion of moral permissibility needs to be developed if it is to be applied to practical problems.

Pattinson says that the first questions we must ask are *what or who matters morally? To whom or what do we owe moral concern?* His answer is that there are two ways an object can attract moral status: 'intrinsically' or 'indirectly'. Who or what, then has '*intrinsic* moral status'? Pattinson says that there are many possible criteria in use: some want to grant moral status to 'living' creatures, 'sentient' creatures, 'humans' or, as in Gewirthian theory, agents, that is, beings able to act for purposes constituting reasons for their actions. But this latter suggests a familiar yet subtle problem, that of the status of 'partial' agents (beings assumed to possess some but not all the characteristics of agency), and 'potential' agents: non-agents who have the potential to become agents.[66] He presents us with a careful analysis of the concepts of 'partial and 'potential' agency, but for the moment, the explanation of a general point is salutary.

There are, says Pattinson, a wide variety of suggestions for determining the criteria for moral status and none have escaped criticism. In the reproductive technology debate (where at some point the issue of the moral status of adult females in relation to embryos or foetuses must be confronted) opinions are sharply divided, and rhetoric appealing to 'more than one criterion for possession of intrinsic moral status is pervasive'.[67] There is, says Pattinson, controversy and diversity here, but this does not imply the indeterminacy or incommensurability of the issues in question. Pattinson's aim at this point is to argue that Gewirth's ethical rationalism is, in general, sound and applicable in particular as a guide to the regulation of reproductive technology, but that the Gewirthian notion of 'proportional agency' (and consequently the proportional entitlement of rights to 'partial' agents) is flawed. Yet, says Pattinson, there are indeed hierarchical levels of agent status even at the human or potentially human level. In following this line of thinking, and with severe *ceteris paribus* conditions, he suggests that the morality of abortion does not reduce to the impasse of a dilemma between the assumed 'rights of the mother and 'the rights of the child'. Rather, the superior 'intrinsic' moral status of the adult female and her possible decision to terminate a pregnancy overrides the inferior entitlements of the foetus. This position would

65 Ibid. p. 14.
66 Ibid. p. 16.
67 Ibid. p. 69.

not, of course, receive universal support, yet Pattinson claims he can provide a logical demonstration of its validity. He says,[68]

> The absence of political consensus has no relevance to the determination of who has moral status at the level of principle. Morality… comprises a set of other-regarding obligations the existence of which is not dependent on their recognition as such. Since my argument is premised on the claim that it is necessarily true that an agent denies that it is an agent if it fails to accept and act in accordance with the PGC, reliance on consensus, intuition, or alternative moral perspectives is to be rejected.

Importantly (for those who might not find his conclusions appealing, or who might want to insist that these issues are simply 'dilemmas', he points out that:[69]

> If the acceptance of the conclusion strikes the reader as being unduly dictatorial, or lacking moral appeal, this can only be because a prior moral framework is being implicitly appealed to.

Let us then turn to some technical detail which Pattinson handles in accomplished fashion. Let us reiterate that this exercise, although a valuable contribution to bio-ethics in itself, is here presented to illustrate what we might learn in general about the analysis of basic moral precepts, their indirect application, incommensurability, and the notion of a moral 'dilemma'. We might look at his treatment of the logical problems of moral status, partial agency, and, of particular importance, tactics for dealing with *multi-causal and multivariable issues.* These latter, one suspects, are the kind of ethical tangles that invite a conveniently swift appeal to the labour-saving device of the notion of 'incommensurability'.

Gewirth claims that the PGC can grant moral status to beings that might reasonably be regarded as non-agents:[70] foetuses, neonates, very young children, the mentally impaired, non-human animals and so on. The suggestion is that a principle of proportionality would grant rights to agents proportional to their possession of agency; the more agency being possessed, the more rights accrue to it.[71] But problems arise with this formulation. Pattinson points out that there are three we should consider carefully. The first is that agent rights under the PGC are 'waivable' will/choice claim-rights and as such only meaningfully possessed by choosing/willing agents. The second is that with rights come correlative duties, and thus the imposition of duties on partial agents is implausible. Thirdly, the original Gewirthian attempt *qualitatively* to transform generic rights into quasi-generic rights (that is, benefit/interest claim-rights) by varying merely the *quantity* of agency assumed to be possessed, and thus evading the first two problems noted above, is logically implausible. These three problems stand in the way of granting

68 Ibid. p. 19.

69 Ibid.

70 Ibid. p. 20 quoting Alan Gewirth *Reason and Morality* (op. cit.) p. 121.

71 Ibid. p. 20.

proportional moral status to *partial* agents; *potential* agents, however – that is, straightforwardly *non*-agents fare even worse.

The PGC, says Pattinson, grants intrinsic moral status exclusively to agents. Who or what, then, are we to identify as agents? Self-reflectively, I have, in Cartesian fashion, a guarantee of my own agency; but again in a Cartesian sense, I cannot be sure that other self-reflective minds are in operation. It would be wise, however, to employ what Pattinson calls a *precautionary principle* to the identification or assumption of the existence of agency based on some straightforward empirical evidence of *ostensible* agency. When other beings display the same ostensibly purposive and communicative behaviour as oneself, the claim that they are agents has, metaphysically, the same epistemic status as the claim that they are not agents, for all the reasons that are to be found in Descartes' system of radical doubt. But, says Pattinson,[72]

> The PGC imposes a framework for interpreting these propositions, because these propositions have significantly divergent moral import. If I mistakenly presume X to be an agent, then, although this will lead me mistakenly to have to restrict my exercise of my rights to some extent, I do not deny my (or any other agent's) status as a rights holder. In contrast if I mistakenly presume X not to be an agent, then I deny X (an agent) is a rights-holder. In short, the consequence of being wrong in one case involve restricting the exercise of my rights, and the denial of all the rights of a rights-holder in the other.

If we establish this precautionary approach to the problems of partial and potential agency we can proceed to a rational second phase of analysis that accommodates the problems of proportional agency and the required hierarchicalization of rights in certain circumstances. We arrive at the idea that, when faced with '... conflict between beings displaying different degrees of agency related behaviour and characteristics, the *criterion of avoidance of more probable harm* provides a hierarchical structure for determining priority'.[73] Similarly, when faced '... with a conflict between different levels of harm or need *the criterion of degrees of needfulness of action* provides a hierarchical structure'.[74] When the problem involves conflict between different degrees of probability with regard to the occurrence of harm, we should again turn to *the criterion of avoidance of more probable harm.*[75]

Despite these formulations, however, Pattinson reminds us that we still face logical difficulty in situations that display *multi-variable* features, that is, conflicts between more than one of the variables mentioned above, that is, moral status, level of harm/need,or probability of harm.[76] We might, perhaps, add to our

---

72 Ibid. p. 23.
73 Ibid p. 68.
74 Ibid.
75 Ibid.
76 Ibid. p. 69.

decision-making repertoire the Gewirthian principles of *intervening action* and also of *prior wrong action.* He says:[77]

> Where someone is at fault for the creation of a dilemma, criteria can be offered to evade the difficulties of weighing what appear to be incommensurable variables.

The *principle of intervening action* first deals with the situation where an intentional intervention by B can be identified as the more direct and proximate cause of some harm Z perpetrated by A, the moral responsibility for Z is removed from A. The *principle of prior wrong action* holds that agents who are responsible for the creation of a dilemma can be *estopped* in an essential sense from claiming priority in the resolution of this dilemma.[78] But although there is much to be said for these guiding principles '... they are of no help in the resolution of many multi-variable conflicts'.[79] Theoretically, says Pattinson, there are three ways of resolving conflicts between the criterial variables of moral status, level of harm/need, and probability of harm:[80]

> (a) introducing criteria for resolving conflicts between the above criteria;
> (b) using a random method ... (e.g tossing a coin); or
> (c) relying on procedural, rather than substantive, criteria for resolution of such dilemmas.

But the incommensurabilist/pragmatist thesis – ambiguously, disingenuously and equivocally, but *effectively* – has argued all along that 'option (a)' is *not* available in any *objectively rational* or *foundational* sense. This means that the incommensurabilist/pragmatist, in the face of moral vacuity sees options (b) and (c) as somehow self-supporting and thus 'authoritatively' applicable. This displays a fundamental misunderstanding of what is required to synthesise legal authority from moral reasoning. Pattinson says:

> If (a) is possible then this is what we ought to aim to do. In the absence of such an approach (or so I shall argue, even in the presence of principles or criteria of dilemma resolution) the third option (c) is a practical necessity which might sometimes result in a solution being derived by random choice.

Let us briefly explain the ethical rationalism that underpins Pattinson's grasp of the situation. First, an objective theory of morality based on the precepts of (Gewirthian) ethical rationalism does not envisage moral omniscience nor the perfection of the moral order. It accepts the inevitability of a plurality of reasonable interpretations of the requirements of the indirect application of the PGC in certain circumstances and especially in the multi-variable circumstances

77 Ibid.
78 Ibid.
79 Ibid.
80 Ibid.

lately discussed. However, Pattinson says, '... the PGC can, without violating its precepts, take into account the reality of the human condition'. He says:[81]

> In practice, some decisions can legitimately be left to the discretion of individuals and other, more problematic decisions, must be delegated to appropriate decision-making bodies or persons. Without procedural measures for dealing with dilemma resolution difficulties, the force of the *uncontroversial implications* of the PGC could be undermined. It goes without saying that any such procedural mechanisms must be constrained by the PGC, as the PGC must not knowingly or avoidably be violated. (Our emphasis)

Pattinson says that[82] 'practical legitimacy [that is, for the purposes of a rational system of dispute resolution and prevention] must be given to the decisions of those, appointed in accordance with PGC-derived procedures [here he cites Beyleveld and Brownsword][83]who seek to make a good faith attempt to apply the PGC with a certain degree of competence ... expending effort that is commensurate with the importance of getting it right'. He goes on:[84]

> If we do not presume the legitimacy of rules or decisions made by those legitimately appointed, competently making a 'good faith' attempt to apply valid moral principles, attempted social regulation will be immoral at the level of attempt as well as achievement.

Principle, Procedure and Authority

In the light of Pattinson's demonstration of first, the possibility of extrapolating substantively and specifically in complex contexts from principles of basic right, and for showing us the logical ordering of principle, then procedural exigency and finally the presumption of authority, let us return to the example we started with, the dilemma of rights surrounding abortion of the foetus. Empirically, a legal decision to extend abortion on demand might make a 'pro-life' supporter less happy than members of some 'choice' groups. But the putative justifications for 'pro-life' views and for 'choice' views might be confused, contradictory, disparate, unreasoned, gender-biased, born of personal sentiment, personal short-term interest, or the espousal of an unquestioned religious dogma – and so too might a putative 'legal' decision from a judge with an axe to grind in this regard. The point is that a legal philosophy worth the name must respond to this problem and its potential for conflict by envisaging a practically feasible and defensible structure of form and principle which allows us to imagine an ideal legal decision – one which can be made transparent (if not pleasing) to all parties. Such a decision

81 Ibid. p. 70.

82 Ibid. p. 70.

83 See Deryck Beyleveld and Roger Brownsword *Law as a Moral Judgment* (London: Sweet and Maxwell 1994) Chapters 7–9, also 'Principle, Procedure and Precaution in a Community of Rights' *Ratio Juris* (Vol. 19 No. 2, June 2006).

84 Shaun Pattinson (op. cit.) p. 70.

would or should transcend the cauldron of conflict and would be based on an attempt to work out a solution to the problem based on a comprehensive theory of basic rights. The pragmatist 'solution', however, appears simply to *describe* the problematic situation, assert *a priori* that values are incommensurable and then tell us that the 'rational' way out is to 'look at the context' and make a 'reasonable', consequentialist decision. This, we can now see, is incoherent, as 'reasonable' can refer only to the search for objectively defensible ethical principles.

The Finnisian view is that as practical reasonableness cannot solve the dilemma, *authority* must. But, as we have seen, this is based on the incoherent notion that there are 'basic' principles of right, but that these principles are static and unserviceably general,with little or no contextual relevance or application. Pattinson's scrupulous analysis disposes of this misapprehension and exposes the vacuity of the assertion that where reason runs out we must simply call down the *deus ex machina* of 'authority' to resolve our conflicts.

On the Incommensurability of Systemic Rules

We have argued that basic or generic goods are not incommensurable, that basic goods can lead us to knowledge of more complex goods, and that we should not, therefore, accept the claim that all value questions of *any* complexity are incommensurable. But might incommensurabilism arise inevitably as a property of any attempt to devise an authoritative system of rules?

It is true that the problem of what Aquinas calls *determinatio* (that is, the indirect application of basic principles of right in complex circumstances, presents us with challenges. Thus it will not be unusual to have to face a situation in which the complexity of legal reasoning will admit of a plurality of alternative and perhaps equally rational solutions. We admit this as a matter of course. And we admit that legal authority must be used to terminate conflict by adopting one solution over another. But we must also emphasize that it would be a mistake to see this issue of authoritative choice as a matter of settling conflicts between incommensurable values. Rather we should theorize these instances as cases of tension or competition between the rules and principles of a legal system. There are two ways of handling such tension in the legal system. The first one relates to a situation where there exists a conflict of rules, and the other relates to a situation where there exists a competition between principles.

Conflict of rules is of a character that we can describe as 'hard tension'. This is because rules are norms which are specifically designed to be fulfilled in the legal system – not merely approximated. The consequence of this is that when rules conflict, it is not always possible to frame a compromise between them. There are only three ways to solve a conflict of rules. The first is to introduce an exception to one of the two rules. The second is to declare one of the rules invalid; and the third is to solve the conflict by the use of *meta* rules (for example, *lex specialis*, *lex posterior*, *lex superior*), which in effect *hierarchicalize* the rules in tension.

It might be said that all legal rules are artificial, by which is meant that no hard and fast rules can be derived directly from morality. Morality always comes in the form of principles. Thus the conflict of rules does not display the kind of deeper tension between moral principles that our previous discussions focused upon. So let us look at competition between principles.

We might refer to competition between principles as 'soft tension' because principles are norms, which (recalling the notions of 'aspiration and duty' or 'basic and flourishing' criteria) might be fulfilled in the legal system to some degree. Alexy calls them 'optimization requirements'. Thus when two principles compete, it may be possible to either decide the case in the form of a balanced compromise between the two principles (for example, a balance between the principle of full compensation for damages and the principle that compensation should only be paid for a proven loss), or to give one principle *conditional precedence*.[85] It is the last of these two solutions to problems of competing principles that is most interesting in this context because it comes closest to pragmatist aspirations without surrendering to the dogma of incommensurability of values. Thus the principle of conditional precedence uses the factual conditions of the case as a basis for generating rational criteria that may be used to create a temporary hierarchical relationship between the values (principles), which are in conflict.

It should be noted that there is nothing irrational about this. The exercise of *creating* hierarchical relations between two competing principles with a view to making a concrete decision in law is in fact an exercise in how to fulfil the obligation to make morality work in practice. Thus the searching out of relevant factual conditions that may be used as a basis for the construction of a conditional precedence should be seen as merely one stage in what we have called *the continuum of practical reason* from the prudential to the moral, and through to the legal – and let us note, on to the logic of political and social institutional design that must arise in and around the authoritative processes of a legal order.

Part 3: Fuller's Proceduralism and the Morality of Law

No-one has made a more straightforward or influential case for the link between procedure and legitimacy as Lon L. Fuller. We noted above that there are two powerful strands of it in Fuller: the Habermas-Alexy nexus and the famous account of the inner or internal morality of law. The former we touch upon briefly in Chapter 5 but here let us try and settle some of the confusion that still persists as a legacy of the Hart-Fuller debates on this matter. In the section of Chapter 2 of

85 This term, again, comes from Robert Alexy, *A Theory of Constitutional Rights* (2002, p. 52) translation from the German by Julian Rivers. As examples to illustrate the use of conditional precedence Alexy points to two decisions from the German constitutional court. One example concerns the impending criminal trial of a person who was in danger of dying from a heart attack if subjected to the procedure; the conflict here is between the principle that everyone must stand trial for his criminal actions on the one hand and the principle of right to life and bodily integrity on the other. Another concerns a conflict between the freedom of speech and the right to privacy (media report of an old crime to be broadcast at the time of release of the convicted person affecting the resocialization of the person in question).

The Morality of Law, subheaded 'Eight Ways to Fail to Make Law' and later in the article bearing the same title, Fuller chronicles the attempts of a well-intentioned despot *Rex* to assume complete control of the promulgation, interpretation, revision and repeal of the laws of his land and in so doing demonstrate the pitfalls of law making.[86] In this illustration Fuller identified eight principles of rational law making that amount to the definitive criteria for identifying a legal system and, presumably, the criteria for legal validity. The story is well known, but here are the eight opportunities for 'failure' listed concisely by James Boyle:[87]

> Rex's bungling career as legislator and judge illustrates that the attempt to create and maintain a scheme of legal rules may miscarry in at least eight ways; there are in this enterprise, if you will, eight distinct routes to disaster. The first and most obvious lies in a failure to achieve rules at all, so that every issue must be decided on an *ad hoc* basis. The other routes are: (2) a failure to publicize, or at least to make available to the affected party, the rules he is expected to observe; (3) the abuse of retroactive legislation, which not only cannot itself guide action, but undercuts the integrity of rules prospective in effect since it puts them under the threat of retrospective change; (4) a failure to make rules understandable; (5) the enactment of contradictory rules or (6) rules that require conduct beyond the powers of the affected party; (7) introducing such frequent changes in the rules that the subject cannot orient his action by them; and finally (8) a failure of congruence between the rules as announced and their actual administration.

A total failure in any one of these eight directions, says Fuller, does not simply result in a bad system of law; '... it results in something that is not properly called a legal system at all, except perhaps in the Pickwickian *sense in which a void contract can still be said to be one kind of contract*'.[88]

The argument that starts here, of course, is that this procedural concept of law is too thin to give us a genuinely critical account of law, for the very simple reason that these precepts of acceptable law making could be employed consistently by the most heinous and vicious regime imaginable. Surely, the trick for those who hold to the possibility of a pragmatic 'third way' is to provide a non-positivistic account of law that provides a platform for our objections to the laws of the rulers but does not require us to subscribe to the objectivism of modern ethical rationalism. Let us first, then, try and get this objection to Fuller in its proper perspective.

Fuller encouraged us to look at law as a purposive activity. His broad suggestion was to begin by defining law as 'the enterprise of subjecting human conduct to the governance of rules'; but to what *end* are we to subject human conduct to the regime of rules? In other words, what is the *external* moral goal

---

86 Lon L. Fuller *The Morality of Law* (New Haven, CT: Yale University Press, 1969) Chapter 1.

87 James Boyle 'Legal Realism and the Social Contract: Fuller's Public Jurisprudence of Form, Private Jurisprudence of Substance' *Cornell Law Review* (78, 1993) p. 371.

88 Quoted in James Boyle (op. cit.) from Lon L. Fuller *The Morality of Law* (op. cit.).

in view. If the answer to this is not forthcoming then we must assume that there is something valuable or worthwhile in rule governance for its own sake, that is, intrinsically rather than internally, and that there is something significant to be gleaned about the reference to rule governance as it stands? But it is characteristic of Fuller to have it both ways here: yes there *is* an end to the enterprise of law; and yes there *is* something important and valuable about making, applying and observing rules as instruments to what, *from a distance*, is a greater end. Law as means and law as an end-in-itself is thus one of the logically elusive if not paradoxical aspects of Fuller's thinking. In *Means and Ends* Fuller says,[89]

> Our best institutions are, I believe, pregnant with beneficial side effects. It is chiefly for this reason that I have so vigorously objected to the view that institutions are mere inert conduits directing human energies … toward certain desirable end-states. Our institutions are part of the pattern of our lives. The task of perfecting them furnishes an outlet for the most vigorous of moral impulses.

We can examine these wider sociological issues in later chapters, but if, for the moment, we substitute laws or 'rules' for 'institutions' here, the point, and the complexity behind it, becomes significantly clearer. When law is conceived exclusively as an instrument, the eight tenets of the inner or internal morality of law appear as a merely neutral procedural technique. This gives rise to the well-rehearsed and plausible Hartian objection that all manner of pernicious ends can be achieved with skill and technique; gruesomely, the poisoner's art is mentioned in emphatic illustration.[90] Both Hartian positivists and Fuller accept the general validity of the distinction between an activity (carpentry/law) and the product or end of the activity, say, respectively, a table or changes in a tax regime. But how, asks Pauline Westerman, does one see the eight rule precepts (even taken as a whole set) as a substantively moral as opposed to a purely technical form of reasoning? She adds, importantly:[91]

> Fuller … omits to argue why the eight requirements, unlike other rules of craftsmanship, are to be regarded as moral standards. In his reply to critics [in *The Morality of Law*] he even argues the other way round by conceding that seven out of those eight requirements [the exception is congruence between official action and declared rule] can be regarded as purely technical ones, merely furthering expediency, not morality. It all seems to depend on the *context* in which the craft of rulemaking is conducted.

This must be so: if the context is one where mutual understandings of the primacy of certain values exist, and where, for the sake of argument, the notions of rights and 'freedoms' operate, then rules that are dissonant with these moral

---

89 Kenneth I. Winston *The Principles of Social Order* (op. cit.) p. 74.

90 Pauline Westerman 'Means and Ends' in Wiliiam Witteveen and Wibren van der Burg (eds) *Rediscovering Fuller* (Amsterdam: Amsterdam University Press, 1999) pp. 146, 147.

91 Ibid. p. 147.

understandings will attract justifiable condemnation from those held to be subject to them. Westerman adds:[92]

> In the context of top-bottom relationships exemplified by what he calls 'managerial direction' these seven requirements are morally neutral. Only in the domain of 'law' defined by Fuller as a framework for the horizontal relations between *free* citizens, and as such distinguished from managerial direction, [do] these requirements gain moral significance.

There is, of course, still scope in this situation for a Legal Positivist argument (and a Legal Idealist/Natural Law one) to the effect that even 'laws' or rules antithetical to accepted (contextual) understandings of morality and rights must, nevertheless, be obeyed, and as such appear effectively 'valid', but this is dragging us away from the problem now brought sharply into focus by Westerman: is it the rules that contain the moral quality, or the context in which they operate – or a combination of both? Westerman goes on to say:

> His argument [Fuller's], however, does not support his theory that the requirements are to be regarded as an 'internal' morality.[93] On the contrary, it seems to strengthen Hart's view that *taken by themselves* these requirements are morally neutral. Instead of arguing that law owes its moral qualities to the eight requirements, Fuller argues here that the eight requirements owe their moral quality to law.

This, we think, is precisely what is going on in Fuller, although the story concerning the *concept* of 'an enterprise of subjecting human conduct to the governance of rules' may yet yield some intrinsic depth. Let us, then, pursue this line of thought briefly.

Does Fuller exclusively *define* law as the set of eight precepts of rule-making? A plausible and textually supportable answer responds in the negative to this. He certainly stands by the so-called precepts of the inner (procedural) morality as a pretty good indicator of the existence of the basis of Good Order and notes that where rulers have attempted to remain faithful to these precepts, Good, as opposed to Evil intention is more often than not attached to it. Let us ask then, whether Fuller has, or has attempted, a definition of the *external* morality of law, or, more directly for our present purpose, an analysis of the moral nature of the context in which the rationality of rule-making must take place? The answer, obviously, is yes; this preoccupation forms the superb introduction to *The Morality of Law*[94] in the analysis of the relationship between morality and duty. Fuller's account of the distinction between the two tells us quite a bit about his approach to ethical analysis.

Fuller says that,[95]

---

92 Ibid.

93 The actual text places dashes either side of the word 'internal, thus '– internal – morality'. Our interpolation assumes a typographical error.

94 Lon L. Fuller *The Morality of Law* (op. cit.).

95 Ibid. p. 5.

> The morality of aspiration is most plainly exemplified in Greek philosophy. It is the morality of the Good Life, of excellence, of the fullest realization of human powers. In a morality of aspiration there may be overtones of a notion approaching that of duty. But these overtones are usually muted, as they are in Plato and Aristotle.

This notion of excellence in life or *areté* offers us two sets of criteria: one aimed at establishing a criterion of right or fitting conduct, and the other to answer questions of political or legal rationality and action. In modern parlance, the later might be captured by reference to criteria for rational institutional design. In other words, the notion of *areté* is in one sense the antithesis of ethical and political thinking in modernity in that, as Nigel Simmonds[96] pointed out recently, the triumph of the notion of *Subjective Right* over *the Good*, gives rise, in Alan Brudner's terms, to the apparently unshakeable principle of 'the lexical priority of Right over the Good'.[97] This principle stems from the modern declaration of the failure of Reason's attempt to secure a rational understanding and demonstration of what is constitutive of the Good, other than in terms of subjective attitudes. The 'morality of aspiration' thus shares with Greek notions of the Good the idea that it is somehow possible to frame an adequate conception of the Good or the excellent life. Fuller accepts that this is a philosophical task of overwhelming complexity but uses the foundational idea to establish a more modest thesis, namely that we might illustrate the distinction between aspiration and duty, and that our better understanding of duty in this regard brings us, in turn, to a better understanding of duty's 'blood cousin', law:[98]

> Where the morality of aspiration starts at the top of human achievement, the morality of duty starts at the bottom, it lays down the basic rules without which an ordered society is impossible, or without which an ordered society directed towards certain goals must fail of its mark.

This is the context, then. There is perhaps enough here, in these first few pages of *The Morality of Law* to suggest that Fuller operates with the idea of moral continuum between the aspiration to create the basic conditions of social order and the pinnacles of ethical, social and aesthetic achievement. But one might also argue, positivistically, that all that is said here is that whether or not morality and the nature of the Good is fathomable, brute necessity requires social order, and duty and correlative enforcement constitute the minimum amount of compliance. This view might reasonably be assimilated to Hart's Legal Positivism or even Hobbes's theory of the sovereign.

There is much more in Fuller, however, to tilt the balance in favour of a moral idealist conception of the legal *context*, and thus we might examine this presently in some detail in relation to his account of the context or 'external morality' of law in the recently unearthed essays dealing with concept of 'affirmative freedom'.

---

96 Nigel E. Simmonds *Central Issues in Jurisprudence* 2nd edn (London: Sweet and Maxwell, 2002).

97 Alan Brudner. *Constitutional Goods* (Oxford: Oxford University Press 2004).

98 Lon L. Fuller *The Morality of Law* (op. cit.).

For the moment, however, we might simply recall Westerman's neat articulation of the logic of the issue at hand. Does a moral conception of the contextual relations between persons impart a moral significance and quality to the rules that aim to mediate and regulate those relations?

Beyleveld and Brownsword offer some guidance here. In *Law as a Moral Judgment*,[99] in the chapter entitled, 'The Idea of a Legal Order' they explain their idealist concept of law as stemming from the acknowledgment that natural rights and duties can be shown to exist as a product of the practically reasonable viewpoint of a prospective, purposive agent (PPA). The Gewirthian imperative applicable to all PPAs is the PGC such that *one must act in accordance with the generic rights of the recipients of one's actions as well as oneself.* This is the foundational principle of morality and governs all rational conceptions of human action and relationships. Consequently, the *prima facie* referent of the concept of law articulated by Fuller, namely, 'the enterprise of subjecting human conduct to the governance of rules' accepted without demur by Beyleveld and Brownsword, becomes, in the *context* of their Gewirthian account of the rational regulation and co-ordination of human relations, a necessarily *moral* conception of rule-making. Of the tenets of legal rule-making laid down by Fuller, Beyleveld and Brownsword say:[100]

> It has been claimed by some of Fuller's critics (see e.g. Hart, 1964 ...) that conditions such as these do not comprise a Morality of law because (i) they may be viewed as conditions of efficient control, not as Moral requirements, and (ii) they may be fulfilled by Morally iniquitous rules. However, from our point of view it does not matter that they *can* be viewed as conditions of efficient control. It only matters that someone who adopts a moral point of view (specifically someone who adopts the PGC) must view them as moral requirements.

They go on:[101]

> It is true that by themselves these conditions [Fullers eight tenets] are formal or procedural and can be compatible with immoral contents. We, however, would not suggest that they are sufficient conditions for law.

Beyleveld and Brownsword add that to provide a sufficient set of conditions the procedural tenets need to be coupled with conditions that state that a rule is law if, and only if:

(a) the rule is posited by an authorized source (a source authorized by the PGC);
(b) the norm posited is not immoral (the behaviour it prescribes does not violate the PGC).

---

99 Deryck Beyleveld and Roger Brownsword *Law as a Moral Judgment* (op. cit.) p. 177.

100 Ibid.

101 Ibid. p. 178.

The general point, then, is that 'procedure' is incoherent without a context, and morally incoherent without a moral context. The particular issue relating to Fuller's so called inner morality of law is that we should not spend too much time debating the self-sufficiency of the 'eight ways'; this is a cause that appears to be already lost. Our attention should be directed to the nature of the *external* morality of law, for it is in trying to capture this in a critical way that we see most clearly the relationship between ethical reason and the methodology of the social sciences and, as a by product, the ambiguities and false dichotomies erected in the course of the misguided conflict between 'Natural Law' and Legal Positivism.

The question boils down to the sociological task of how we characterize relationships between persons. To characterize them 'positivistically' in a sociological sense is to attempt to construct models of persons and institutional order without value judgment. The aversion to ethical objectivism has pushed us into a search for a methodological panacea in the form of Pragmatism, Incommensurabilism and Proceduralism in Sociology and Legal Theory. They are self defeating strategies in that they do not achieve coherence without assumptions of guiding moral principle. If such a principle can be found, we no longer need desperate alternatives to operate in their stead. In the following chapter, we pursue the search for a critical context for law: its *external* morality. We do this by examining Fuller's general conception of law as a morally appropriate framework of regulation and coordination between intrinsically valuable, free persons. This is the beginning of our attempt to locate an interface between the methodological contributions of Fuller's work with our confidence in the achievements of Gewirth. We will argue that we can make common cause between these approaches in showing that the project of law is really the project of sustaining morally appropriate institutional relations. This is indeed a craft requiring a procedural structure, but it is a craft that can be practised only with the aid of substantive principle.

Chapter 2

Means, Ends and the Idea of Freedom

In 1958 Fuller delivered the *Edward Douglas White Lectures on Citizenship* at Louisiana State University under the title of 'Freedom and the Nature of Man'. These three lectures survive in parts: the first as the full written text, the second a mixture of text and short phrases, and the third as a few hand written notes that Kenneth Winston, in his commentary on the revised edition of *The Principles of Social Order* presents under the provocative title of The Case Against Freedom'.[1] In these lectures Fuller launches an attack on some of the complacencies of traditional liberal thought, particularly on the idea that the propagation of individual freedom is beyond criticism. He proposes to examine a sacred theoretical cow: the idea that freedom is first, a comprehensible and unproblematic notion, and secondly, that it is *intrinsically* valuable. Fuller asks us to reconsider J.S. Mill's and Hayek's defence of freedom as mere 'absence of constraint' – what Fuller refers to as *negative* freedom – and asks why we ever managed to swallow such a creaky and obviously incomplete account of what is supposed to be our most prized moral possession. Of Mill's *Essay On Liberty*, Fuller says,[2]

> With each re-reading I found my doubts increasing – doubts not merely to the adequacy of the analysis, but doubts as to integrity. After a short introduction *The Essay* states that its object 'is to assert one very simple principle … [T]hat principle is, that the sole end for which mankind are warranted … in interfering with the liberty of action of any of their number, is *self-protection*.' The individual's 'own good, either physical or moral, is not a sufficient warrant' for interfering with his liberty. [(You) can interfere with a man's liberty, if he is going to hurt you, but not if he is about to hurt himself.]

Fuller goes on:[3]

> Some seventy pages later we read: 'I fully admit that the mischief which a person does to himself may seriously affect [others]'. Why – one asks – did seventy pages have to intervene before the *one very simple principle* to which *The Essay* is dedicated received this rather obvious qualification?

1 Kenneth I. Winston *The Principles of Social Order – Selected Essays of Lon L. Fuller* (Oxford: Hart Publishing, 2001).

2 Fuller in Winston, ibid. p. 317.

3 Ibid.

This is not, of course, an attack on the idea of freedom *per se*; it is an attack on an impoverished conception of it that appears to have gained ascendancy in political and sociological thinking. Fuller explains:[4]

> As an advocate arguing against freedom I should have to make two contradictory arguments: (1) freedom is a meaningless goal of social policy, (2) freedom is a meaningful goal, but a mistaken one ... Instead of taking the posture of devil's advocate, I decided to assume the role of a judge – a judge who wishes conscientiously and fully to state the arguments of the litigant against whom he is deciding – for I assure you that my decision will ultimately be that freedom is both a meaningful and a valid standard for the ordering of human relations.

These *Edward Douglas White* lectures were to serve as the basis for a book on the concept of freedom that, for various reasons and in the face of strong diversions, was never completed. But the ideas contained and hinted at in these papers have led some to suspect a shift in theoretical emphasis away from the traditional bone of contention between, on the one hand, the positivist insistence that law aims at order, and, on the other, the Natural Law or Legal Idealist tenet that law must *necessarily* aim at justice, towards the more contemporary sounding notion that 'institutional design' is intimately concerned with the promotion of freedom, and that the very concept of freedom is therefore in need of elaborate inquiry. Winston, in his introduction to Fuller's essay says,[5]

> Fuller appears to abandon the idea that justice is the inherent, general aim of legal institutions; instead he conceives of them as diverse vehicles of freedom ... Fuller conceives of freedom as effective agency, that is the capacity to realise one's choices in the world. The forms of legal order are the central ingredients of that capacity. Accordingly, in all the Eunomical essays (which were written from this period into the late 1960s), Fuller's principal focus is the nature of citizens' participation in the decisions that affect their lives.

There is a great deal to be said about the relationship between justice and freedom, and we should not hastily endorse the view that a shift from the former to the latter has taken place. In fact, in our view, taking the idea of the role of freedom as the point of departure in thinking about institutional design sharpens the focus on the issue of justice. Let us consider Fuller's thinking here in more detail.

Negative and Affirmative Freedom

Fuller's preoccupations with interaction and social order should provide a clue to the gist of the argument contained in the 'The Case Against Freedom': his suggestion is that we must become more agile in our understanding of the interplay

---

4 Ibid. p. 316.
5 Ibid. p. 315.

between, on the one hand, the obstacles to choice presented by institutionalized forms of social constraint and social channelling, and on the other, the facilitative power that the system of constraints provides to individuals to exercise various liberties. He makes the point that the words 'freedom and liberty' are derived from terms which originally had connotations similar to those which now attach to the word *enfranchised.* He says:[6]

> If in the intervening centuries there has been a gradual shift in meaning, so that to be free now means primarily to be *unfettered,* I believe this is due to an increasing – and I believe, dangerous – tendency to take for granted the facilities offered by an organised and functioning society, and to take for granted the forms of participation that society accords to us. We can say, I believe, that the original meaning of freedom was an *affirmative* one.

In the history of ideas The nineteenth-century debate between Mill's 'negative' conception of freedom and James Fitzjames Stephen's 'affirmative' or sociological account of it resulted in a resounding defeat, in terms of philosophical influence, for the latter.[7] These basic oppositions, of course, have been reproduced in the debate between Liberals and Communitarians[8] and more recently in the 'culture *versus* individual rights' discussions that have energized the debate on multiculturalism and what has been referred to as 'The Politics of Difference'.[9] There is no way we can avoid the difficulties involved in attempting to achieve a synthesis in this regard, but there might be a way of framing an approach to it that prevents us from becoming ever more tightly jammed in the confined spaces to which we are lured by one-sided thinking.[10] Fuller reminds us that if freedom *is* valuable, then we have to explain *why* it is valuable. And if we are to value freedom and encourage it, we must ask what values must condition the social relations that support it and how might these values be interpreted, maintained and applied in the dynamics of our social practices.

Winston, let us recall, tells us that:[11]

---

6 Ibid. p. 323.

7 See James Fitzjames Stephen *Liberty, Equality, Faternity* [1874] (Chicago: University of Chicago Press, 1991).

8 See pp. 93–99 *infra.*

9 See pp. 153–162 *infra.*

10 By this we mean that the typical liberal emphasis in political discourse of freedom from state interference tends to develop into a caricature when faced with the fact of the complex economic and political arrangements that make up the modern welfare state – the welfare systems which, in turn, function not only as a care-provider for individuals, but also as a means of facilitating corporate business in a way that no minimal state could ever do. Likewise, the multiculturalist insistence on the cultural groundedness of human identity, and hence the need for enhanced respect for culture in all its guises tends to develop into a caricature when faced with the liberating, and in some sense anti-cultural ethos of the idea of modern statehood. See Chapter 6 infra for a more comprehensive discussion.

11 Kenneth I. Winston (op. cit.) at p., 315.

> *Fuller conceives of freedom as effective agency, that is, the capacity to realise one's choices in the world. The forms of legal order are the central ingredients of that capacity.* [our emphasis]

This is of fundamental importance to the orientations of sociological jurisprudence. The conscious acknowledgment of the logical and moral implications of the conditions under which *effective agency* can be secured and employed provides the principle on which we have based our understanding of the critical rationale of social theory in general and the concept of law in particular. We have expressed this over the years by way of an endorsement of Gewirth's theory of agent rights and duties and of Beyleveld and Brownsword's application of Gewirth's ideas to legal theory.[12] A Gewirthian version of the idea that Winston present above is in no way antithetical to Fuller's approach. On the contrary, we would argue that the ethical objectivism defended by Gewirth, and the rationalist methodology built upon it, is better suited to explicating and applying Fuller's insights than the incommensurabilist/pragmatist programme that has sprung up so vigorously around them[13]. Fuller's critique of un-sociological and unengaged conceptions of individual freedom is an emphatic reminder that we still face the impasse brought about by eulogizing about individual (negative) freedom whilst ignoring the regulatory, co-ordinatory and communicative social structures required to sustain it. If we are to hold fast to a defensible and socially located conception of individual freedom in a Fullerian sense, we must be prepared to enter the sphere of complexity that attends the attempt to give an account of these structures, and it is here that the close relationship between the idea of freedom and the idea of justice becomes apparent.

The role of a theory of justice is to give an account of the body of principle that provides the general underlying *rationale* to a body of rules and decisions. But, as Fuller reminds us frequently, the rules and decisions in question are not to be understood exclusively as established formal-legal rules and decisions; what we ordinarily acknowledge as *the legal* evolves from the the pragmatics of social interaction in the quest for viable forms of order in human association[14]. If we are to create a *Eunomically* reflective understanding of this process – that is, a normatively critical *theory* of it – and allow this theory to inform present and future *praxis*, then we must endeavour to provide the essential *rationale* for Good Order over the entire normative institutional framework of society. If these fundamentals principles relate to 'affirmative freedom' understood as '... effective agency, that is, the capacity to realise one's choices in the world ...', and if the evolution of 'the forms of legal order' are 'the central ingredients of that capacity', then formally, justice appears as the mediating *rationale* between law and freedom, and its substantive *normative content* is to be found in an ethical and

12 See for example Henrik Palmer Olsen and Stuart Toddington *Law In Its Own Right* (Oxford: Hart Publishing, 1999).

13 See Chapter 1 *supra*.

14 See Fuller's essay 'Human Interaction and the Law' in Kenneth I. Winston (op. cit.) pp. 231–266.

sociological analysis of what rights and obligations attend the institutionalized guarantees of that freedom.

Institutional Design: Means, Ends and The Concept of Freedom

Fuller's message is that if political and legal philosophy is to make progress in its defence of liberty, then the opposition between *affirmative* and *negative* freedom should play a central part in our deliberations.[15] What we might be able to grasp more easily in the light of the above discussion is that the practical-logical status of the 'negative' conception of the value of freedom as an *intrinsic* end is quite clearly deficient. This is not simply because it seeks to make arbitrary individual choice the ultimate ethical value – even though, as we shall argue, this is a very difficult idea to defend – but rather because a conception of freedom as mere 'absence of constraint' *presupposes*, institutionally speaking, static *con*straint and active *re*straint in the relational guarantees and inter-subjectively understood boundaries of action and choice required to make even the idea, let alone the actual exercise, of freedom socially feasible.[16] Negative freedom is after all freedom *from* something, and for the concept of freedom to be meaningful, we must be in a position to understand what this something is and why it is important to be free from it. This much, of course, is admitted in Mill by way of the so-called 'harm principle'. He says, famously that[17]: '... the sole end for which mankind are warranted ... in interfering with the liberty of action of any of their number, is *self-protection*'. The individual's 'own good, either physical or moral, is not a sufficient warrant for interfering with his liberty'. But far from this being merely and negatively a 'necessary evil' of interference with the 'freedom' of others, Fuller reminds us that Mill himself later admits[18]: '... that the mischief which a person does to himself may seriously affect [others]'.

We must not proceed too rapidly here, but there are significant implications for social and political organisation contained within these minimalist remarks. Although Fuller talks about affirmative freedom as the capacity to 'participate', and also about 'citizens participating in the decisions that affect their lives' we should not leap from speculations at the most basic level of social organization to assumptions more appropriate to the institutional dynamics of a fully fledged

15 See Fuller's essay 'Means and Ends' in Kenneth I. Winston (op. cit.) pp. 61–81.

16 That is, any conception of state and society must rely on some form of normative social framework, which works as the background for freedom (negatively conceived).

17 John Stuart Mill *On Liberty*, quoted from Fuller in Kenneth I. Winston (op. cit.) p. 317.

18 Ibid. The full consequences of this might be narrowly or widely conceived. On a minimalist reading it could mean, for example, merely that 'mankind' has a duty to interfere if a father fails to take proper care of his children because he is an alcoholic or a drug addict. On a more extensive reading, it could mean that we ought to have a duty of education and supply a proper educational system through which this duty may be fulfilled. Either way it implies a regulatory public framework of some description.

and ready made system of participatory democracy. Our discussion of freedom should not simply assume a fully operational system of civil society if it is to do the theoretical job that Fuller intends it to do. We must remember, of course, that Fuller's 1958 lectures were entitled 'Freedom *and The Nature of Man*'. The issue of human nature implicated here has in recent years, and for a variety of reasons, only received scant attention. But the ideas of freedom and agency are significantly coloured depending on the philosophical anthropology that attends them – for example, whether we adopt a Rousseauian or a Hobbesian conception of the 'State of Nature', and we discuss this dimension of the problem briefly in Chapter 3 *infra.* For the moment, and resolving not to import political and civil extravagances into our basic deliberations, we can still say safely that even on a 'simple' as opposed to a 'complex' conception of society, the ideas of freedom as effective agency require that we accept some important prudential implications for regulatory and co-ordinatory organisation. These arise not only from the fundamental 'harm principle' associated with negative freedom, but it seems – and on the basis of Mill's own admission – on its concomitant, let us call it the 'harm-correlative' or 'Eunomic' principle, that freedom entails that we attend to the institutional propagation of forms of association that are conducive to an individual's well-being – even if our motivation merely lies in the general protection of 'freedom' as 'effective agency'. This being said, let us reconsider the link between Fuller's critique of Mill's conception of freedom and their shared concerns with the analysis of 'means and ends'.

The relationship between the concept of freedom and the model of law and society based on Fuller's contrast between 'the morality of duty' and 'the morality of aspiration' is of vital importance here. It confronts us directly with what is at issue in the attempt to characterize the foundational orientation of Fuller's philosophy and method to moral reason, namely, how, from the perspective of Eunomics, we are to understand the relationship between social means and ends? Are we first, in Aristotelean fashion, to assume some understanding of the *ends* of human excellence and virtue and approach law and institutional design as forms of organisational *means* to these ends; or are we to abandon the metaphysics of 'ends-in themselves' and, in support of some form of matrix of co-ordinated (but not collective) 'subjective freedom', acknowledge the priority and diversity of individual choosing? Nigel Simmonds in his *Central Issues in Jurisprudence*[19] speaks of a fundamental divergence of perspective that turns upon what Hegel called 'the pivot and centre of the difference between antiquity and modern times' – 'the right of subjective freedom'.[20] This observation, says Simmonds, allows us to establish a useful dichotomy. He contrasts Aristotle's conception of *Politics* with contemporary liberal attitudes to law and governance. Of the Aristotelian conception, Simmonds says:[21]

---

19 Nigel. E. Simmonds *Central Issues in Jurisprudence* 2nd edn (London: Sweet and Maxwell, 2002).

20 Ibid. p. 6.

21 Ibid.

> One tradition of political philosophy, drawing its inspiration from Aristotle's *Politics* ... regards as fundamental the question of what counts as an excellent, valuable life for a human being. Having arrived at such a conception of excellence, a philosopher within this tradition will then describe the social and political institutions capable of fostering such excellent lives. The family, the forms of economic production, and the forms of governance will all be viewed from this perspective.

A rival tradition, he goes on to say, giving centrality to 'subjective freedom', emphasizes '... the importance of each individual deciding for him or herself upon what counts as a good or excellent life'.[22] But crucially, this emphasis on subjective and individual freedom breeds a heavy dependence on that which it appears to abhor, namely, coercive constraint:[23]

> Within the Aristotelian type of theory, law occupies an important but not necessarily pre-eminent place. By contrast, law assumes *absolute centrality* within the later type of theory that emphasises 'the right of subjective freedom'. For individuals can be provided with the opportunity of pursuing their own conception of a good life only if they possess clearly demarcated domains of liberty within which they are free from interference; and it is the law that must demarcate such domains of liberty. In this way, political debate in such a community is dominated by essentially juridical notions such as 'rights', 'justice' and 'equality' (rather than by non-juridical notions such as 'well being' or 'the common good').

The relevance of Simmonds' account to Fuller's thinking is twofold. First, and as we noted in our discussions of 'the morality of duty' and 'the morality of aspiration',[24] Fuller's understanding of a general ethical framework (what he calls 'the morality that makes law possible', or the 'external' morality of law), is undoubtedly derived from an Aristotelean model of institutional design. Secondly, what Simmonds says about the litigious tendencies of the politics of subjective freedom resonates very powerfully with Fuller's intense opposition to the preoccupations of legal scholarship with the formal legal process at the expense of an understanding of informal regulatory and co-ordinatory social practices. But before we face up squarely to this theoretical choice (or address the issue of whether this is indeed an 'either-or' situation), we need first to try to disentangle the problem surrounding *the concept of freedom* from the practical-logical problem of *the means-ends relation*, and for this task it is well worth taking some time to consider the precise nature of the logical difficulty that arises here. For it is in an attempt to overcome it that Fuller invests so much energy and rhetorical enthusiasm in developing the metaphor of 'architecture'.

22 Ibid.

23 Ibid. p. 7.

24 See Chapter 1 *supra*. pp. 59–65.

The Metaphor of Architecture

Fuller, in his article *Means and Ends*, quotes J.S. Mill as follows:[25]

> All action is for the sake of some end, and rules of action, it seems natural to suppose, must take their whole character and color [sic] from the end to which they are subservient. When we engage in a pursuit, a clear and precise conception of what we are pursuing would seem to be the first thing we need …

If institutions are normative channels, which are supposed to serve as means to desired ends of social and political life, we need, it seems, a 'clear and precise conception' of those ends. Fuller, in his introductory remarks to the essay *Means and Ends*, however, remarks that Mill gave us 'no explicit answer' to the problem raised so clearly in the above argument.[26] But this is not so. Mill, gives a very explicit answer. It is not one that is helpful to the cause of establishing a science of Eunomics, but it is clear nevertheless:[27]

> Questions of ultimate ends are not amenable to direct proof. Whatever can be proved to be good, must be so by being shown to be a means to something admitted to be good without proof. The medical art is proved to be good by its conducing to health; but how is it possible to prove that health is good? The art of music is good, for the reason, among others, that it produces pleasure; but what proof is it possible to give that pleasure is good?

Mill's central argument in his *Utilitarianism* is that, in relation to the question of which human ends are *intrinsically* worthwhile, we must face the fact that there is but one, happiness, and that this notion is held to be radically subjective. This does not, of course, prevent Mill from later attempting to de-radicalize it and reduce it to his own idiosyncratic views on the higher virtues of the study of Geometry and Greek over board games and lavish dining. But Mill erected his entire theory of Utilitarianism on the Epicurean principle that practical reason was powerless to determine the rationality of ends-in-themselves. Rather, practical reason begins its employment only when supplied with an end in view. Given an end or goal to strive for, practical reason must confine itself to the task of fathoming the most effective and efficient means to achieving that end. And in this task, the human employment of practical reason excels.

We thus have the logical basis of the two great schools of political thought: subjectivists who accept that Reason cannot fashion justifications of ends-in-themselves, and objectivists who believe in our capacity to defend conceptions of intrinsic human worth and articulate them in a universal understanding of the Good. Although it would be going too far to say that without the latter belief, our

25 J.S. Mill, *Utilitarianism, Liberty and Representative Government* [A.D. Lindsay ed.] (New York: Dutton, 1951) p. 2 quoted in Kenneth I. Winston (op. cit.) p. 63.

26 Fuller in Kenneth I.Winston (op. cit.) p. 64.

27 J.S. Mill *Utilitarianism* John Stuart Mill and Jeremy Bentham *Utilitarianism and Other Essays* [Alan Ryan ed.] (Harmondsworth: Penguin, 1987) p. 275.

political and moral practices would be rudderless, we do need to acknowledge, that they would be incapable of universal justification. Indeed the whole concept of universal justification – apart from the justification of the 'universal subjectivity of practical reason' appear as 'metaphysical', pre-modern and ultimately, perhaps, ideological or arbitrary.

Fuller was impressed by the force of the anti-metaphysical objection to the idea of 'intrinsic ends' and seemed to realize that if Eunomics was to offer any hope of justifying ultimate *ends* towards which, politically and legally, we might employ institutional *means,* it could not proceed without some alternative to the orthodox understanding of the practical problem. Fuller's suggestion, as we are aware, is that we consider the analogy of *architecture.*

Fuller says that although architecture is a practical art existing for the satisfaction of the human ends of Utility and Beauty, the *means* by which the art is practised, and the criteria by which we judge the excellence of the practice, do not depend upon complete clarification of the definition of Utility or Beauty. A survey of what is possible precedes that of what is desirable, and some limitation of means is in fact necessary to liberate the creative spirit. But this is not all. We need furthermore to be careful not to turn the whole logic upside down. Fuller says:[28]

> ... because it is a mistake to assign an unconditional primacy to ends over means in thinking about creative human effort, it does not follow that the mistake can be rectified by a turn of 180 degrees .... Some vague conception of architectural ends at the outset is essential to define the range of means worthy of consideration for architectural purposes. In the development of architecture it is safe to assume that an obstinate quest for new forms of beauty and utility has sometimes led to the discovery of means capable of realizing them, so that firmly held ends stubbornly pursued can sometimes create means that were previously non-existent.

Fuller goes on to articulate his unease about the way 'negative' conceptions of freedom have brought a new language of liberty and choice in to play and has recast our *ends* or *ethical objectives* in Nietzschean terms as our value 'preferences' which in turn might be given practical-technical expression in some simple form of utility calculus. These rhetorical observations are meant to strengthen our resolve in the search for the rationality of institutional design. But the implicit assumption that there are real important and fundamental ethical ends that we ought to attend to as opposed to mere value preferences skates over a bigger problem than is fully acknowledged by Fuller. Blaming J.S. Mill and Nietzsche for encouraging subjectivism, individualism and nihilism is one thing, but defeating their views is quite another. The ethical problem lying behind Fuller's unease, of course, is the one described so brilliantly in Macintyre's *After Virtue*. It is the problem of finding a defensible replacement for the ethical ends of human excellence that the Aristotelian notion of virtue formerly provided. But if God and Virtue are dead in our 'emotivist' world, then there really are only 'value preferences', and consequently no firm ethical distinction between *any* ends.

---

28 In Kenneth I. Winston (op. cit.) pp. 65–66.

This lament is a prelude to a sustained attempt by Fuller to subvert the troublesome logical relationship between means and ends that appear to frustrate the attempt to make critical progress in the theory of institutional design:[29]

> No abstractly conceived end ever remains the same after it has been given flesh and blood through some specific form of social implementation ... an end takes its 'character and color'[30] from the means by which it is realised.

But even if this (perhaps simplistic) severance between means and ends is accepted, we often conveniently overestimate our capacities to achieve these ends, and simultaneously assume the 'infinite pliability of social arrangements':[31]

> Curiously, though the technicians capable of devising the apt means for social ends are never identified, it seems to be assumed that their competence is unlimited. There are signs by which we know a good carpenter, one of them being his knowledge of the limitations of the materials with which he works.

But perhaps the most important passage in this sequence of reasoning about means and ends is Fuller's objection to the conceptualisation of institutions in general. His remarks here are designed to arrest our linear trajectory in thinking about practical reasoning both in modelling institutions and in our understanding of the 'architectural' task of social policy. He says,[32]

> We should not conceive of an institution as a kind of conduit directing human energies toward some single destination. Nor can the figure be rescued by imagining a multipurpose pipeline discharging its diverse contents through different outlets.[33] Instead we have to see an institution as an active thing, projecting itself into a field of interacting forces, reshaping those forces in diverse ways and in varying degrees. A social institution makes of human life itself something that it would not otherwise have been. We cannot therefore ask of it [that is, the institution] simply, *Is its end good and does it serve that end well?*

This is an extremely important observation: ends derive from reasoning about human nature and the human predicament, and we may devise means that are to serve these ends as efficiently and effectively as possible by understanding the environment in which human life unfolds. But when the means in question are capable of transforming the environment, and even the conditions under which sustained reflection about human nature and so on takes place, then surely we cannot use a simple means-ends matrix as a system for devising good institutional

---

29 Ibid.

30 This is a reference to remarks in Mill's *On Liberty*.

31 Fuller in Winston (op. cit.) at p. 70.

32 Ibid. at pp. 68–69.

33 This is a reference to Stephens' *Liberty, Equality, Fraternity* (op. cit.) which contains a vigorous critique of Mill's *On Liberty*. Stephens was much given to hydraulic analogies.

order. But there is more complexity awaiting our inquiry, for neither, says Fuller, should we attempt to 'arrange human ends in a hierarchical order' and design social policy as 'a schedule of ends in the order of their urgency'.[34] He goes on:[35]

> ... human aims and impulses do not arrange themselves in a neat row of desired 'end states.' Instead they move in circles of interaction. We eat to live and we live to eat. We love that we may be loved, and we want to be loved that we may love freely. The pattern of our private desires reflects itself in the pattern of our social institutions. We keep up with public affairs so that we may vote intelligently, and we believe in democracy partly because it gives us an incentive to keep informed. We take legal measures to insure the impartiality of jurors, and we defend the jury system because it tends to inculcate a habit and taste for impartiality.

This certainly makes us reconsider the convenience of employing simple distinctions between, on the one hand, norms or institutionalized policies as means and, on the other, the outcome of these policies – or its values – as ends. There is, undoubtedly, inevitable and usually unexpected 'overspill' or 'externality' in any policy direction as soon as one moves from policy *formation* to policy *implementation*. This is so plainly evident in attempts to implement economic policy that economists have provided us with these very terms of art. Furthermore, and what is reflexively important to the logic of institutional design, there is, as Fuller says, a curious and interesting merging of means and ends once we realize that there is a form of 'virtue' in the creative attempt to shape a policy direction or to modify an institution for the purposes of accommodating freedom. This is so, not only because institutions, as we have seen, cannot be characterized as mere means, but also because the very act of engaging in this kind of activity has positive side-effects; let us recall Fuller's words:[36]

> Our best institutions are, I believe, pregnant with beneficial side effects. It is chiefly for this reason that I have so vigorously objected to the view that institutions are mere inert conduits directing human energies ... toward certain desirable end-states. Our institutions are part of the pattern of our lives. The task of perfecting them furnishes an outlet for the most vigorous of moral impulses.

In the reception of these imaginative reflections on the relationship between means and ends, we must bear in mind two things. First, that Fuller begins this phase of his writings as an attempt to make some logical and theoretical progress into a profoundly difficult philosophical problem, that of showing how it might be possible to bring practical reason to bear on the evaluation and adoption of ends-in-themselves. The main aim of the idea of 'architecture' is a thus a *rhetorical* attempt to undermine the firm logical objection expressed so powerfully by Mill.

---

34 Fuller in Kenneth I. Winston (op. cit.) p. 68.

35 Ibid. p. 70.

36 Fuller in 'Means and Ends' in Kenneth I.Winston (op. cit.) p. 72.

Secondly, at the empirical level of action and consequence, as well as at the psychological level of consciousness, there is certainly much that is of relevance and importance here. But logically and methodologically, the decision to subvert the distinction between means and ends, and to reject the notion of a 'hierarchy of ends' might lay up more problems than it solves. The former, the distinction between means and ends, is, as we shall explain, indispensable to an understanding of the structure of practical reason and thus to the possibility of concept formation at the level of sociological method. The latter, the objection to 'a hierarchy of ends', begins to look incoherent if we recall the implicit distinction made between 'ethical objectives' and mere 'value-preferences, and, can only hinder us in our attempt to avoid the pitfalls of incontinent notions of incommensurability.[37]

Means, Ends and Sociological Method

Fuller's essay 'Means and Ends' offers an opportunity to reconsider Weber's reflections on the problems of method that introduced social theory to the device of the Ideal Type and thereby the related concerns of Selznick's articulation of the sociological indispensability of the Master Ideal.[38] There is certainly some agreement between Fuller and Weber on the central methodological obstacle, namely that of the intractability of institutions to convenient characterisation for the purposes of sociological analysis. At the empirical level of action, one could imagine Weber and Fuller in complete agreement, but methodologically there is almost a complete opposition. Weber argued that *because* of the infinitely complex flux of history, the ambiguity and ambivalence of conscious subjectivity, and the multiple and amorphous intermingling of the posited and inferred means and ends of institutions, social phenomena precludes itself from systematic explanation. However, he advanced the view that *aspects* of social action might be illuminated and rendered artificially discrete, and that our cognitive interest in them satisfied to some extent, by ideal-logical modelling of the practical activity associated with social institutions. In short, we might make artificial but instrumentally uncontentious assumptions about purposive social action in general, and draw inferences about the rationality of means employed to intelligible reconstructions of various ends. The key to understanding social life, according to Weber, lies in an understanding of the practical core of social action, and this seems readily to translate into the examination of the institutional expression of social norms (means) and the values (ends) that contextualize and, it seems, motivate normative action. Embracing value-phenomena in this way does not, in Weber's opinion, mean judging the intrinsic worth of ends implicit in our values. His conception of 'value-free' or 'value-neutral' method suggests that on the basis of ideal-typical hypotheses we might instead offer an approximate account of the way values (in the form of conditional or hypothetical goals and ends) shape the historical and social landscape in terms of institutional striving, and, given an awareness

37 For a discussion of this see Chapter 1 *supra* pp. 35–40.

38 See Chapter 1 *supra* pp. 31–33.

of the objective and material *context* of action, lead us – with a bit of luck – to further insights into why certain institutions prevail or why certain individuals act as they do.[39]

Weber's work is an important advance in the direction of our sociological thinking (particularly away from the confusions of sociological 'psychologism' and naturalistic or 'nomological' abstractions),[40] but the question that has been asked of this supposedly 'value-free' method is, 'how is it possible without caprice in the selection of institutional elements, to construct a defensible model of the ends or goals of a complex institution – say of law, or of the family or of education?'.

This is precisely the question we posed earlier in relation to Selznick's notion of the Master Ideal[41] – a device that we take to be directly analogous to Weber's notion of the Ideal Type. This is the central problem that arises methodologically in relation to the logic of means and ends, and Fuller's analysis is not helpful in this respect. The logical problem raised explicitly and intentionally by Mill above, and the logical problem of the 'value-freedom' of the ideal-type arising in Weber's (and in Selznick's) theorizing are untouched by Fuller's admittedly accurate observations that means–ends social action appears very messy at the level of actual experience. So Fuller acknowledges the problem, and appears to appreciate its complexity at the deeper normative level of analysis, but he does not tackle it – or at least he does not tackle it in any satisfactory way.

What, then, is the best reading of Fuller's methodological reflections and of his 'architectural' rhetoric? It seems that stricken by the intractability of the means-ends problem and facing the demoralizing duality of the prospect of the demise of sociology on the one hand and the triumph of 'the salesmanship of value-preferences' on the other, Fuller concedes defeat and abandons the (Weberian) hope of targeted methodological concept formation in social science (that is, abandons the hope of an ethically and logically systematic characterisation of social institutions).

In salvaging what integrity and ethical hope there is left for the future of sociological jurisprudence, the potentially fatal critique of *intrinsic* conceptions of practical reason (the alleged incoherence of defensible conceptions of 'ends-in-themselves') is avoided and instead Fuller diverts our attention away from logical collisions to a world of not merely plausible, but genuinely inspirational, metaphors. Specific means require specific ends, and the absence of specifically defensible ends is not merely inhibiting, but methodologically speaking, debilitating. Fuller thus urges sociologists to postpone their fate and put their rational energies into developing the much more general insight that *ideally* there

39 See Stuart Toddington *Rationality, Social Action and Moral Judgment* (Edinburgh: Edinburgh University Press, 1993) Chapter 2.

40 By 'nomological' Weber meant the 'covering law' or 'hypothetico-deductive' model of explanation which had been suggested (by, inter alia, J.S. Mill) to be appropriate to both the natural and social sciences. Weber's method of verstehen is the rejection of this approach in social theory. The technical details of this discussion can be found inToddington *Rationality, Social Action and Moral Judgment* (op. cit.).

41 See Chapter 1 *supra* pp. 30–33.

is a very close relationship between freedom and the idea of perfecting institutions. Freedom then becomes closely linked to the activity of institution formation and the activity of amending and reshaping institutions, and it is in this light that the concept of *affirmative* freedom takes on a more specific meaning.

Freedom and the Source of the Legal Impulse

The piece unearthed by Winston and named 'The Case Against Freedom' might thus be 'inserted' into Fuller's essay 'Means and Ends' at this point to great effect. For Fuller shows precisely how endorsements of *negative* freedom underpin, perhaps innocently, flawed ideas of institutional design based on convenient distinctions and simplistically hierarchical conceptions of social policy. In approaching the conclusion of the third section of 'Means and Ends' Fuller says:[42]

> In a tacitly assumed hierarchy of ends, freedom is accorded a high position – perhaps the highest position – this ranking being assigned to it, *not because of any assumed structural relation with any other ends*, but because of an attributed *intrinsic* value. [Our emphasis]

Fuller's brief, but, with Winston's reconstructive contribution, now fortunately expanded discussion of freedom ends here with the remark that this conception of the intrinsic worth of freedom is unrelated to an understanding of the structural exigencies of social ordering – other than to concede (*à la* Mill) the need for the 'necessary evils' of some constraint. This view, says Fuller, can only '... encourage and appear to legitimate what may be called the salesmanship of value preferences'.[43]

In relation to Fuller's engagement with the orthodox issue of explicating a concept of law in terms of the divide between Natural Law theory and Legal Positivism[44] we now have a better understanding of what Fuller intends as the relationship between the 'external' and the 'internal' morality of law.[45] The 'external' morality of law, or the external *context* of legal rules as we referred to it earlier, is a morality constituted by a striving to create an institutional environment appropriate to our aspirations to productive freedom in the pursuit of a form of excellence.[46] In other words, the linear problem of means and ends is transformed in a subtle way into a reflexive consciousness of the ways in which we might contribute to a vision of what the architecture of *freedom* might look

---

42 In 'Means and Ends' in Kenneth I. Winston (op. cit.) p.72.

43 Ibid. p.74.

44 See, for example, Lon.L. Fuller, 'Positivism and Fidelity to Law – A Reply to Professor Hart' *Harvard Law Review* (Vol. 71, No. 30, 1958) p. 632.

45 Lon L. Fuller *The Morality of Law* (New Haven, CT: Yale University Press, 1969) pp. 95–151.

46 See our discussion in Chapter 1 *supra* pp. 59–65.

like. The evolution of *formal* legal processes from *informal* ones seems to receive its impulse from a developing consciousness that the *essential* aim of the legal enterprise is the practically reasonable supervision and development of the procedures by which the institutional commitment to freedom (in its enhanced affirmative sense) is regulated and co-ordinated. Rather than being as Winston plausibly suggests, a shift in theoretical emphasis from the concerns of *justice* to the promotion of *freedom,* we can see just how Fuller's analysis of freedom is integrally relevant to the institutional theory of law as 'Good order and workable arrangements'.

But, perhaps we are some way from a firm understanding of the substantive picture of the anti-Positivist, anti-Realist standpoint that emerge from Fuller. We do know that it lies in a conception of human nature which is essentially Aristotelian insofar as it requires us *to contemplate what could be meant by human flourishing.*[47] If cognitive and practical engagement in addressing this question requires an understanding of what *affirmative freedom* means, then it seems that we have a small part of the answer: the ethico-philosophical orientation to the problem of human association is *in itself* part of the primordial impulse to the human striving for well ordered social institutions, which in Fullerian terminology is what the business of Eunomics is about. The Good of arrangements allowing or encouraging the expression of affirmative freedom appears as a second-order *presupposition* of thinking and talking about the problem of institutional design, not as a substantive first-order problem relating to one of the sub-sets of ends subsumed by the idea of human flourishing. Affirmative Freedom, in Fuller's thinking, it seems, thus belongs to a higher set of Goods than those 'value-preferences' that might figure normatively, in policy terms, in the questions raised by the practical rationality of the implementation of institutional means and techniques. Our understanding of Fuller's message is that if this higher good underlies all our regulatory and co-ordinatory strivings, then the architecture of *freedom is* the architecture of *justice.*

Fuller, Gewirth and the Idea of Effective Agency

If we try to pursue Fuller's reasoning a bit further, can we not say then, that a reflexive analysis of the problem yields something like the idea that there are levels or orders of the problem of social regulation in relation to human purposes, and that regardless of the specific orientations of choice, there is something very significant about the very having of purposes *per se* and of the general activity of striving for purpose fulfilment? And, as we noted above (and without making unsupported presumptions about aspirations and virtue, or about the modern, pluralistic complexities of choice and identity), is there not a general *end* apparent in the very idea of the project of constructing a social order, namely, that of facilitating the expression of voluntary purposivity? We must answer

---

47 See the discussion *supra* of N.E. Simmonds' (op. cit.) juxtaposition of Aristotle's conception of Politics with contemporary liberal attitudes to law and governance.

this affirmatively, we think; but, despite Fuller's assistance in bringing us to this point in the analysis, there remains a gap in our deliberations. Where Fuller talks about the 'enfranchisement' of individuals and 'participation in decisions that affect their lives', he need not immediately be assumed to be taking modern civil and democratic institutions and rights for granted, because this conception of freedom and enfranchisement is, in principle and widely in actuality, applicable to simple, 'pre-legal' or 'customary' forms of association.

But there is, in Fuller's conception of the relationship between freedom and institutional design, an assumption that guaranteed and rational participation in decision-making is a basic *interest* of human beings. We would not, of course, dispute this; the point, however, concerning the attempt to construct a theory of legitimate and workable social order from a conception of freedom is that one must show that *each* individual has an interest in, or some reason to respect and provide the guarantees and opportunities for *others* to participate in decision making that affects their (others') lives. The sociological-jurisprudential gap is created by the absence of sociological or ethical warrant for the operative assumptions of *the equality of persons* and of the existence of *reciprocal rights and duties* accruing to individuals to respect the capacities for voluntary purposive activity of other persons. In other words, from the conjunction of propositions that persons can be conceived of as actors collectively and individually, and that individuals and groups are capable of framing and pursuing purposes voluntarily, and that all or some persons are capable of reflecting upon institutional design conducive to the protection and expansion of this voluntary purposive activity, and even that these facts are mutually communicable,[48] it does not follow that we might now romp *Eunomically* towards the rationally necessary demonstration of the universalized, egalitarian and participatory model of Good Order. This is because despite the Fullerian guidance in our reflections on freedom as affirmative and effective agency in making the case for basic order, the prudential and purposive calculations of individuals or groups have nowhere been shown to require *necessarily* the taking into account of the freedom-related interests of *other* individuals or groups. In other words, the definitively *moral* question from the perspective of the individual: 'Why should *I* regard *your* capacity for freedom as being as valuable and worthy of the same protection and possibilities of expansion as *mine*?' is not answered in a way that significantly affects our *Eunomic* understanding of the *structural* location of freedom. The 'internal' morality of law does not provide an answer (rather, it presupposes one); the 'external morality of law' or 'the morality that makes law possible' as a framework of duty and aspiration does not provide one – in fact, in Aristotelean provenance, this is a notoriously *inegalitarian* model.[49] We might also note that where, hitherto, we have used 'affirmative freedom' and 'freedom as effective agency' interchangeably, there is a subtle priority in

48 For a more comprehensive discussion of this point see Stuart Toddington 'The Moral Truth About Discourse Theory *Ratio Juris* (Vol. 19, No. 2, June 2006) pp. 217–230.

49 Aristotle's theory of slavery is found in Book I, Chapters iii–vii of *Politics* and in Book VII of *Nicomachean Ethics*.

operation here. 'Negative' freedom is 'freedom from constraint' asserted to be *intrinsically* valuable; 'affirmative freedom' is Fuller's antidote that stresses the idea of freedom as an integral and vital part of a set of Eunomic social-structural relations. Now while the *structural* implications of negative freedom, are seen as negatively implicated in the sense that they are mere 'necessary evils', freedom understood as effective agency (that is, affirmative freedom) stresses that these 'necessary evils' should rather be theorized as vehicles for the general advancement of equal access to engagement in self-directed purposive activity. This of course is not a *carte blanche* that gives unlimited access to realize one's choices in the world, for this, without more, would be identical to a *negative* and structurally free-floating conception of freedom that would simply be a restatement of the 'necessary evil'-thesis. Instead we need an argument that can show why it is rational for individuals to participate in freedom enhancing activities for other people than themselves. Only through this type of argument will it be possible to construct rational models for the institutional and collective pursuit of affirmative freedom, and hence of justice.

Winston tells us that Fuller's notion of 'freedom to realize choices' is undoubtedly related to a 'participatory' notion of order. Winston is right about this and the textual evidence is clear in Fuller's famous essay, 'The Forms and Limits of Adjudication'. This essay predates the Habermasian analysis of Communicative Action in locating the legitimacy of institutionalized adjudication in the alleged reciprocity of rights and duties that flow from the basic human interest to give and receive reasons.[50] But again, this makes no progress in establishing the case for a *Eunomic* social structure unless, as noted above, we demonstrate that the individual's *interests* in establishing and securing forms of communicative co-ordination and reason-based adjudication *logically entail* these fundamental mutual and reciprocal participatory rights and duties.

Our suggestion is that the reading of Fuller's conception of Eunomics erected upon the vital critique of negative freedom is significantly enhanced if the moral presuppositions that underpin it are first identified and then candidly exposed to epistemological analysis. This, of course, is the role we envisage for Gewirth's ethical rationalism. A detailed explanation and defence of Gewirth's argument can be found elsewhere,[51] but here let us state it as the basis of our understanding of what *Eunomics* must adopt as its operative conception of 'affirmative freedom'. Gewirth argues that all agents – that is, all those who voluntarily employ means to ends – must as a matter of practical necessity acknowledge the indispensability of the basic and generic wherewithal to act, regardless of their purposes. They must pro-actively value the set of generic goods comprising this wherewithal: a set of

50 Compare the analysis of fundamental interests in discourse theory – for example Jurgen Habermas *The Theory of Communicative Action* (Cambridge, MA: Polity, 1998) with Lon L. Fuller 'The Forms and Limits of Adjudication' *Harvard Law Review* (92, 1978) 353–409.

51 See Alan Gewirth *Reason and Morality* (Chicago: Chicago University Press, 1978) and Deryck Beyleveld *The Dialectical Necessity of Morality* (Chicago: Chicago University Presss, 1991).

goods that Gewirth refers to as 'freedom and well being' or the generic features of action. This proactive valuing entails, from the viewpoint of the prospective, purposive agent, and on pain of contradiction, an effective rights claim to the generic features of action. This rights claim arises from the property of agency, and *any* agent must thus accept that *all* agents must make this claim to their 'freedom and well being'. This, from the perspective of any agent *vis à vis* any other agents, amounts to the acknowledgment of a duty. Hence, all agents must assent to the imperative: 'act in accordance with the generic rights [that is, the right to freedom and well-being] of the recipients of your actions as well as your own', this being the Principle of Generic Consistency or PGC.

The adoption of the PGC will benefit our future deliberations in several ways. The first, is that we can establish the notion of *Eunomic* order as an architecture of justice on the basis of an egalitarian notion of primordial (as opposed to 'positive', 'derived' or conveniently assumed) individual rights inhering in the very notion of 'freedom as effective agency'. This allows us to see that freedom and morality are inextricably linked. Freedom as a presupposition of effective agency is a notion that, dialectically, from the standpoint of the agent, shows how *other-regarding* interests feature as an integral part of prudential practical reason. Explicating this result frees us from the reliance on rhetorical and metaphorical allusions to altruism and innate rights that might have become hostages to fortune in relation not only to 'architecture', but, moreover, certainly in relation to central aspects of the Aristotelian and Platonic models of 'the morality of aspiration'. It frees us as social and legal theorists from a disingenuous reliance on the appeal to common-sensical and destructively ambiguous 'liberal' values in order to achieve completeness and coherence in the critique of existing institutional arrangements.

Secondly, in incorporating the Gewirthian analysis of agency we establish firmly the theoretical indispensability of the existence of conceptual orders or levels of human goods. In this regard, in relation to incommensurability theory and recalling Fuller's implicit distinction between defending principles of institutional design and 'the salesmanship of value-preferences' we might reiterate our conception of the orderly relations that pertain between references to 'Goods', 'ends', 'means and ends', 'norms' 'values', value-preferences', 'rights' and 'interests'. Where incommensurability theory speaks plausibly of the 'intransitivity of goods', where 'goods' are the objects of acts of choosing or preference, this analysis loses much of its appeal when we shift, as logically we should, to initially speaking of voluntary purposive action rather than 'choice' of 'goods'. Defending the significance of incommensurability becomes more problematic when we then emphasize the distinction between, on the one hand, those *generic* goods that comprise the essential wherewithal to function *feasibly* as a purposive being, and on the other, the panoply of goods that feature as the focal objects of choices to pursue certain courses of action aimed at securing certain desired outcomes. Once this distinction is made, a hierarchy of, we might say, *second order* or *generic* goods appears defensible, and the question of the 'incommensurability of goods' operates coherently only in the realm of 'first order' choices. But more than this, the rights and duties implicated in the agent's relationship to the *generic* goods of Gewirthian 'freedom and well-being' are not merely static and 'basic', they expand logically and contextually in a continuum of practical reason to allow us to synthesize much more complex rights and duties and thus condition and structure, in principle, the entire range of, and the very rationality of, human choosing. The simple truth is that once 'I' become apprised of the necessity of pro-actively valuing certain goods whatever purposes 'I' may wish to pursue, and of the moral implications of this categorical valuing, then the actual pursuit of some of my putative purposes will then be seen to be rationally impermissible. The static model of, on the one hand, a small and dialectically necessary (or, as some would perhaps prefer 'self-evident') table of Basic Goods (and thus basic rights) juxtaposed on the other to a vast territory of complex and incommensurable options and values insulated from and unrelated to the former, is thus shown to be entirely misleading. We shall return to this in our discussion of some of the currently pressing issues arising from the influence of pluralist and multiculturalist critique in Chapter 5 *infra.* In the following chapter we attend to several issues arising from what might be seen as the 'politics' of the notion of 'affirmative freedom'.

Chapter 3

The Politics of Affirmative Freedom

Fuller surely points us in the right direction in steering us towards a confrontation with the sociological demands arising from the eulogy on freedom; he also presents us with a clear illustration of the intimate connection between freedom and justice. The break with 'negative' conceptions of liberty is, however, merely the first push that overcomes the moral and sociological inertia of the 'means-ends' conundrum. Some difficult issues remain. Three such will occupy our attention in this chapter: (i) the fundamental issue of freedom and responsibility in opposition to a model of determinism; (ii) the problem of evaluating the 'instrumental' as opposed to the 'intrinsic' conception of freedom and the related issue of the priorities of individual *versus* communal 'ends'. This latter is perhaps the heart of the Liberal/Communitarian debate. Finally (iii), the idea implicit in Fuller's critique of J.S. Mill that freedom requires not only a settled institutional environment, but the engaged and collective creation and acceptance of authoritative norms and individual obedience to them. This is to say that the idea of *affirmative* freedom implies a social contract model of authority. This is of great logical importance because Mill, the archetypal 'negative' libertarian, would be most reluctant to accept this claim. Mill is famously opposed to the idea of a social contract, yet, as we have explained, the 'harm principle', implies it. Some coherent resolution of this position is urgently required at this stage of the discussion.

Our model of law and of freedom (though not our epistemology of moral reason) presupposes the necessity of a contractarian model of the rationality of consent to institutionalized authority. We will argue that the account of 'institutionalized right' is the pivotal *logical* if not historical moment in what we have called *the continuum of practical reason,* whereby prudential reason can be shown to imply moral reason, and where moral reason can be shown to imply the rationality of the creation of legal structures and beyond. Thus before concentrating (in Chapter 4) on the logical detail of the notion of such a continuum, let us pause to explore some of the issues arising in the relationship between freedom and the demands of a model of a social contract. Through this examination we can make some genuine progress in responding to the problems raised in all three areas noted immediately above.

Hume and Mill on the Social Contract

Both Hume and Mill expressed their antipathy to the idea of a social contract. In his *Man and Society* John Plamenatz announces that Hume rejected not only Natural law but also 'the notion of a social contract, not merely on historical grounds, but as a tool of explanation'.[1] But, as we shall presently see with Mill, if this is true, it is a subtle and complex rejection. There is considerable scope for confusion and cross-purpose discussion when speaking of the social contract: is it to be understood as a heuristic device rather than an account of historical development; is it as a pronouncement upon the fate of human nature, is it simply an embellished description of the fact of political and legal authority seasoned with a hint of reciprocity to explain our supposed obligations? We should bear in mind that the long history of social contract theorizing, as GDH Cole remarked, offers merely a *formula*, the substantive values and variables of which we might contest in various ways.[2] These variables are profoundly contentious and relate to motivational models of human agency, the material organizational context of social and economic relations and, as we see dramatically in Hobbes and Rousseau, no less than a 'philosophical anthropology' offering an 'affective' account of human nature.[3] Substantively, this trio of variables presents us with a range of profound philosophical and sociological problems, but methodologically, this is a 'plus' rather than a 'minus' for the heuristic application of the idea of the social contract. Its formal structure allows us to organize complex claims and hypotheses into an ideal-typical framework of contextualized rights and obligations, and there should be no serious objection to this useful methodological feature. Form and substance do indeed come together in social contract arguments to make dramatic claims about authority and obligation, and if the approach is to offer more than a heuristic orientation it must be capable of responding to objections which strike at the heart of its operative assumptions about legitimacy. We must, then, be clear about whether it is the substantive aspects of the social contract claims that we find objectionable or the formal idea of the framework itself, but admittedly this tidy division is not always as straightforwardly apparent as these brief remarks might suggest. Hume's famous objections illustrate the potential for ambiguities.

There are in Hume two main sources of dissatisfaction to social contract theorizing. One is his understandable contempt for the disingenuous allusions to consensus which attach themselves to notions of an 'original' contract. In this he is undoubtedly right and we should take the opportunity to endorse his views in this regard. A mature and sociologically respectable account of the social contract

---

1 John Plamenatz *Man and Society*: *Vol.I* (London: Longman, 1963) p. 300.

2 See the invaluable commentary to *The Social Contract and Discourses by Jean Jacques Rousseau*, translated with Introduction by G.D.H. Cole (London: J.M. Dent and Sons, 1913).

3 Erich Fromm's explanation of the 'affective' dimensions of social and political theory offers a valuable contribution, see, for example, *Man For Himself* (New York: Rinehart, 1947).

does not require them. The other concerns his aversion to the very ideas of natural 'laws' of morality, preferring instead, to treat the institutions of morality, and institutions of government founded upon them, as pragmatic conventions arising from natural sympathies and the exigencies of association. In giving an account of government in this way, it is not so much that he engages with the apparatus of Natural Law and the Social Contract, but rather that he offers a less fanciful route to their sufficient explanation for the purposes of establishing a theory of political obligation.

'Of the Original Contract'

Hume devoted an essay bearing this title[4] to the issue of the nature and function of consensus in the account of the genesis and continuing legitimacy of government. In this he has a fairly easy target. The idea that human beings, variously located, did at some point naturally consent to place the authoritative administration of their affairs under the *aegis* of some sovereign person or body of persons is, of course, implausible. And just as we cannot adequately theorize an empirical transitional moment between natural (animal) and (human) social existence in human affairs, we cannot and should not assume that social order arises from chaotic and dangerous conflict and is settled at a stroke by some act of consensual submission to an overarching authority. The idea of more or less ordered relations of reciprocal expectation in interaction is a starting point for social theory, not a discrete event to be explained 'historically'. Hume's observations, in *Of The Original Contract*, are not so much aimed at the naive historical assertion of the coming together of savage peoples to opt for civilization and central government, but are an expression of his scepticism of the idea that the process leading to the establishing of government is a *consensual* matter which thereby legitimizes the ensuing authority.[5]

> I maintain, that human affairs will never admit of this consent, seldom of the appearance of it; but that conquest or usurpation, that is, in plain terms, force, by dissolving the ancient governments, is the origin of almost all the new which were ever established in the world. And that in the few cases where consent may seem to have taken place, it was commonly so irregular, so confined, or so much intermixed either with fraud or violence, that it cannot have any great authority.

There is the suggestion of an uncomfortable regress implicated in this reference to the existence of the 'ancient governments' which provide convenient structures for the usurper to put to new uses. But Hume does have a reply to this obvious inquiry to which we can turn presently. We must note first, however,

---

4 David Hume *Of the Original Contract* [1748] Sir Ernest Barker (ed.) in *Social Contract: Essays by Locke Hume and Rousseau* (Oxford, Oxford University Press, 1960) pp. 147–166.

5 Ibid. p. 154.

that his remarks are not a rejection of the idea that consensus *can* provide a 'just foundation for government'; consent, he says, '... is surely the best and most sacred of any';[6] his difficulty lies with the romantic fictions which the historian of 'the original contract', or the apologist for the present regime is prone to create.

Thus it is not history *per se*, or the idea of a contract, but it is the idea of an historical act of consent or a natural process leading to consensus which Hume rejects. But Hume has a 'more philosophical refutation' of this principle of the original contract. He suggests that all moral duties are of two kinds.[7] The first are those which are found as natural instincts in men, such as the love of children or pity for the unfortunate. These sentiments are unreflectively felt to be proper, and the exercise of such natural forbearances is an obvious advantage to the functioning of society. The second type of morals are performed from a sense of obligation which is produced by reflection on what is required for the possibility of social life. It is from reflections upon the justice of respect for property and the necessity of honouring promises that obligations arise and are acknowledged as authoritative. These obligations, Hume says, are functions of prudential reasoning which flow from the logic of self-love:[8]

> For as it is evident that every man loves himself better than any other person, he is naturally impelled to extend his acquisitions as much as possible; and nothing can restrain him in this propensity but reflection and experience, by which he learns the pernicious effects of that license, and the total dissolution of society which must ensue from it.

This reflection, carried a little further, leads us to understand the source of political or civil duty.[9]

> A small degree of experience and observation suffices to teach us, that society cannot possibly be maintained without the authority of magistrates, and that this authority must soon fall into contempt where exact obedience is not paid to it.

It is important that we acknowledge this qualitative shift in the analysis of the description and justification of the basis of the contract. We are not being presented with an historical account of what certain beings thought or did, but rather, we might say, we are offered an ideal-type of prudence which suggests that, given the kind of motives and desires human beings in general possess, and given their context of action, it thus appears as reasonable to give allegiance to an authority set up to enforce the institutions held to be appropriate to the pursuance and provision of the 'interests and necessities of human society'.[10] But is not this precisely the insight that identifies the idea of the social contract?

---

6 Ibid. p. 154.
7 Ibid. p. 159.
8 Ibid. p. 160.
9 Ibid.
10 Ibid. p. 161.

There is no reason, according to Hume, to struggle to ground the duty of allegiance on the idea of the intrinsic morality of a promise arising from an act of consent to submit to authority. We are not bound to obey our sovereign because of the sacred worth of a promise, but, rather, because the great advantages of commerce and social intercourse 'can have no security where men pay no regard to their engagements'. Because the obligation to obey (allegiance) is prudentially as powerful as the obligation to keep our promises (fidelity), there is nothing to be achieved, says Hume, 'by resolving the one into the other'. There is, however, some considerable logical advantage in formulating the matter in respect of allegiance as opposed to fidelity. Hume says that those who attempt to ground the argument in the intrinsic value of promising are embarrassed when asked for a reason as to why one ought to keep one's promises. If the answer is likely to rest upon the assertion that society would be chaotic without the institutionalized dependence upon the performance of reciprocal expectations, then Hume's point is well taken. The more pressing issue, according to Hume is: '*But to whom is allegiance due? And who is our lawful sovereign?*'

Hume's suggests that an inquiry into the determination of property rights, and the succession and rights of princes and governments is philosophically 'uncertain, ambiguous and arbitrary'[11] In the light of Hume's historical accounts of a variety of despotisms arising from deception, treachery, lust and greed, it is, he suggests, wise to consider, if not in too scrupulous detail, the most advantageous method of stabilizing the continuation of sovereign authority. Hume says:[12]

> The general obligation, which binds us to government is the interest and necessities of society; and this obligation is very strong. The determination of it to this or that particular prince, or form of government, is frequently more uncertain and dubious. Present possession has considerable authority in these cases, and greater than in private property; because of the disorders which attend all revolutions and changes of government.

This is so much like Hobbes that we can safely conclude that Hume, far from being a critic of the idea of the social contract *per se*, is, historically and logically, as competent a proponent of the argument as we are likely to find. Hume's idea might be expressed as an acceptance of the unfathomable processes in and through which political and economic relationships take shape, power becomes distributed and property allocated. Whether the initial causes or actions leading to these states of affairs might, in some sense be rationally regarded as legitimate or otherwise, is highly debatable. However, like Hobbes, the idea that the radical righting of wrongs is a cure far more painful than the disease is clearly at the forefront of Hume's analysis of prudence and the idea of obligation. If this is a sound point then a model of the social contract should incorporate it.

11 Ibid. pp. 161–162.

12 Ibid. p. 165.

J.S. Mill's 'Critique' of the Social Contract

J.S. Mill was certainly sympathetic to Hume's account, but, as we saw clearly in Fuller's examination of the account of liberty, Mill was already slipping into logical arrears with the sociological implications of his thesis in this regard. This is confirmed when we look closely at his objections to the idea of a social contract. Let us consider the following remarks. In *On Liberty*, Mill dismisses social contract theory thus:[13]

> Though society is not founded on a contract, and though no good purpose is answered by inventing a contract in order to deduce social obligations from it, everyone who receives the protection of society owes a return for the benefit, and the fact of living in society renders it indispensable that each should be bound to observe a certain line of conduct towards the rest.

In this one sentence there are four discrete declarations, three are merely asserted, but the last takes the form of a conditional argument. The first, in an empirical-historical sense, and as Hume maintains, is almost certainly true: '*society is not founded on a contract*'. The second, '*no good purpose is answered by inventing a contract in order to deduce social obligations from it*' is, however, false if the third: '*everyone who receives the protection of society owes a return for the benefit*', is true. The fourth, namely that '*the fact of living in society renders it indispensable that each should be bound to observe a certain line of conduct towards the rest*' leaves us no choice but to re-examine the meaning of the entire passage, for this now appears as almost intentionally contradictory. The following passage confirms these misgivings:[14]

> This conduct consists, first, in not injuring the interests of one another, or rather certain interests which, either by express legal provision or by tacit understanding, ought to be considered as rights; and secondly in each person's bearing his share (to be fixed on some equitable principle) of the labours and sacrifices incurred for defending the society or its members from injury and molestation.

This passage contains all the conceptual ingredients of a social contract theory. It does not use the term 'sovereignty' but it alludes heavily to a fixed and formidable source of authority; it speaks, one must assume, of interests rightly protected as opposed to mere subjective expressions of interests; it alludes to a positive and coercive legal system; it endorses (oddly, given Mill's eulogies to non-conformity and experimental living) individual deference to an institutional structure of extant and unspoken cultural norms or traditions ('tacit understandings'); and finally, it takes as self-evident the need and duty to establish a protective state apparatus: a public sphere of internal and external policing and security, presumably to be

---

13 J.S. Mill *On Liberty* in H.B. Acton (ed.) *Utilitarianism, On Liberty and Considerations on Representative Government* (London: J.M. Dent and Sons Ltd, 1972) p. 132.

14 Ibid.

staffed, funded and supported by the efforts of all according to some equitable method.

Where do all these ideas come from? The obvious rejoinder (that is, social contract theory) would be facetious, but the answer inherent in the fragments of Mill's text we have before us lies in the grounds of the truth of the proposition that '… the fact of living in society renders it indispensable that each should be bound to observe a certain line of conduct towards the rest'. From here we have some warrant to suggest that, for example, but perhaps most importantly, that this conduct consists, '… first, in not injuring the interests of one another …' and that these duties suggest that, '… each person [should bear his share to be fixed on some equitable principle] of the labours and sacrifices incurred for defending the society or its members from injury and molestation' because clearly, '… everyone who receives the protection of society owes a return for the benefit …'.

To return to the first of Mill's remarks quoted immediately above, what fact or facts of society are these which provide, it seems, a necessary justification for a series of duties and obligations in respect of our conduct towards others? In other words, what '*is*' of society is supposed to generate these '*oughts*'? If there are such '*oughts*', or at least if we wish to proceed in designing and defending institutions on the basis of the assumption that there are – as does Mill – we must, it seems, take up a contrary position, namely, that although society is not founded on a contract, a good theoretical purpose *is* answered by inventing one. Liberalism, after all, is just such an invention.

Liberalism: Individual Freedom and Public Authority

Mill's contribution to liberal thought, despite its problems, has been as enduring as anything we can point to in the modern history of ideas. The same will be said about John Rawls's version of it. For although Liberalism is more than John Rawls, and even more than an amalgamation of the Old Rawls and the New Rawls, no-one in the latter half of the twentieth century has managed to exert such a profound influence on our thinking about individual freedom and institutional justice than he, and he is rightly taken as the most accomplished and comprehensive proponent of modern liberalism. And despite the wide range of interests and theoretical positions which might be found in the work of writers now retrospectively labelled as 'communitarian', this strand of thinking is almost defined by its attitude to Rawlsianism.

Rawls is a Kantian insofar as he sees the primary importance of the idea of autonomous agency as giving us the key to understanding justice and freedom. A person is a person and an intrinsically valuable thing because it is a thing capable of framing ends in general, not because it has adopted or might adopt certain ends in particular. In an older, but still very relevant language of ethics and of persons, it is not because a person is virtuous or has aspirations to virtue, that he or she is a uniquely valuable thing. Rather, the capacity to choose (or reject or change one's mind about) an *orientation* to the good, not the goods chosen, constitutes the most valuable aspect and, Rawls suggests, the *highest* interest, of the person. In this respect all persons are equally valuable. This, however, does not imply a complete and unrestrained liberty. Rather, from the viewpoint of the idealized framer of ends it points to the rational necessity of accepting universal principles of government. The state, according to Rawls, is to be organized in a way that gives priority to the individual's capacity to choose its own ends. It must refrain from attempting to impose upon persons specific and substantive conceptions of the good or from officially discriminating in favour of certain goods whilst denigrating others. In the parlance, this is the principle that the state must remain neutral between conceptions of the Good.

Rawls' strategy is to ask us to consider persons abstracted from their historical and biographical identities, actual preferences and values in society, and on the assumption that they are all equally and minimally free and rational (in the sense of minimally and prudentially rational as prospective framers of ends anxious *above all things* to remain as such) to imagine them in an 'original position' behind a 'veil of ignorance', completely unaware of any talents, deficiencies or proclivities they might have, or any social and economic advantages that might contingently accrue to them. Rawls suggests that all would 'agree' that society should be regulated on the basis that each person is to have:[15]

> ... an equal right to the most extensive total system of equal basic liberties compatible with a similar system of liberty for all.

and that:

> Social and economic equalities are to be arranged so that they are both (a) to the greatest benefit of the least advantaged, and (b) attached to offices and positions open to all under conditions of fair equality of opportunity.

Arrangement (a) rests on the idea that individuals would optimize their situation by choosing equality from behind the veil of ignorance as a guarantee that they might limit their worst-case scenario on entry into an actual social location and identity. This is an ingenious account of how simple prudence might justify the idea of equality, maximization of liberty and a pluralist state. Moreover, if the assumptions about, and definitions of, persons, the characterization of purposive value-choice, and the identification of interest priorities underpinning it are true, then it would be difficult to reject it.

But communitarians (and many others) have asked whether this conception of the person – this autonomous framer of ends but of no end in particular – can be coherently employed. Problems arise from the Rawlsian conception of the individual as something fully formed yet antecedent to society, and from the assertion that it is not *ends* that are important, but rather, the choice itself and the capacity to choose, reflect, and change our ideas about 'the Good'. We can refer to these objections respectively as relating to the problems of (i) abstraction, and (ii) of the arbitrariness of preferences.

---

15 John Rawls *A Theory of Justice* (Cambridge, MA: Belknap Press, 1971) p. 302.

(i) The Abstracted Self

Charles Taylor offers two theses about the person which challenge Rawls' device of the individual and of the idea of an original position. The first is a fairly orthodox sociological account and thus is susceptible to orthodox objections itself. He suggests that the very idea of personhood depends upon identity, and that identity is formed directly from our social location in a matrix of value orientations within a linguistic community. Human animals are basically 'self-interpreting' animals, but there is a cultural context and a structure antecedent to the self-interpretive potential. The capacity for the creation of self is given shape and substance in personhood by virtue of its location as a thing within this structure. In other words, as a thing within this matrix of language and value orientations, it is possible to exist consciously in many ways, but it is not possible to exist consciously other than in the form of a thing which adopts some orientations to ends framed *in terms of the extant linguistic and conceptual resources of the community*. Individuation then, occurs, when one has adopted a sufficiently well-oriented and systemically viable set of ends. But this is not a purely random or subjectively arbitrary process. Taylor suggests that ends or value commitments not only *can* be articulated and defended, but that they *must* be so articulated and defended if they are to count genuinely as ends or values in the context of conscious agent choices as opposed to mere automatic physical or emotional reactions to the world. He refers to the idea of 'strong evaluation' as opposed to mere unqualified, unintellectualized likes or dislikes.

Taylor says:[16]

> We are not selves in the way that we are organisms, or we don't have selves in the way we have hearts or livers. We are living beings with these organs quite independently of our self-understandings or interpretations, or the meanings things have for us. But we are only selves insofar as we move in a certain space of questions, as we seek and find an orientation to the good.

The way Taylor defines this process makes it impossible to conclude anything other than that community is prior to, and constitutive of, the self. For it is the community that, in the quest to arrive at selfhood, provides the space, the vocabulary, the 'space of questions' and thus the options to explore. On the face of it, this is, as noted, a plausible and familiar sociological account amounting to the claim that society shapes our identity. But the devil is in the detail; and when it comes to reconciling structure and action in a comprehensive account of the person, one suspects there is something not wholly coherent or wholly 'authentic' about the suggestion that persons can forge 'strong evaluations' of individuated selfhood from within what more orthodoxly might be seen as a pre-constituted 'socializing' environment. Taylor's point against Rawls, however, would be that we must start from the idea of community, and not the individual, and that the idea

16 Charles Taylor *Sources of the Self: The Making of the Modern Identity* (Cambridge, MA: Harvard University Press, 1989) p. 34.

of a significant yet unsocialized core of choice-framing self-hood is unserviceable as the basis for our ethical and political philosophy.

Michael Sandel arrives at a similar conclusion.[17] In a sense his is perhaps a more powerful criticism for the reason that it draws out an immanent tension in Rawls' account of the person rather than imposing, as Taylor does, an alternative sociology of the self upon it. Sandel, like Taylor, is unhappy with the idea of a disembodied (he says 'unencumbered') self cut off from any specified ends. He speaks of Rawl's attempt to 'deontologize' liberalism by investing a neutral (as opposed to a substantive) idea of Right or justice with a supreme value. Sandel suggests that only by constituting all hypothetical individuals as a community in the first place – and a very special type of community affirming certain specific conditions of association – does it make sense for Rawls to speak of the value of co-operative and structured equality and justice. The community in question, says Sandel, must first be assumed to be united on the basis that they might share a cultural and political space equally, and also on the basis that all would prioritize their individual capacities to frame diverse but unspecified ends.[18] This, of course, entails that they are content in the knowledge that this would create a multiplicity of personal orientations to the good and that this condition is itself desirable. It is this last point that, if accepted, would scupper the Rawlsian project insofar as it offers an alternative to traditional deontology: a project that we might define as the attempt to establish a defence of values, yet which does not itself presuppose or appeal to values. For is there any theoretical improvement on asserting the Rawlsian basis of the ultimate Good as opposed to earlier conceptions of virtue? Is the former not itself a *substantive* claim?

(ii) Arbitrariness of Ends

Of the issue relating to what we designated as 'the arbitrariness of ends', it is Alasdair MacIntyre who raises the most disconcerting objections and, perhaps, points the way to their eventual resolution. In *After Virtue*[19] MacIntyre begins by agreeing with the liberal and pluralist description of the ethos of choice that characterizes the social condition we presently inhabit. This he calls the 'emotivist'[20] society: a *milieu* in which it is generally true to say that the *belief* that there are intrinsically valuable ends or an objectively defensible hierarchy of aspirations is indeed, long dead. But rather than celebrating the emancipation of the individual that allegedly arises from this realization, MacIntyre makes the sensible if somewhat deflating observation that we seem to have produced a

17 Michael J. Sandel *Liberalism and the Limits of Justice* (Cambridge: Cambridge University Press, 1982) Chapter 1.

18 See ibid. and also H. Benjamin Shaeffer's review of Michael J. Sandel *Public Philosophy: Essays in Morality and Politics* (Cambridge, MA: Harvard University Press 2005) 292 in *Essays in Philosophy* V(ol. 8, No. 1, January 2007).

19 Alasdair MacIntyre *After Virtue* 2nd edn (London: Duckworth, 1985) pp. 11–14.

20 The term 'emotivist' is borrowed from Ogden and Richard's linguistic empiricism.

multitude of choice-making individuals free to invent conceptions of the Good, but, he asks, why should anyone take any notice of them? What is more, he asks, what value or worth is there in 'liberty' already agreed to be, in moral terms, worthless and directionless.

For Rawls, let us remember, two axioms about the self create the framework of liberal pluralism: (i) the individual is a thing which values *above all else* the capacity to choose and (ii) it is an individual who subscribes to *the truth* of a version of incommensurability theory: that is that there is no objectively determinable *Good* and, in relation to competing conceptions of the Good, no '*better*' life. This, taken at face value, and at least in its effects, is close to a reproduction of the 'emotivist' impoverishment of the individual's moral choices that MacIntyre asks us to consider in his critique of Rawls in *After Virtue.* In *Whose Justice? Which Rationality?*[21] MacIntyre expands upon this observation:

> Desires of course had always been recognised as motives for action, and someone could always explain his or her action by expressing the desire which had motivated it by means of some such expression as 'I want'. Nor was there anything new about it being believed that it is good to satisfy certain desires or that the pleasure in so satisfying them is good. What was new was the transformation of first-person expressions of desire themselves, without further qualification, into statements of a reason for action, into premises for practical reasoning. And this transformation, I want to suggest, is brought about by a restructuring of thought and action in a way which accords with the procedures of the realms of the market and of liberal individualist politics.

MacIntyre's point can be rendered concisely if somewhat technically by saying that we have abandoned the metaphysics of a teleology of freedom, for an allegedly presuppositionless discovery of the *intrinsic* value of liberty. Ethics, the ancients suggested, is the business of identifying the Good: that which is valuable for its own sake. And freedom in this scheme of thought is a pre-condition of a striving toward ends of genuine value: virtue and dignity. The ancient teleology of *areté* is indeed contentious, but the modernist strategy asks us to relinquish the *telos* of virtue, replace it first with a universal acknowledgment of the delusional quality of the Good, and then postulate that the *capacity* to pursue 'the Good' is, above all things, that which each and all of us should value in ourselves and in others. For the moment let us simply note the blunt collisions: Is freedom a means to something genuinely valuable in human terms, or is it an end in itself? Is the community historically, psychologically and morally prior to and productive of the individual? Is the idea of community and a commitment to the integrity of community a value that is presupposed and logically prior to a commitment to the valuing of individual persons and individual freedom?

---

21 Alasdair MacIntyre *Whose Justice? Which Rationality?* (Notre Dame, IN: University of Notre Dame Press, 1988) pp. 338–339. Fuller's lament in this regard is that, 'Where we once judged a man by the cast of his character, we now inquire about his 'value preferences'. From his essay 'Means and Ends' in Kenneth I. Winston (ed.)*The Principles of Social Order – Selected Essays of Lon L. Fuller* (Oxford: Hart Publishing, 2001) p. 71.

Thinking about Institutional Design

In Chapter 2 we said that Fuller's endorsement of the idea of affirmative freedom is not a solution to the problems of institutional design, but rather a more promising starting point that might allow us to reflect upon the apparent intractability of some foundational problems about freedom. These are the problems of relating the individual to the social and natural whole in terms of a meaningful selfhood, and the problem of reconciling the heterogeneity of individual liberty and identity with, we can now say, the value of the quest for a vital form of homogeneity in community. We have said enough to show us that opting for one or the other aspect of social existence is neither a rational nor even an emotionally satisfying option. We can characterize these tensions as 'dialectical', but should we, perhaps, acknowledge them more candidly as 'contradictions'?

It would certainly be a contradiction to hold as simultaneously true, for example, Rawls' account of the primacy of the individual *and* Taylor's theory of the communal self. But it is not a contradiction for an individual to come to the realization that he or she is, by virtue of consciousness, part of the world of nature and humanity, yet essentially separated from the world and from all other beings in it. This is a fact about the self (or self-consciousness) and the world; and far from being a contradiction, the awareness and acceptance of this fact as an essential aspect of the human condition, is, as Erich Fromm has urged us to acknowledge, a crucial pre-condition of overcoming the disorienting and potentially destructive tendencies engendered in the personality by this initial state of alienation.[22]

And neither is it a contradiction for an individual to desire or to hope to experience the exhilaration of liberty and the affirmation of self on the one hand, *and* also desire the opportunity to experience community and the selflessness of duty on the other. We can go so far as to say that it is not a contradiction to suggest that these desires and their fulfilment in experience might *occur* simultaneously. If individuality and society, and order and freedom *were* contradictions it would be impossible to construct a coherent theory that embraced, justified and valued both. Our starting point is, therefore, simply and intuitively dialectical in that we know that whatever the case might be, plumping exclusively for order against freedom, or for individuality against community, will always turn out to be irrational.

This is not to say that contradictions in institutional thinking do not exist or that the discovery of contradictions does not provide us with opportunities for theoretical and practical progress. A somewhat pedestrian approach to logic serves us best here: The Socratic dialogues, for example, can be interpreted plausibly as showing us that the nature of the reality we seek to apprehend seems to be characterized by oppositions, antitheses and apparent contradictions, and that the hapless proponent of a one-sided conviction always ends up looking rather foolish. We need not rush to the conclusion, however, that what we learn from dialectical critique is that the secret of successful philosophizing is never

22 See, for example, Erich Fromm *The Sane Society* (London: Routledge and Kegan Paul, 1956).

to miss a particular opportunity to restate the general problem by contriving as many contradictions and ironies as possible in the process of inquiry. Neither are we required to ontologize the cognitive experience of theoretical tension by congratulating ourselves on the fact that our confusions are in fact accurate representations of a 'contradictory' reality. We can simply say that faced with apparent antitheses, tensions and exclusivities, we should not adopt a one-sided and partisan enthusiasm, but instead, acknowledge that our task as social scientists or merely as informed observers and commentators is to strive theoretically and practically to overcome them.

Affirmative Freedom and Human Nature

Given the complexity of the attempt to theorize a universal account of society and the individual in other than exclusive or non-dialectical terms, we should not be surprised, then, to find that philosophical and anthropological speculations on some common source of human nature have played a major role in attempting to construct all-embracing theories of political and legal obligation. These have focussed on more concrete psychological attributes of human beings as opposed to the ethereal and abstract capacities of idealized agency which we considered above in the discussion of Rawls and Kant. Some of these accounts of the fundamental dispositions of humanity, we might note, from Plato to Hobbes and on to recent times, have been quite disappointing to the liberal-minded, alleging and emphasizing as they do the incorrigibly illiberal tendencies and traits of human beings. This is a pessimistic one-sidedness in thinking that is as unhelpful as over optimism – but perhaps not as dangerous. Let us consider briefly what we might take from the cautious and pre-emptive view of authority in overcoming this impasse in theorizing a model of personality or human nature.

In Hobbes, Locke and Rousseau, the idea of Civil Society is based upon the notion that a negotiated form of ordered, cultural and economic interrelatedness has grown out of an assumed savage or 'natural' stage of human existence. Hypothetically, this transition is modelled on the assumption that historically, viable human association is dependent on the actual existence in some sense of an associative contract or compact. This compact serves as a logical springboard for the idea of a deliberate and consciously designed contract of government in more complex circumstances of association. Arising from this common premise, however, are not only major divergences concerning the nature and functions of the institutions of civil society in relation to 'the state', but also conflicting and confusing images of the logically pivotal account of what constitutes the primordial, 'natural', or 'pre-legal' environment.

Accounts of the natural condition vary dramatically; from a predatory war of all against all in a sea of normlessness, to a gentle and reciprocally respectful Golden Age of happy and mutually respectful beings. Famously in Hobbes and to some extent Locke, we are to imagine a jungle where the meek and the weak often in isolation, sometimes loosely and precariously brought together, scrape a miserable subsistence, living constantly in fear of the predatory aggressor.

By contrast, in Rousseau, and, we are often told, as a consequence of his more sanguine conception of the human personality, we see a well-ordered, co-operative and happy association of primitives, well-disposed to each other and free of the vices that, with the advent of complexity, property and sectional interests, are later to corrupt them. Ostensibly, then, it is from these divergent accounts of the original condition and equally disparate understandings of the psychological and moral dispositions of its inhabitants, that disparate prognoses and prescriptions for our present, complex condition are held to arise.

The account of the natural state is, therefore, logically crucial. And let us recall that, as we noted in our discussion of Rawls, once the scene has been set, it appears as a simple and compelling step to offer an account of the function and limits of 'the state'. Sandel, we recall, took exception to this in Rawls' account of the individual, suggesting that there was a prior 'loading' of the subject in terms of interests (in respect of autonomy and choice, predispositions to co-operation, tolerance and appreciations of diversity) as well as in motivations. The claim was that Rawls had already constituted his abstract individual as a collectivized and politicized being. This is identical to well rehearsed and forcefully developed criticisms of Locke's account, and it looks like there is something in the logic of this type of social contract theorizing that predisposes us towards this error.

In Locke, it is barely disguised. The Natural Law account of society and the person is traditional and explicit, even the account of property is mediaeval but, of course, in the historical circumstances was delivered with some revolutionary implications. Quite apart from these implications, the logic of Locke's argument from the idea of property is simple and sound. Locke says, as had Natural Lawyers before him, that individuals in a 'state of nature' are clearly God's creation, they are not put here to perish but have a duty to preserve themselves. To do this they must labour; the physical and mental faculties that enable them to labour, and the fruits of that labour, are necessary means to this preservation.[23]

> The labour of his body and the work of his hands, we may say, are properly his. Whatsoever, then, he removes out of the state that nature hath provided and left it in, he hath mixed his labour with it, and joined to it something that is his own, and thereby makes it his property.

From this idea of property in a state of nature, prior to all government, laws and protections, comes the idea of a natural right to defend it and thus a right to punish and deter those who would contrary to the natural law, attempt to deprive another of it. Locke's theory of legitimate government and reciprocal obedience to it is, then, built upon this idea: In effect, a system of government which regulates and codifies punishment and property rights on the basis of these natural rights. And how remarkably close this idea is to Herbert Hart's, concept of a 'minimum content of natural law' underpinning the procedural and validating institutions

23 Peter Laslett (ed.) *John Locke The Second Treatise of Government* [1690] (Cambridge: Cambridge University Press, 1991) S. 27, p. 287.

of' the union of primary and secondary rules' that emerge to 'remedy the defects' of a 'pre legal' (that is natural or customary) condition of society.

The problem, given that there appears to be considerable common ground in these texts concerning the basic needs of human subsistence and the finitude of resources, is that these differences appear to turn upon the affective (emotional) and cognitive (prudential-rational) aspects of the motivational profile of the hypothetical individual faced with what is, broadly speaking, an economic problem in the 'state of nature'. Social contract theory appears as an attempt to integrate a general philosophical anthropology with political economy and jurisprudence as it attempts to articulate the nature and scope of rights and obligations of the hypothetical individual so conceived.

But despite common orientations to the explanation of the emergence of the phenomenon of sovereignty, Hobbesian, Lockean and Rousseauian views of the world (for example) appear markedly distinct if not irreconcilable. Furthermore, contemporarily, as we have noted, at the level of systematic theory and even at the level of personal political attitudes, references to these great divides persist. These differences arise from disagreement in three foundational areas of speculation. Let us examine their durability in the language of more recent concerns.

G.D.H. Cole, as we noted earlier, warned us of the contentious variables required to give substantive status to the *formula* of a social contract model. We mentioned there that these were, in general, problems concerning accounts of agency, material context of action, and the 'affective' account of the personality. These categories, however, are usually found tacitly merged in a package of assumptions. Let us separate them and say a little more about them.

The first, the problem of agency, is absolutely central to our account of the concept of law and, of course, is pivotal in Fuller's philosophy. It concerns the idea of the individual as agent and the conception of the nature of practical rationality assumed to be constitutive of this agency. We have seen that there is a strong objection to assuming, for theoretical and justificatory purposes, the coherence of a disembodied agent simply in possession of some form of purposive consciousness. 'Rawls *versus* the Communitarians' raises some fascinating dimensions to this debate. But this issue also encompasses a range of difficult philosophical problems concerning the relationship of purposes to the source of the desires which framed them. Thus problems about free will and determinism, in sociology and in moral philosophy, and disputes about the conditions under which autonomy and moral culpability might exist, confront us immediately. So too do the attempts to model conceptions of instrumentally-rational economic behaviour, especially with regard to the relationship between self-interested 'prudence' and 'other-regarding' morality. We have suggested that Gewirth's model of the agent is minimal and non-contentious, assuming no complex dispositions or 'affects' other than the pro-active valuing of purposes. This, however, leads us to a synthesis of rights and duties. The potential in Gewirth's argument to the PGC for achieving a theoretical resolution of what we can see as the liberal/communitarian conflict is, therefore, of immense importance.

The second problem, that of orienting ourselves theoretically to the material context of action, is, of course, intimately related to the first, and concerns the attempt to interpret and respond to the inherent problems of social and economic organization. We could hardly imagine a broader category of phenomena. Generally it concerns the situation assumed to provide the context of the agency – whether individual or collective. It might be framed in terms of large scale historical-sociological accounts of the dynamics and major transformations of modes of production including more technical concerns about the division of labour and social differentiation, class and the conditions of production, distribution and capital accumulation and thus power relations. At different levels of generality a fairly blunt collision of views on this matter could be offered by the example of Marx's view of history and economic development in opposition to Hegel, or equally importantly, Marx's great rifts with the economic theories of Smith and Ricardo. Sociologically, Marx features as a good example again of the antithesis, in a fundamental or ontological sense, of Durkheim (or almost any non-Marxist): is society a dialectically evolving structure comprised of conflictual class relations and heading towards the abolition of private property and the state, or is it a self–regulating organic unity tending towards equilibrium and an ever more responsive and pluralist state apparatus? Both Marx and Durkheim, however, share common ground in characterizing the individual and individual economic behaviour as almost epiphenomenal to the great structural forces at work in the historical-social process. And this structural approach, merely to reinforce the point about the scope for profound disagreement in this area, would be antithetical to the great individualists like Bentham and Mill and in direct opposition to 'actionist' schools of sociological thought.

The third element concerns the explanatory and subsequently the unavoidably prescriptive and justificatory function of the theoretical incorporation of a 'deep' motivational or 'affective' model of the personality assumed to be implicated in the response. We find the most overt and dramatic investigations into this problem in psychoanalytical schools of thought. Psychoanalysis or psychology are convenient labels here, but, in the case of, for example, Jung, Freud, and Fromm, these inquiries are explicitly theological, mythological, historical, political and anthropological – and not, it seems, related in any important sense to the present concerns of 'psychology'. In fact the divergence of views between Jungian, Freudian and Post-Freudian schools of psychoanalytical thought are closer to the sphere of disagreement between Hobbes and Rousseau. In this regard we might also consider the gulf between Benthamites and Kantians in the language of utility versus moral essentialism, or between Kant's articulation of a Will to (rational) Autonomy through obedience to the immanent moral law, and Nietzsche's (and subsequent post-philosophical) rejection of moral reason as a disingenuous Will to Power. In various combinations and possible permutations even of this small, if prestigious, assembly of thinkers, motivations and sentiments, behaviours and reactions, hatreds and devotions might be reduced variously to the delight of the sexual frissson, the desperate need to be at one with the world either in death, destruction or love; Diffidence, Greed and Vainglory; the blend of pity and self love; freedom through participation in the universality of the rational and the moral, or freedom through existential courage and the imposition of the superhuman will on the world. Let us also note that we have not attempted to fathom the 'psychological' assumptions operating in supposedly non-psychological accounts such as those of Marx and Durkheim.[24]

Towards a Synthesis

If it is the case that these great constellations of disagreement in social and political theory arise from the fundamental problems of reconciling order with freedom, we should find the three elemental components of ontology and method implicated in any comprehensive account of society. These concerns are certainly not confined to post-enlightenment or contemporary discourses. And neither are cleavages in these fundamental areas products of modernity. Zeno's anarchic Republic was, it seems, the perfect antithesis of Plato's authoritarian vision of the State and the Noble Lie that perpetuated it. John Carey tells us, that:[25]

> The Republic shows his [Plato's] admiration for the iron discipline of the victors. Other philosophers of his day were preaching freedom. They dreamed of a past golden age of communal happiness with no government and no inequality. Zeno, founder of the Stoics, wrote a Republic (now lost) in which, apparently, temples, law courts, schools and money were abolished. In place of such benign idealism, Plato proposes rigorous control.

This is very familiar. Two millennia are not enough, it seems, to exhaust the resources of political philosophy in its production of brilliant, passionate, and mutually exclusive descriptions of one or the other side of the dialectic of human nature and its prognosticated destiny. A more phlegmatic and informative account is to be found in Dahrendorf.[26] He speaks of a journey along what he calls the 'Road to Anomia'. Following the Romantic Rousseau, this journey begins with the adoption of an optimistically one-dimensional model of the personality offering a celebration of the self and a denunciation of the corruption and repression of social institutions. The line of reasoning seems to be that, because there is no objective standard of good or bad, we cannot be judged; and even if there were such standards, it is institutions that make us bad, and thus we are not to be blamed.

Dahrendorf argues that when this type of speculation migrates into the mainstream of political culture and social policy its effect is to weaken the institutional framework of society from within. We reach the first stop on the 'Road to Anomia' by creating what Dahrendorf calls, 'the condition of impunity'.[27] This condition of moral paralysis accelerates institutional decay. Because normative institutions are the repositories, refineries, and ultimately

24 See, in this regard, Alex Inkeles in Robert K. Merton *Sociology Today* (New York: Basic Books Inc., 1960) p. 252.

25 John Carey (ed.) *The Faber Book of Utopias* (London: Faber 1999) p. 12.

26 Ralf Dahrendorf *Law and Order* Reith Lectures (London: Stevenson, 1986).

27 Ibid. Chapter 1 'The Road to Anomia'.

effective expressions of social norms, once this sustaining environment deteriorates, norms, and the reciprocal expectations they engender, dissipate. The terminus is normlessness or *Anomia*. But the cure, says Dahrendorf, is worse than the disease.

The false but predictable 'cure' for the immense distress caused to the fragile psyche by exposure to this dangerous condition of *Anomia* is the simplistic and brutal institutional 'quick-fix'. The 'quick fix', always regressive, tends to totalitarianism and builds upon slogans of a return to some notion of fixed and immutable values. This condition cannot be summarized more succinctly than in the title of Dahrendorf's remarkable chapter on the concept of impunity: 'Seeking Rousseau, Finding Hobbes'. This irresistible formulation (although, as is now customary, unfair to Hobbes) is the fate of creating the conditions under which authoritarianism appears as the consequence of a naïve and reckless quest for 'Rousseauian' self-regulation.[28]

Dahrendorf's message is that our attitudes to, and our understanding of legitimate institutions must be sought in a more reflectively sober model of the personality and thus a re-evaluation of the dynamics of our institutional existence. Authority must be judged by the degree to which a good faith attempt is made to turn the legal enterprise to the task of promulgating and defending institutions that offer scope and guarantees for *socially sustainable* personal autonomy. Institutional design must embrace a model of the personality which is dialectically complex, and which is dangerously misrepresented by one-dimensional conceptions – optimistic or otherwise – of human nature.

This analysis of *Anomia* seems to offer us orientation to the problem of conceptualizing a *Eunomic* social order: authority resides in normative and regulatory institutions that can function in mutually appropriate ways to preserve both the autonomy *and* security of human beings. This is another way of expressing Fuller's message that social power is legitimate and should be entrenched and preserved when it is exercised in accordance with human interests; and that genuinely 'prudent' individuals have a direct and profound interest in collective institutional design.

The Complexity of 'Eunomic' Freedom

Fuller, of course, counselled us against the convenience of operating not only with the assumption that institutions are simple vehicles (means) to the production of ends, but also that there is no clear divide in this context *between* means and ends. We should have the utmost respect for this observation, but, eventually, life without these basic practical distinctions becomes, without auxiliary aids to exposition and analysis, impossible for the theorist of institutions. Institutional design is all about constructing a normative framework of society. But let us think about this in first and second order terms of understanding the issues.

---

28 Ibid. Chapter 2 'Seeking Rousseau, Finding Hobbes'.

The 'first order' understanding is perhaps the naïvely instrumental grasp of the problem that Fuller criticizes in his essay 'Means and Ends'. It assumes that norms are means and values are ends, and nothing sensible can be said about appropriate means unless we have an understanding of appropriate ends. This is where Fuller introduces us to the metaphor of architecture and the 'second order' subtlety and generality of designing an environment compatible with what we now know in the light of this brief reflection upon it, is the very complex notion of human freedom. We can agree with Fuller that a reflexive practical awareness of the scope of this project is in itself an absorbing and rewarding focus of human thought and action. But the technical or instrumental *rationale* for norms, sociologically speaking, is grasped in terms of *means* by which we might arrive at certain *ends* or realize certain values, and in many instances of ordinary policy discourse as well as the level of concept formation in sociological method, this is a perfectly coherent way of thinking about means and ends. The trick is to know when first and second order discourse and analysis are optimally appropriate.

In thinking about law and freedom in modernity, it is sensible to imagine institutions as entrenched strategies of normative regulation or channelling that purport to express more or less legitimate – or habitually accepted – ways of achieving or sustaining more or less legitimate ends. That the transgression of some institutionalized norms attract codified and pre-determined punishments might be a clue to their identity as laws in the form of regulatory components of the apparatus of the modern state; but the absence of some official punitive response in similar circumstances of normative transgression, or conversely, the absence of overt endorsement or reward for compliance, does not imply that the norms in question are not regulatory, nor that they ought not to be considered, in a subtle yet critically defensible sense, as functioning elements of the apparatus of order. This ambiguity of the formal and the informal, of course, hints at the level of difficulty in separating the ideas of 'state' and 'civil society' and explains why some of our most influential thinkers have exhorted us to resist the temptation of this classificatory convenience.

This understanding not only allows us to acknowledge the importance of avoiding a first-order 'naturalization' of certain institutional forms, it also shows us how acute is the problem of the intrusion of *evaluation* in the attempt simply to *describe* social phenomena. We discussed this at length in Chapter 1 and noted that, in our illustrative examples, to be male, to be female, to be a parent, to be young is, of course, partly a matter of physical contingency, but importantly, it concerns one's attitude to the normative propriety of the occupancy of roles.[29] Conceptual analysis of these examples of family, gender, and youth as institutions, therefore, takes on a contentious moral and political character. The repertoire of roles and the norms embedded within these institutions can be seen as means (that is accepted or favoured pathways) to particular ends. With the use of the sociological imagination we can see how and why apparently 'natural' institutions might be identified as regulatory strategies, the *motives* and purposes or professed *ends* of which now become ripe as the potential subject matter of moral and

---

29 See Chapter 1 *supra* pp. 15–19.

political debate concerning conceptions of human interests. If the sociological imagination can awaken us to the possibility of critique in this way, it is the legal imagination that will lead us to design the institutional guarantees under which this 'debate' might take place in accordance with what Fuller and, we would argue, Gewirth would understand by the idea of freedom as effective agency.

Chapter 4

Natural Law, Sovereignty and Institutional Design

Hobbes is regarded as the thinker who brought an end to the era of traditional Natural Law-based social contract accounts of sovereignty. He did this not by denying the existence or validity of Natural Laws discoverable by reasoned reflection, but instead, rather than echoing the divine and altruistic rights of property, sociability, and reasonableness, presented a blood-curdling account of the dreadful prerogatives of nature springing from the exigencies of self-preservation. In addition, he exposed the secondary importance of, and the equivocations present in, the convenient consensualist account by laying bare the genuine logic of the notion of sovereignty and its functions.

There are two powerful strands of argument in Hobbes that replace previous medieval or even Graeco-Roman accounts. The first is a matter of change of emphasis rather than substantive disagreement in relation to previous accounts of Natural Law. Hobbes stressed the over-riding importance of a need for a sovereign authority not primarily to endorse, encourage or bring about any particular divine or natural instantiations of the Good, but simply because as creatures with appetites we would, without such an authority, inevitably endanger and brutalize ourselves and others in the simple process of attending even to the partial fulfilment of those appetites. This concern was, of course, evident in previous accounts, but the dramatic emphasis on security and self–preservation stand out as the overwhelming *prudential* basis of the move to social incorporation under a protective and regulating sovereign, notwithstanding the entire corpus of Natural Right previously expounded. Secondly, because all rules or laws, whatever their provenance, require interpretation, Hobbes demonstrated that even if we accepted the existence and truth of eternal principles of ethical Natural Law, sovereignty or genuine supremacy would still be located precisely with the human person or persons possessing the final authority to determine and propound *the meaning* of a rule or a law and thus the scope and nature of its application in a given set of circumstances.

If the traditional social contract view at its most coherent was that sovereignty, although indispensable to the practical functioning of society, is exercised legitimately only with the *imprimatur* of Natural Law (and this invariably included the idea that the implied consent of the ruled is tied to a deal which guarantees or at least strives to secure the well-being of the ruled) then this still envisages a situation where an act of the sovereign might be alleged to be contrary to a principle of Natural Law. *Who*, asks Hobbes, would be competent to assess and evaluate the situation; *who* would frame and articulate the appropriate rule, and *who* would judge that the sovereign was in breach of it, and thus of the notional contract. The answer seems to point to the distinction between Natural Law as a set of authoritative ethical principles on one hand, and on the other, to some person or persons (hitherto subject to the sovereign) as the *interpreters* and *appliers* of that principled authority *against* 'the sovereign'. The question inevitably appears to focus on the political or personal *who* rather than the philosophical *why,* and Hobbes makes it clear that the sovereign power must be a human power and not a principle or maxim of the theory of Right.

Thus the traditional Natural Law account of the social contract theory of sovereignty lands us with two problems: one concerns the supra-positive mysteries of the process by which we are to glean the ethical principles themselves, the other concerns the identity and status of a human person or group deemed to be authorized to make such a judgment over the head of what, initially, the account suggests is 'the sovereign'. Even if such a selection process can be shown to be feasible, the traditional, pre-Hobbesian Natural Law account presupposes a *super*-sovereign authority that might be wheeled out to check the now clearly misnamed 'sovereign' and this, says Hobbes, is a contradiction. But is this a genuine problem? Can we not simply sidestep this objection to the Natural Law account of the contract by pointing out that the ethical background of principle leading to the institutionalization of sovereignty can be understood as a *constitutional framework* that clearly lays down *the limits* of sovereignty? This, however, is not as simple as it seems.

Constitutionalism and the Locus of Sovereignty

The rhetorical role played by the general maxims of Natural Law historically has been of immense importance. Principles of Natural Law have been held up as paragons or templates of reasoned right against which to measure the rationality of rightness of positive laws issued by mortal sovereigns even if they have not been held to *override* or displace positive commands. But the important point for our understanding of the logic of sovereignty (as it relates to the concepts of Natural Law and of the constitutional issues raised by the model of the Social Contract) concerns the *duality* of the concept of *normative supremacy:* what is alleged to be ethically overriding or supremely authoritative in terms of *ethical obligation* is settled by recourse to a *supreme normative-theoretical principle*; the normative supremacy attaching to politico-legal sovereignty and *legal obligation*, however, is best understood, first and foremost, as an organizational *strategy*.

It is a strategy that accords with the logic and reasoning of the Natural Law tradition, but it is qualitatively different from ethical reflection on the nature of human association. Sovereignty is a supreme 'allocation of the say' requiring the institutionalization of a powerful and effective source of decision-making that operates as the juridical terminus of dispute or deliberation. Acknowledging the appropriateness and legitimacy of this terminus of dispute as a 'fact', however, is not the same as accepting the philosophical or 'epistemological' terminus of inquiry into the truth or 'validity' of one or another normative principle of Natural Law.

We might insist that the ethical reflections of Natural Law should inform the proper exercise of sovereign authority, but we err in articulating the nature of the relationship between politico-legal Sovereignty and Natural Law if we assume that they are types of normative supremacy similar in kind, or if we hastily assume that *sovereign* authority *actually* resides *within* the ethical (Natural Law) principles themselves. A moment's inattention here produces even more confusion: we can rapidly and plausibly be seduced in to holding the view that 'the sovereign' rules with the tacit consent of 'the people' or 'the community' but within the bounds of propriety laid down by the *higher authority* to be found in the basic principles of Natural Law. In other words, we are now equivocating, and in danger of shifting back and forth, here and there, between several accounts of the *locus* of sovereignty.

The Persistence of the Hobbesian Objection

In English and European radical political thought of the late sixteenth and mid-seventeenth centuries, let us remember that the claims of 'constitutionalism' took the form of *anti-monarchist* ideologies claiming sovereignty of 'the people'. In Holland, England and Scotland in this period (1588–1649) the strength of these movements resulted in the deposition and/or execution of monarchs for alleged tyrannical breaches of the social contract contrary to the laws of God. France, in this period, despite the turmoil of constitutional 'conflict' did not see events progress quite to this point. The 'constitutional' rhetoric in play had the contemporary ring of the cause of 'democratic' individual freedom and liberty ranged against 'absolutist' tyranny. Hobbes, of course, is usually seen as a proponent of this form of unconditional and anti-democratic obligation to a sovereign power. But the historical and theoretical irony here is that the unfortunate monarchs in question[1] were all replaced by assemblies *claiming sovereign authority*. Hobbes's personal preference was for monarchical government, but his theory of sovereignty – and more importantly his critique of 'constitutional' limitations, applies perfectly consistently irrespective of whether, for example, Charles alone as monarch, or Cromwell's parliament or assembly, might be, or might claim to be, the sovereign incumbents.

The point is that constitutional bodies cannot, without some equivocation, claim to limit or control a sovereign without themselves taking on the attribute of sovereignty. This does not preclude constitutional design of a commonwealth incorporated under civil law. But this design is *internal* to the system of sovereign authority: constitutionality is public law interpreted by the sovereign's appointed judges charged with the task of articulating the *authentic* will of the sovereign. A constitution cannot, as Kant pointed out and as we shall proceed

1 Charles I in 1649, Mary Stuart in 1566 and Phillip II in 1581.

to discuss, contain a public law that permits the sovereign to be overridden.[2] The constitutional principle (and Hobbes's central maxim) is that the law is the authentic will of the sovereign and the judicial task is to determine what this is.[3]

The Power to Interpret the Laws

The analysis of the consequences of conflictual and appetite-driven human nature seems almost enough to clinch the argument for sovereignty. For even if we accept a promise of ethical eternal truth as the basis of human affairs, and even if we press the claims of Natural Law, we face the demand for a sovereign to interpret such, or, *ex hypothesi,* face what we now *know* to be an appetite-led bias in the individuals or groups who take over the power of interpreting and applying natural law. Thus we have two problems:

1) a straightforward societal-managerial problem of security, co-ordination and protection arising from the existence in competitive association of even the well-intentioned, let alone the malicious; and in addition to, and independently of this state of affairs,
2) the substantive ethical problem of determining what the moral or ethical content of Natural Law *is*, and interpreting and applying *natural* laws in respect of a sociological and ethical account of institutional design in accordance with it, and of *judging* the fidelity of sovereign authority to this design.

The fact that the ethical or moral demands of a Natural Law have, historically, achieved a high profile when ranged against the Positive Laws of Sovereigns and Monarchs does not mean that Natural Law is inherently and inevitably opposed to Positive Law or the idea of legal order. On the contrary, the logic of Natural Law brings us to the point where we are urged to move to obedient incorporation under a positive sovereign authority. In broad historical terms, the problem, as we have seen, is that, *post-incorporation*, (that is, as we move into 'civil society' under a 'social contract') and as we experience the shift in the context of authority and obligation, the ethical substance of Natural Law and its influence in relation to conduct appears, in the light of Hobbes, to render itself inappropriate and

---

2 Kant, Immanuel *The Metaphysics of Morals* Mary Gregor, (ed.) (Cambridge university Press, 1996) p. 96.

3 Hobbes says: 'For it is not the Letter, but the Intendment or meaning; that is to say, the authentique Interpretation of the Law (which is the sense of the Legislator,) in which the nature of the Law consisteth; and therefore the Interpretation of all Lawes dependeth on the Authority Soveraign, and the Interpreters can be none but those, which the Soveraign (to whom only the Subject oweth obedience) shall appoint. For else, by the craft of an Interpreter, the Law may be made to beare a sense, contrary to that of the Soveraign …'. Thomas Hobbes *Leviathan* C.B. Macpherson (ed.) (Harmondsworth: Penguin, 1968) Part II Chapter 26, pp. 321–322.

ineffective. Thus the ethical resources available as a source of *critique* of positive law and positive obligations become suddenly depleted. Simultaneously, of course, Modernity provides the opportunity for the rise of technical-managerial and organizational *rationales* for Legal Order. Particularly in the context of the emergent nation-state, technical or 'positivistic' accounts of legitimate authority and legality assume an overriding importance and tend to fill entirely the vacuum created by the demise of Natural Law reasoning.

Let us try and work through the emerging continuum of issues by first assuming that the Hobbesian consequences of the account of the relationship between Natural Law and Sovereignty is essentially correct. Obligations are transformed in civil society and perhaps it really is the case that the *rationale* underpinning sovereign authority is one of an urgent self-preserving *prudence.* But does the focus on 'prudence' and the affirmation of the logic of sovereignty force us to interpret Hobbes as an uncompromising absolutist barring the way to the idea of *constitutionality.* In the light of our discussions above, this surely cannot be the verdict we would want to deliver on such a complex and accomplished thinker, notwithstanding his apparent preference for monarchical forms of government. And what we must also bear in mind is that there is a complicated philosophical relationship between Hobbes, via Rousseau, to the most profound of moral rationalists, namely, Immanuel Kant; and that the latter reproduced Hobbes's theory of the unquestionable supremacy of the sovereign – even in the face of immoral commands – in almost identical fashion. What is the reason for this? It is certainly not because Kant's intention was to rule out the possibility that we might coherently affirm and guarantee 'natural' and inalienable human rights, including the right to democratic participation in the business of a sovereign state. In fact, in Kant, as we shall see, we find quite the reverse.

Rather we should examine the idea that practical reason has a dynamic attribute of continuity and that prudence, moral obligation and legality do in fact reside in a coherent set of relations. But this position cannot usefully be articulated through equivocation on the implications of established sovereignty. We cannot have our incommensurabilist cake and eat it by complaining first, about the authoritarianism that allegedly lurks in the ideas of the moral objectivity of 'Natural Law', and then, when it is purged by a Hobbesian 'prudence', take fright at the prospect of an indispensable and absolute sovereign acknowledging no moral bounds.

The Prudential, the Moral and the Legal

In examining Fuller's treatment of the problem of means and ends we touched upon the logical anatomy of practical reason. It will be useful to revisit that discussion in some detail at this point. A closer examination of practical reason might allow us to establish some agreement on non-contentious forms of the simpler practical phenomena, and thereby make progress in understanding what we take to be the *moral* implications of *prudential* reason.

By practical reason we mean, in general, reasoning about the relationship between means and ends. The idea of *instrumentality* appears as a basic notion in this regard, whether we refer to technical, prudential or moral purposes. We are familiar with instrumental reasoning in the form of 'hypothetical' or 'conditional' imperatives of the form:

If you want to achieve end *E*, then you must do *m*.

Here *m* refers to some instrumentally required action or set of actions that constitute the means to the end, purpose or objective, *E*. Instrumentality presupposes *a causal relation* between means and ends. Means are instruments; their deliberate employment as causal factors in the self-conscious pursuit of ends is what is meant by instrumentality or instrumental reason. I can, for example, employ my feet, my money, my power of communication and command of automotive machinery as means – as instruments – in the pursuit of my desire to travel from A to B. The instrumental employment of these powers and objects in changing my position in the world is merely my conscious and technically informed manipulation of causality; the same causality that, when not consciously and successfully manipulated and directed (exclusively) by me, might account for the same automotive machinery ending up at location C (embedded in a motorway bridge support) at time *t*, as opposed to location B (Aunty Mabel's driveway) at time *t+20*. Messing about in the world of causality in a deliberate and goal-directed way fashions causal relations into potential instruments, and directing these instruments towards *ends* turns them into *means* to our ends. We can note this merely to establish the fact that, for purposes of discussion and analysis of some of the higher order practical concepts, a conscious practical attitude to the world transforms inanimate materials into practical phenomena, and an absence of a conscious practical attitude leaves them inanimate.

The instrumental employment of means to *given* ends (as in the initial example above of 'hypothetical' or 'conditional' imperatives) appears to pose no serious logical difficulties. The ends are indeed *given* in the sense that they are merely reported, regarded as unproblematic, unobjectionable, intelligible and so on. The practical-logical issue discussed at length in Chapter 2 focuses exclusively on the technical question of *how* to achieve the end rather than *why* we should adopt that end. It is important at this stage to emphasize that this type of technical, or hypothetical-technical reasoning is useful in illuminating the basic idea of instrumentality in practical reasoning, and *not* to give a comprehensive account of what is entailed by prudential reasoning. Prudence might turn out to be much more complicated than first appeared to be the case.

Moral reasoning, as distinct from hypothetical-technical reasoning, suggests unconditional, or categorical ends: 'intrinsic ends' or 'ends-in-themselves' as we have previously referred to them, and raises entirely different and much more difficult problems. The focus shifts at warp speed from mundane judgments about technique and skill to the realm of the deontological: judgments about what is intrinsically good or intrinsically virtuous, or what should be the subject of categorical duty. Prudential reasoning conceived as technical reasoning is assumed not to be implicated in the issues of intrinsic and categorical ends, and appears before us, by definition, as complete with its own self-defined or *given* ends or goals: being prudent in this sense is to act in an instrumentally efficacious fashion in pursuit of one's own stated and preferred ends. This understanding of the problem often leads us to conflate the ideas of hypothetical-technical reasoning with prudential reasoning, and to oppose *the prudential* to *the moral* on the basis that prudential reasoning is uncontentious instrumental reasoning about means to (self-defined) and thus (taking 'self-defined' ends as unquestionable) *given* ends, whereas morality is understood as contentious speculation about *intrinsic* ends. The situation worsens when we accept and acknowledge the supposed infallibility of our understanding of our own self-interest, but immediately characterize any imperative alluding to 'other-regarding' interests as an example of a sphere of reasoning diametrically opposed to the immediate, unquestionable, given experience of self-interest. Prudential reasoning becomes an almost instant justification of self-regard; morality becomes the allegedly unjustifiable sphere of regard for *others*.

This, with unhelpful familiarity, situates morality and prudence *in opposition to each other* rather than at different points along *a continuum of practical reasoning*. The conventional and almost axiomatic assumption of the incompatibility of the prudential and the moral must be avoided if we are to make any progress towards understanding the relationship between the two. Rather, we will suggest that the phenomenology of prudence reveals the concept of instrumentality as the substratum of *all* practical reasoning, and that rather than thinking of prudence and morality as ever diverging destinations of practical thought – the East and West of *self*-regarding opposed to *other*-regarding reason – let us consider another way of looking at the problem.

In our discussion of the relationship between Natural Law and Sovereignty we made the observation that, despite a great deal of talk about *morality*, political philosophy and jurisprudence has given us a great deal of impressive argument showing that there are some compelling prudential, psychological and simply organizational reasons to establish legal sovereignty, and that the consensus of opinion leans towards the view that none of these elements in isolation – even undisputed moral rightness – manages to complete the entire picture in terms of a convincing and comprehensive account of legal obligation in civil society. Rather than working with spurious oppositions (such as law/morality) or exclusive disjunctions (for example, morality or order/ efficiency) in these matters, let us ask how the undeniably inter*related* practical dimensions of prudence, psychology and morality might be *integrated* with each other under the penumbral concept of *obligation.*

We might start with two distinct but logically related conceptions of prudence: a narrow conception and a broad conception. 'Narrow' referring to our immediate self-regarding *wants and preferences* and 'broad' referring to our deeper and wider *interests* perhaps in emancipation, freedom and equality, as well as psychological health. Thus *broad* prudence might include rationally compelling obligations to take into account *the interests of others* in just as instrumentally-rational terms as the simple gratification of hunger gives rise to the technical imperative to find sustenance. And if this proves to be the case, this does not rule out the possibility that, in addition, and notwithstanding our prudentially based obligations, there might also exist modes of practical reason which are 'pure' (in the Kantian sense), of giving rise to duties which are simply intrinsic to reason itself.

A narrow, instinctive conception of prudence should be seen as a phenomenological first step and not a fully developed account of practical reason and self-interest. It is an intuitive basis or point of departure for subsequent reflective analysis of practical reasoning not because of its non-contentious nature, but because as conscious, appetitive *and* purposive beings we have an instinctive *and intuitive* awareness of the relationship between our interventions in the world and the fulfilment of wants. If and when these wants and desires and the strategies appropriate to their fulfilment are elevated intellectually and by reflection from phenomenological immediacy into abstract categories in systematic thought, only then are we in a position to begin an analysis of the nature of practical reason. And from this point there are constant pitfalls to be avoided in mapping our phenomenological experience on to a system of concepts and language suitable for philosophical reflection. The most immediate and debilitating is to fail, conceptually, to differentiate subtle yet significantly discrete and diverse aspects of our experience. This leads inevitably to the error of employing unwieldy concepts that distort the representation of phenomena, and the related failure to develop an adequately flexible and responsive terminology of analytical expression. These deep-rooted errors are crystallized at the surface of theoretical discourse in the form of inadequately precise definitions. Worse, in critical terms, errors can be put to use as ideologically contrived stipulations. Attempts to rectify these errors thus must follow the reverse route from first, the dissatisfaction with words, to the conceptual and then phenomenological differentiation that lies behind them.

There is no clearer example of this conceptual inadequacy than in discussions of the relationship between practical reason and prudential interests. Here, in the political language of 'choice' and 'value-preference' the nature of the individual's wants are aggrandized as willed products of a highly evolved sense of self. But we might refer to value-preferences or choices as mere appetites occurring in the human organism and then point out that there is an extravagant assumption that these appetites originate from *within* that organism, and further that this origin is assumed to be unique, autonomous and evidence of self. Where projected or anticipated gratification of these appetites rapidly find themselves defined as 'interests' of that self, we are not a great deal removed from purely biological accounts of prudential behaviour. This type of discourse offers little prospect of drawing out any significant implications in the direction of morality.

The idea of prudence can, of course, be presented and explained in terms of general strategies that identify pragmatically successful and efficient methods of ensuring gratification. And the condition of wanting, and the decisions to initiate causal interventions as means in response to the ends expressed in the wanting can be conveniently referred to as autonomous or self-activated practical action. But even if this is the phenomenologically immediate account, it requires some reflection to render it consistently. For employing the notion of causality (as we must to account for the instrumental rationality of means and ends) is at odds with the decision to render the appearance of the want or appetite with the notion of a *spontaneity* of want or desire arising within the self, and it is even more odd to invent the idea of *autonomy* and *free-choice* to account for it. Let us remember that the most influential and profound discussions of autonomy and freedom have been invented in order to allow us to escape from the overwhelmingly compelling sociological accounts provided by *causal determinism.*

As appetitive beings with a capacity for thought and language, we come to be acquainted abstractly with the concepts of gratification as an end, and our causal capacities as means; thus we might grasp the idea of instrumental action in relation to our wants and their prospective gratification in the way that a ravenous shark probably does not. But where the concept of the *instrumentality* of the process bringing about gratification of the appetite of a shark is exactly the same logical concept applied to the means-end relationship of appetite and gratification as applied to an Aristotle, the concept of prudence is not. This is because prudential reasoning is not about the gratification of my appetites, it is about the systematic and harmonious realization of my *interests* given that I might generate them *freely and autonomously.* Unless the notion of interests is reduced to the processes of gratification applicable to the 'interests' of a shark, the concept of *prudence* cannot be reduced to a conception of instrumental gratification applicable to a shark. The first task of an analysis of prudence, therefore, is to separate qualitatively the notion of *appetite* from *interests* on the basis that appetites are *caused* (unfree) and interests arise from autonomous reasoning. Practical reasoning must be conceptually separated from instinctive human gratification, and the crucial and qualitatively distinct elements of reflection, autonomy and choice combining to produce *voluntary agency* must takes it place in the discussion.

The first casualty of this phenomenological review is the luxurious license which formerly tolerated the idea of contradictory 'wants'. If these 'wants' are to be incorporated in the account of prudence as 'interests' of the 'self' their mutual antagonisms simply show that one or another of them must be against my interest. Whilst I can appear instrumentally rational in pursuit of one or the other 'want' in isolation, prudence requires me to act in my best interests. I must necessarily have a plurality of interests, and the pursuit of one entailing the destruction of another must be imprudent, or if it is not so regarded, then the thwarted end cannot genuinely have been in my interest in the first place. My best interests are clearly not served by failing to realize that I have contradictory, antagonistic and mutually exclusive aspirations. And the actions and decisions I take in the light of this realization must henceforth be instrumentally appropriate.

Prudential reason (in fact any aspect of practical reason imaginable) is then, a form of instrumental reason. To be prudent means simply that I must *consistently* employ instrumental reason in pursuit of my best interests. What constitutes a person's best interests is, let us concede, a philosophically intractable question. However, this concession does not mean that we can side-step this classical formulation of an ethical question and transform it into an apparently technical one by equating 'best interests' with the entire range of subjectively self-defined goods or accepted preferences. We can, of course, make instrumental and prudential reason as complex as we wish by introducing hypothetically ingenious subjective orientations to notions of interests. But, whatever the content of practical reason turns out to be, we now see that the general relationship between means and ends requires instrumentality to remain as its *substratum*, whereas the qualitative differences between types of *ends* correspond to different modes of practical reasoning conditioned by different interest perspectives and correspondingly different modes of obligation. Basic (animal) appetites are, as we have seen, usefully distinguished from autonomous or agent-generated prudence, and the immediate task is to see whether the *narrowly* prudential relates in any necessary way to the broader aspects of prudence.

The most illuminating discussion of the nature of human interests arises in relation to the notions of power and consent. It is true to say that power, as opposed to genuine consent, can often be exercised *against* the interests of people, where consent seems to define *ipso facto* the interests of people. We would rather say that genuine consent in various forms of regulated association is a necessary, but not sufficient, condition of power being used in one's interests. This raises separate issues, but, as Steven Lukes pointed out many years ago in his classic analysis of the concept of power,[4] it seems to be a well understood aspect of sociological *theory* that genuine consent as opposed to indifference, mere absence of resistance, or an uninformed and perhaps mistaken acquiescence, can arise only in relation to some active discussion of (if not pristine knowledge of) *genuine* interests. We might not be able fully to settle the issue of what constitutes genuine human interests, but we should not contribute to the confusion caused by insisting that consumer choices are definitive of it.

Let us make two points. The first is that it would be difficult to find many adult persons who would not agree that it is often the case that there are many things which are the object of passionate desire which are clearly 'not good for us' or, we might say, the possession or consumption of which are 'not in our interests'. The list of objects producing this confusing utility profile ranges from boiled sweets to economic policies, and, for example, Marx's entire analysis of history and economics is based on the recognition of this dichotomy between what we may refer to as 'false 'and 'real' interests. The criterion that would enable us to identify the one from the other is, of course, in many cases but not all, a matter of profound philosophical conjecture. But because the question is onerous, this should not prompt us to abandon the analysis to a relativism of unreasoned preference which, by virtue of its very simplicity, is unlikely to be true. Rather, because such a relativism of wants implies that no-one, anywhere, at any time, in relation to any matter of judgment under any circumstances could possibly be mistaken about what is good for them, we can be fairly sure that it is false.

The second is that as soon as we locate the notion of human interests in a theatre of interaction, wants which affect others can no longer be accorded sovereign status on the basis of inviolable and infallible subjective choice. If I want to do or consume something that produces displeasure or discomfort on the part of another, then it becomes contradictory to elevate the subjective choice on *my* part over that of another if *subjective choice* – and not, simply, *me* – is to be the

4 Steven Lukes *Power: A Radical View* (London: Macmillan, 1974).

criterion of real interest. For this same reason we cannot complain that subjective perceptions (perhaps mistaken ones) of harm or discomfort on the part of those who are implicated intentionally or accidentally in our choices and wants is merely 'subjective' and thus should not override our wants. There is an important point to be made here, especially if it is assumed that this critique of subjective desire begs a moral question. That is, we do not have to establish the moral argument for equality and moral forbearance to show the failings of an amoral self-interest: Even if we are to affect a belief in the sovereignty of individualized preferences, 'I want x' is entirely cancelled out by another person asserting that 'I don't want you to have x'. Here we have wants of equal value which ought, therefore, to translate into interests and presumably, 'rights' of equal value. To suggest that one ought to recognize this equivalence is not a subjectivist abstention from a theory of the good (i.e., each person is the arbiter of what is good/right/valuable etc.) it is a moral judgment, and one that requires a hefty dollop of philosophical justification. To hold fast to subjectivism yet deny the equal worth thesis does not, however improve or legitimate the subjectivist position: the sheer existential refusal to recognize only the validity of one's own desires has much less going for it logically than the reasonable hunch that the desires of others appear, certainly to them, as, *prima facie*, of equal worth to one's own. To sidestep this one must now adopt a more precise belief in the primacy not of merely *subjective* preferences, but to a personalized and *solispsized* subjectivity rejecting the validity or worth of other sources of potentially obstructive or competing subjective wants.

This is why an unqualified utilitarian or liberal conception of 'pluralism' as a social and political sphere of diverse and competing interests must, if it wishes to avoid this philosophical problem of theorizing the Good in terms of the realization of interests by asserting that the individual is the best judge of his or her interests, contend with the no less complicated problem of theorizing what is *not* Good. In other words, if social life is to support the existence of a sphere of individual utility choices, then, as Mill propounds so straightforwardly and Rawls explains more elaborately, there must be limits to the liberty to exercise choice or satisfy our wants, and those limits are, or logically should be, defined by what is harmful to the liberty of others. What is harmful in this sense should be prohibited.

This, of course, is Mill's theory of the state, and it is often said that Mill is hot on defining the Good in terms of utility, but omits to explain what might constitute harm to others and thus, crucially, what are the precise boundaries to our own liberty. But this is not entirely true. Mill does have some forthright ideas in this regard. We find this in an interesting quote, a portion of which we encountered earlier:[5]

> What, then, is the rightful limit to the sovereignty of the individual over himself? Where does the authority of society begin? How much of human life should be assigned to individuality, and how much to society?

---

5 J.S. Mill *On Liberty* in H.B. Acton (ed.) *Utilitarianism, On Liberty and Considerations on Representative Government* (London: J.M. Dent and Sons Ltd, 1972), pp. 131–132.

> Each will receive its proper share, if each has that which more particularly concerns it. To individuality should belong the part of life in which it is chiefly the individual that is interested; to society, the part which chiefly interests society.
>
> Though society is not founded on a contract, and though no good purpose is answered by inventing a contract in order to deduce social obligations from it, every one who receives the protection of society owes a return for the benefit, and the fact of living in society renders it indispensable that each should be bound to observe a certain line of conduct towards the rest. This conduct consists, first, in not injuring the interests of one another; or rather certain interests, which, either by express legal provision or by tacit understanding, ought to be considered as rights; and secondly, in each person's bearing his share (to be fixed on some equitable principle) of the labors and sacrifices incurred for defending the society or its members from injury and molestation. These conditions society is justified in enforcing, at all costs to those who endeavor to withhold fulfillment. Nor is this all that society may do. The acts of an individual may be hurtful to others, or wanting in due consideration for their welfare, without going the length of violating any of their constituted rights. The offender may then be justly punished by opinion, though not by law. As soon as any part of a person's conduct affects prejudicially the interests of others, society has jurisdiction over it, and the question whether the general welfare will or will not be promoted by interfering with it, becomes open to discussion. But there is no room for entertaining any such question when a person's conduct affects the interests of no persons besides himself, or needs not affect them unless they like (all the persons concerned being of full age, and the ordinary amount of understanding). In all such cases there should be perfect freedom, legal and social, to do the action and stand the consequences.

Let us note that it is ironic, first, that Mill fetishizes 'express legal provision or … tacit understanding' as an infallible repository of freedom in what is a blunt contradiction in relation to his critique of the rigidified and parochial locus of prejudice and conformity that he suggests characterizes modern society. Again this is important:[6]

> … society has now fairly got the better of individuality; and the danger which threatens human nature is not the excess, but the deficiency, of personal impulses and preferences. Things are vastly changed, since the passions of those who were strong by station or by personal endowment were in a state of habitual rebellion against laws and ordinances, and required to be rigorously chained up to enable the persons within their reach to enjoy any particle of security. In our times, from the highest class of society down to the lowest every one lives as under the eye of a hostile and dreaded censorship. Not only in what concerns others, but in what concerns only themselves, the individual, or the family, do not ask themselves — what do I prefer? or, what would suit my character and disposition? or, what would allow the best and highest in me to have fair play, and enable it to grow and thrive? They ask themselves, what is suitable to my position? what is usually done by persons of my station and pecuniary circumstances? or (worse still) what is usually done by persons of a station and circumstances superior to mine? I do not mean that they choose what is customary, in preference to what suits their own inclination. It does not occur to them to have any inclination, except for what is customary. Thus the mind itself is bowed to the yoke: even in what people do for

6 Ibid. 'On Individuality' Chapter III p. 119.

> pleasure, conformity is the first thing thought of; they like in crowds; they exercise choice only among things commonly done: peculiarity of taste, eccentricity of conduct, are shunned equally with crimes: until by dint of not following their own nature, they have no nature to follow: their human capacities are withered and starved: they become incapable of any strong wishes or native pleasures, and are generally without either opinions or feelings of home growth, or properly their own. Now is this, or is it not, the desirable condition of human nature?

Mill thus sees 'tacit understandings' – presumably arising from the subliminal communication of the herd where 'peculiarity of taste, eccentricity of conduct, are shunned equally with crimes: until by dint of not following their own nature, they have no nature to follow' – as compatible with his prescriptions for vital and critical individuality. This reading of Mill, of course, changes dramatically if we re-examine and contextually reinterpret his conception of the very purpose of liberty as a precondition of the pursuit of something greater than liberty itself.

With Rawls, as we noted earlier, defining self-interest with criterionless and ultimately incommensurable conceptions of wants and preferences creates a similar problem in that theorizing the justification of institutionalized forbearances similarly requires an objective valuing on the part of *all* individuals of the subjective choice-making freedoms of *other* individuals. This can be achieved only on the basis of the pre-loaded argument for *prudence* as a minimization of the worst case interest scenario behind the veil of ignorance. What we can say is that the idea of *affirmative* freedom is not an *alternative* to 'negative' conceptions of liberty, it is entailed by it because affirmative freedom and structurally relevant boundaries have always been implicit in the idea of the desirability of valuing, expanding and guaranteeing individual subjective choice.

A Continuum of Practical Reason

Prudential reasoning is a form of practical reason and all genuine references to practical reasoning, as opposed to metaphorical allusions to it or analogical reconstructions of it in relation to mechanical or animal processes, presuppose agency. All agent reasoning implies self-conscious employment of means to ends. All means-ends reasoning (technical, prudential, moral, spiritual, legal, medical, magical etc.) presupposes instrumentality. It is imprecise to say that the instrumental, like the prudential or the moral, is a *type* or *mode* of practical reasoning; the notion of instrumentality does not designate a *mode* of practical reasoning, it is, rather, its *substratum*. It is upon this substratum that we want to describe how prudential, moral, legal reasoning – and beyond – might be situated on a *continuum* of practical reason.

A practical *continuum* arises from the logical effects of one more or less general form or mode of practical reason on another, more specific, mode. The idea of an *integrated continuum* of practical reason suggests not merely a loose association of modes of purposive thought but a progression of modes of practical reason moving from the simple to the complex, giving rise to each other, transmitting general imperatives through the chain of practical reason where one mode necessarily utilizes principles of, and remains conditional upon, previous modes, and where one particular mode is incapable of coherent expression in the absence of, or in opposition to, these interdependencies.

Kant provided us with an illustration. He gives us a useful (if contentious) model of a practical continuum from the prudential, to the moral, to the legal and beyond to the political. The chain of reasoning employed is broadly structured as follows: Analytically, the idea of morality presupposes freedom. The possibility of choosing alternative courses of action voluntarily, and of employing means to various chosen ends, gives us an understanding of what it means to be an agent. Importantly, these basic reflections also give us an understanding of prudence and thus of what it might mean to act in a prudentially rational fashion. *Prima facie*, acting prudently means choosing an end and employing instrumentally appropriate means to its realization.

Kant's Third Antinomy arises because we *know* that as empirical objects in the world of causality we are subject to exceptionless laws of causality; more precisely, we are subject to the laws of determinism understood as an all-pervasive, transitive, material causation. To inhabit simultaneously the 'Kingdom of Ends' as genuinely free beings we must somehow transcend causality and transform the phenomenological illusion of choice into the form of a truly autonomous Will explicable as such. With a heavy debt to Rousseau's principle that the freedom of one is conditional upon the freedom of all, the seemingly impossible idea of the uncaused *spontaneity* of the Will leads us, says Kant, to discover the *form* which, hypothetically, a free will must take: I must transform the *particular* nature of my self-interested purposes into what might become *universally* valid prudential activity. The universality of the will as a condition of its freedom is achieved by resolving to will only on the basis of maxims which one would wish to see instantiated as universal laws. This, of course, is the Categorical Imperative we must accept as our own *prudential* imperative for freedom. But the universal form of The Categorical Imperative implies *other-regarding* conditions for the exercise of my will thus transforming prudence from *particular self*-interest into a conception of autonomy which shows that the *integral* relationship between prudence and other-regarding duty, or what is the same thing, morality.[7]

Prudence thus shows us the route to freedom through the moral law in the form of the Categorical Imperative, but this imperative is a practical–moral principle of maximal generality. Epistemologically, this imperative, for Kant, is immanent in the individual phenomenology of *praxis* and prior to society. In this sense, and contrary to much that had been maintained by Hobbes and to much that is to be found in recent thinking that views rights and duties as products of social or 'dialogical' interaction, it might be said to show the existence of morality and thus rights and duties within a hypothetical 'state of nature'.

7 There is a great deal to be said about the uncertainties and defects of the argument for morality in Kant. For the moment however, we employ it merely to show what a conceptually necessary move from the prudential to the moral looks like. Gewirth's argument aims at establishing the same necessary connection.

In Kantian language, the moral law as a potential of human reason exists in a pre-civil or pre-legal state of nature. But, says Kant, attempts to exercise rights under such a general principle *unilaterally,* would *necessarily* lead to disputes incapable of resolution through the principle itself. Thus freedom and the Categorical Imperative give rise to the idea of Right, and in so doing generate another practical-moral imperative, that of the need to bring about the Institutionalization of Right, and with it another mode of practical-moral reasoning appropriate to this new *civil* condition, namely, legal reason.

This latter, as Coke reminded us, is indeed different from moral reasoning and, in the sense that morality appears as a *natural* form of practical reason, is clearly an *artificial* type of reason. But this reference to artifice should not lead us to assume that it is somehow arbitrary or inauthentic. The artifice of legality is the rationally inevitable product of a simpler, more phenomenologically immediate, mode of natural and unilateral moral reason, just as this latter superseded the phenomenology of immediate or narrow prudence. Legal reason is an integral product of moral reason and thus demonstrates further the richness and scope of the modalities within what we suggest is seen as *the continuum of practical reason.*

Kant's analysis of the ramifications of practical reason does not end with legality, but spreads inexorably into the account of the organization and role of the state, the constitution, the meaning and form of its *necessarily* democratic basis, and famously his suggestion for a *General History with a Cosmopolitan Intent* – the urgent requirement of establishing the moral-legal basis of a *Perpetual Peace* in international relations. But for the moment, if we can grasp in general, and purely for the sake of argument, the nature of the integral relations between the prudential and the moral, and beyond to the institutionalization of legality, and imagine them situated as points on a continuum of practical reason, we have a useful illustration of not only what is *meant* by references to a continuum, but also what it would mean to assert that there is *a necessary connection* between law and moral reason. But let us first suppose that this kind of continuity does *not* exist.

The Discontinuity Thesis

In rejecting the account of a continuum as presented in Kantian style above, many writers would, in effect, endorse the view that the technical and the prudential comprise, if not the entire universe of practical reason, then the *alpha* and *omega* of the logic of obligation as it might concern *the agent*. For *the moral* is not, we are told, underpinned by rationality at all. Rather, and depending on how profoundly the condition is characterized, it is a delusion, a manipulative strategy, a purely personal optional extra or at best – and nearest to the idea of objectivity – appears as a public by-product of what is an essentially personal prudential strategy.

Who might qualify as candidates for membership of the League of Discontinuationists? In various and selective passages we could cite Epicurus, Hobbes, Hume, Nietzsche, Bentham and Mill, Marx, Weber, Logical Positivists,

Emotivists, Post-Modernists, Hart, and Raz? But their individual idiosyncrasies and equivocations make classification in this regard an extremely contentious exercise. Eschewing biography then, we can say that Discontinuationists understand the rational basis of practical reason in prudentially instrumental terms, but, perhaps curiously when we consider it bluntly, regard the sphere of the moral as a *fiction*.

That is, they reject the idea that there exist rationally defensible imperatives which are at once both categorical and other-regarding. This is not to say that they do not accept the reality and importance of moral conviction or moral belief or moral aspiration, but simply that they do not accept that such phenomena can be grounded in any generalisable and non-arbitrary form of practical reason, and thus, would reject the idea that moral obligation could be shown to arise *necessarily* from the simpler forms of the prudential as we have suggested earlier.

This is not to say that a Discontinuationist conception of prudence does not imply a concept of justice or Right. A Rawlsian account, for example, might show us that ideal-typical prudence implies an 'other-regarding' condition of 'justice as fairness'. Similarly, Gauthier's game-theoretic idea of 'morals by agreement' relates binding duties to others to the concept of medium and long term benefits and self-interest – what is easily identified as 'prudence'.[8] These conceptions might quite properly and justifiably be referred to as examples of 'moral theory', but for the Discontinuationists it is not morality which arises in an epistemological synthesis; it is a *normatively enhanced prudence* which *contingently* is made to take account of the interests of others, the better to serve itself.

But is this subtle distinction between morality as a form of 'enhanced prudence' as opposed to genuinely 'other-regarding' imperatives of vital importance to us? That is, it seems that not only if morality is, in rational terms, a fantasy, but even if, to the contrary, it could be objectively grounded in practical reason and shown somehow to be conceptually related to legality, three pivotal issues remain apparently untouched by the philosophical furore. The first is that there still appears to be an abundance of psychologically, sociologically and economically *prudent* reasons why we should create, develop and maintain fully functioning 'legal' systems, all of which we have touched upon in our previous discussions. The second is that objective morality still leaves us with an apparently intractable problem in relation to the discretionary scope for the promulgation, selection, interpretation and application of norms posited as laws. The third is that in our most profound and influential works of philosophy, the greatest of idealists and democrats, and the most worldly of pragmatists and absolutists, agree that morality cannot sanction disobedience even in the face of the tyrannical abuse of laws. Thus it seems that pragmatically we can, and perhaps do, get by without morality, and theoretically, it appears to makes little difference.

What then, is the relationship between this prudential account of 'morality' and legal reasoning? Law, in Discontinuationist accounts (perhaps, for example, Hobbes, Hume, Durkheim, Hart), appears as external, binding, and universal, but this bindingness (legal obligation) is justified again in purely prudential terms

8 David Gauthier *Morals By Agreement* (Oxford: Oxford University Press, 1986).

– usually in terms that assimilate prudence to the exigencies of the relationship between the individual and the social whole, sometimes stressing the direct benefit accruing to the individual, sometimes more indirectly arguing that the production and maintenance of an orderly social whole is, in the long run, in the best interests of all and any (or in Marx's ideological critique of the concept, of course, a *minority* of) individuals. This is, we assume, in contrast to the broadly Kantian or 'Continuationist' strategy which, whilst accepting and endorsing the general self-interestedly or even cynically 'prudential' arguments for a move to peaceable association, purports to show that it is a moral duty to bring about the condition of a civil society under law. But, as we noted in enumerating the three problems which still remain for legal theory even admitting the most extravagant of rationalist and objectivist claims for morality, both camps appear to share a great deal of common ground: there are all manner of important and convincing arguments for establishing institutionalized regulation; there is little help on offer from maximally general principles of morality like the categorical imperative, and there appears to be very little on offer from morality to counter the absolutist terminus of thought when it comes down to the bitter issue of exempting us from legal obligation in the face of immoral or tyrannical laws. Using Kant as an illustration once again, and bearing in mind what has gone before in our account of Hobbes and Rousseau's conclusions, let us try and show how we might incorporate morality in an understanding of law and legal obligation which goes beyond the traditional impasse.

Kant's Concept of Obligation

It is not social usefulness or even happiness or security which forms the rationale for the establishment of a legal system, it is rather the exceptionless dictate of moral reason which, in the form of the supreme principle of morality, the Categorical Imperative, reveals to each individual the existence of Right and the equality of our potential for freedom and autonomy in conformity with it. This principle, according to Kant, necessarily directs each one us to leave, and if necessary, impel others to leave, the state of nature and institutionalize Right in the form of public, rather than private judgement. The resulting union of the multitude under laws of right and its rational configuration of legislature, executive and judiciary dedicated to act in accordance with the laws of freedom is, in its purely rational form, a state (*civitas*). But, says Kant,[9]

> By the well-being of a state must not be understood the welfare of its citizens and their happiness; for happiness can perhaps come to them more easily and as they would like it to in a state of nature (as Rousseau asserts) or even under a despotic government. By the well-being of a state is understood, instead, that condition in which its constitution conforms most fully to principles of right; it is that condition

9 Immanuel Kant *The Metaphysics of Morals* (Mary Gregor ed.) (Cambridge: Cambridge University Press, 1996) pp. 90, 91.

> which reason, by a categorical imperative, makes it obligatory for us to strive after. (Original emphasis and parentheses)

The purely moral categorical imperative is, therefore, of fundamental constituting importance; even though, it seems, it will not guarantee our welfare or happiness. This relates quite directly to the first of the three points of convergence which we suggested remained inert to the 'positivist' or 'managerial' *versus* the 'idealist' or 'Natural Law' distinction in that happiness, or simplicity and predictability of life, might be better reasons for legality than morality. But what about the second point raised: does moral reason perhaps guide us more securely and peacefully in our affairs and associations than might, for example, Hobbesian or Humean prudence? This seems unlikely. One formulation of the Categorical Imperative suggests that:

> Any action is right if it can coexist with everyone's freedom in accordance with a universal law, or if on its maxim the freedom of choice of each can coexist with everyone's freedom in accordance with a universal law.[10]

The state of nature, that is, 'the state of external lawless freedom', says Kant, allows only for a unilateral interpretation of this principle in the form of a rights claim.[11] Without the mutual reciprocity of claims guaranteed by the institutionalization of Right, this condition, still leaves us, as Jeremy Waldron has said, in '... a situation in which force will be used unilaterally – in fact, if not in spirit – by different factions to support their different views about what justice really requires'.[12]

But is the supreme principle envisaged to be more edifying in the hands of the legislator or the magistrate? Does this distinction – that of the *unilateral* as opposed to the incorporated or collective (public) *omnilateral* application of the categorical imperative – offer a significant improvement over general 'prudential' accounts in the theoretical and practical understanding of interpreting and applying positive laws? Kant aside, the Categorical Imperative does not immediately strike us as being a breakthrough in the theory of interpretation and adjudication.

---

10 Ibid. p. 24.

11 There is more irony here; and not just in relation to Hume. In relation to Hobbes, Kant's entirely antithetical analysis and description of a state of nature and source of natural right amounts effectively and prudentially to the same problem Hobbes identifies. Hobbes tells us that the state of unrestrained competition in the state of nature is to be expected where each man is '... the judge of the justnesse of his own feares'. Kant says that '... before a public lawful condition is established individual human beings ... can never be secure against violence from one another, since each has its own right to do what seems right and good to it and not to be dependent upon another's opinion about this'. Without involving Locke or Rousseau (or Plato) or a dozen others, we already appear to arrive at the same destination (the practical necessity of legality) from at least three different starting points and three different accounts of practical reason.

12 Jeremy Waldron 'Kant's Legal Positivism' *Harvard Law Review* (Vol. 109, No.7, 1996) pp. 1535–1566.

In respect of the third point of convergence, does not a moral idealist account of legality (as opposed to a 'positivist' or at least a narrowly prudentialist account) at least purport to furnish us with the ultimate, suprapositive authority of Natural Law? Unlike Hume's suggestion that we might, for a prudentially quiet life, make all manner of accommodations with bandits and usurpers, we can at least expect from the Legal Idealist a demonstration of the grounds on which we might justly overthrow an immoral sovereign. Can we say that constitutionalism therefore lies with the Idealist or Natural Law tradition, and Absolutism with the positivists?

We are, of course, more often than not disappointed in this regard. Kant, echoes – in fact surpasses – Hobbes, Hume, and other non-moralists in his spirited rejection of the idea that disobedience, let alone removal of the sovereign by force, can ever be legally or morally justified. Citizens may 'complain' about abuses'[13] but they must not 'resist' legal authority or question its fundamental legitimacy. Here are some examples of the short shrift one might expect to receive from the greatest of moral rationalists:[14]

> If a subject, having pondered over the ultimate origin of the authority now ruling, wanted to resist this authority, he would be punished, got rid of, expelled (as an outlaw, *exlex*) in accordance with the laws of this authority, that is, with every right.

or:[15]

> Indeed, even the constitution cannot contain any article that would make it possible for there to be some authority in a state to resist the supreme commander in case he should violate the law of the constitution, and so limit him

or:

> The reason a people has a duty to put up with even what is held to be an unbearable abuse of supreme authority is that its resistance to the highest legislation can never be regarded as other than contrary to law, and indeed as abolishing the entire legal system.

And so on.

It appears (admittedly on our selective sample) that we are likely to end up at the same place with the same problems whether we adopt the prudential route or the moral route. The grand 'continuum of practical reason' might end, humbly, with simple, unheroic prudence. Obligations might arise just as strongly however, from prudence as they were pompously and metaphysically thought to do from morals; and interpretations and adjudications might be equally reasonable or equally indeterminate, equally well-received or equally contentious either way. Finally, prudence and morality might both leave us practically and theoretically

---

13 Immanuel Kant *The Metaphysics of Morals* (op. cit.) p. 95.

14 Ibid.

15 Ibid. p. 96.

helpless in the face of harsh and unjust dominion. Perhaps, as Pragmatism would have it, *there is no difference that makes no difference*. But there is another way of looking at the problem: what if our expectations have been too low; what if the continuum turned out to be wider, richer, and more dialectically complex than the integral but linear version suggested?

To return to Kant as our stock example of a Continuationist, we can note the curious phenomenon that although his reputation as a thinker is unsurpassed, it is simultaneously the case that his ideas are regarded not only as abstruse and contentious but are the ones most often and most unequivocally rejected. Two of these ideas in particular are worthy of our attention The first, more an observation than a criticism depending on one's academic allegiances, is that (despite fitting the bill neatly as a Legal Idealist in terms of our account of the continuum of practical reason), his jurisprudential contribution has been received as a form of legal *positivism* on the grounds that he advocates the thesis of 'the separation of law and morals'. The second comes from scholars who are concerned to advance the claims of democracy over Kant's alleged authoritarian conceptions of both morals and laws. Let us comment briefly on these claims.

The first criticism, (notably formulated by Jeremy Waldron) and in the light of preceding discussions, shows us how logically odd this debate can be even though one might see a sense in which the alleged separation occurs: namely, that immoral laws do not cease to be laws or release us from our obligations to obey them. But this is not a unique version of Legal Idealism or Natural Law thinking. We could defend it by saying that, morality implies the Institutionalization of Right; that the pure concept of valid Public Right (law) ought logically to cohere with morality; and that failures (intentional or accidental) of this coherence and thus failures of *validity* are (theoretically) possible. This appears to suggest (in the Continuationist/Idealist scheme), and again, apparently at odds with Kant's defence of state authority, that immoral laws are not valid laws. But, as we have argued elsewhere, making an issue of validity in isolation from the issue of obligation is rarely edifying. Let us skip the issue of validity in the abstract and cut straight to the matter of obligation.

Perhaps the legislative, executive or judicial failure to preserve the coherence between the Categorical Imperative and positive right in the production of norms might better be explained as a *moral* failure or more generally a failure of practical reason in the sphere of legality. Aquinas and his modern expositors (at least in relation to the ideas of validity, basic right and the problematic notion of *determinatio*) talk like this as a matter of course. And unlike a normative failure of this kind between private individuals in a state of nature, or an 'internal' reflective failure of self-legislation in the individual, the transformation of the imperative properties of natural morality in the process of the Institutionalization of Right might be such that the failure in this context – that of public, institutionalized right (law) – does not necessarily (as it surely does in the foregoing instances) imply the corresponding abrogation of duty (the failure to bind) on the part of the addressee of the norm (the legal subject or citizen). Thus because of this, the Continuationist/Legal Idealist might consistently assert, as does Kant, that some, or even all and any norms posited as law, even if in some sense morally deficient and deserving of criticism, still bind the citizen. This account, and especially this last remark about criticism and citizenship, is important in relation to the second criticism of Kant noted above.

This criticism, relating to the anti-democratic tendencies of the Kantian system, illuminates yet more irony. In the same way that Kant, despite stressing above all the necessary and conceptual continuity between morality and law, has managed to end up being tagged as a proponent of the classic positivist separation thesis, it is similarly odd that his logic of individuality in commonwealth, freedom and equality is not more imaginatively construed as illuminating a link to a yet more extensive practical continuum: linearly from prudence to morality and law, and, necessarily and integrally, democracy and, thence (perhaps dialectically) to their crucial interrelations. Let us note that theorists such as Hobbes and Hume see no *necessary* and intrinsic connection between lawful sovereignty and democracy. Hobbes prefers monarchy but is prepared to accept other forms as valid, Hume, of course is the great Tory but appears ethically and politically indifferent even to banditry in his account of legality. Kant, however, is at great pains to integrate the practical, the moral, the legal and the political (and beyond) and it would be foolish to assume that he would have been content to destroy clumsily and unequivocally the moral continuity of this system in order to square a point about legal validity on the side of officialdom. We should at least take a second look.

Our analysis is not, of course, primarily about Kant, it is about the role of moral philosophy in legal theory, and if Kant is in error then so be it. But, as idle and guiltless post-moderns we might as well take advantage of whatever spade work has already have been done for us. Kant says, echoing Rousseau:

> ... only the concurring and united will of all, insofar as each decides the same thing for all and all for each, and so only the general and united will of the people, can be legislative ... The members of such a society who are united for giving law (*societas civilis*), that is, the members of a state, are called citizens of a state (*cives*). In terms of rights, the attributes of a citizen, inseparable from his essence (as a citizen), are: lawful freedom, the attribute of obeying no other law than that to which he has given his consent; civil equality, that of not recognizing among the people any superior with the moral capacity to bind him as a matter of right in a way that he could not in turn bind the other; and third, the attribute of civil independence, of owing his existence and preservation to his own rights and powers as a member of the commonwealth, not to the choice of another among the people.[16]

The only qualification for being a citizen, he goes on to say, is that of being fit to vote; and this in turn presupposes the independence of someone who, as one of the people:[17]

> ... wants to be not just a part of the commonwealth but also a member of it, that is, a part of the commonwealth acting from his own choice in community with others.

---

16 Ibid. pp. 91,92.

17 Ibid.

Notoriously, and most inconveniently for our argument here, he excludes from this active community, women and those who, in the context of economic and familial relations are dependent for support and protection on others must be seen as 'passive' and not 'active' citizens. This political inequality, however, does not affect 'the freedom and equality they possess as human beings'. and even as 'passive' parts of the state, they can still 'demand that they be treated by others in accordance with the laws of natural freedom and equality'. However, says Kant, it does not follow that they have the right as active members to guide the state, to organize, and to work for the introduction of particular laws. What does follow, according to Kant, is that:[18]

> ... whatever might be the kind of laws to which the citizens agree, these laws must not be incompatible with the natural laws of freedom and with the equality that accords with this freedom ... namely that everyone be able to work up from this passive status to an active status.

If we can leave the biographical Kant – especially those contingent aspects of arrangements for suffrage which are no longer in serious contention – and abstract only the pivotal conceptual moves from prudence to morality, and thence to law and democracy, we might be able to rehabilitate the cause of Idealist theorizing. That is, the convergences which nullified and made obsolete and redundant the role of morality in the account of legality and legal obligation, now appear as divergences of considerable consequence when seen from the perspective of an *expanded* continuum of practical reason; a continuum which now encompasses political rationality – and which identifies this mode of practical reason as necessarily, unavoidably, democratic in nature.

Positivists (like Waldron) have claimed that the 'obedience (to unjust laws) thesis' is a mark or criterion of Legal Positivism. This has been received as an argument that only a 'Natural Lawyer' or Legal Idealist *can* advocate disobedience to unjust laws, and the inference from this proposition here is that Legal Idealists (or constitutionalists or anti-absolutists) *should* advocate disobedience to unjust laws. But Moral Rationalists, Legal Idealists and Natural Lawyers should not equivocate on the issue of sovereignty and obligation. This is not a time for the Legal Idealist to retreat but to show how the continuum of practical reason extends *beyond* legality.

Humiliating and irrevocable obligations in the face of unjust laws appeared as the empty end-point of Legal Idealism within the continuum of practical reason. But the point is, that in regard to these inevitabilities within the legal system, and in relation to the apparently identical and equally miserable consequences of the most cynical non-moral accounts, what a Legal Idealist or 'Continuationist' analysis of prudence, morals and legislation provides is an insight into a continuum of practical responsibilities in which the entire configuration of the Separation of Powers is integrated with the development of individual and communal institutions of democratic will-formation. These moral responsibilities – now

18 Ibid. p. 92.

operating institutionally within the sphere of the political – do not mandate us to advocate disobedience to 'immoral laws', rather, they rationally oblige us to do what we can to ensure that we do not passively allow or actively empower the legal process to impart the coercive properties of positive right to immoral norms which are then unleashed upon us with the force of the state apparatus. It is either disingenuous or simply fatuous to make empty anti-absolutist gestures when faced with the question of obedience to immoral laws. Let us look at what is entailed by the claim.

When Locke, famously, advocated the right of resistance to 'laws' in the cause of parliamentarianism he speaks of responses to a revocation of trust in two distinct senses. One, in relation to the specific and historical topicalities and technicalities of his time, is where in a 'mixed' constitutional order of Prince, Lords and Commons, the legislature is illegitimately altered by, for example, the overweening political and financial influence of the prince. Such a change in the very structure of authority in the commonwealth is, technically, an illegitimate breach of the covenant with The People. How is this rupture in the fabric of authority in the commonwealth brought about?[19]

> … when such a single person or prince sets up his own arbitrary will in place of the laws which are the will of the society declared by the legislative, then the legislative is changed …
>
> … when the prince hinders the legislative from assembling in its due time, or from acting freely, pursuant to those ends for which it was constituted, the legislative is altered …
>
> … when, by the arbitrary power of the prince, the electors or ways of election are altered without the consent and contrary to the common interest of the people, there also the legislative is altered …
>
> … the delivery also of the people into the subjection of a foreign power, either by the prince or by the legislative, is certainly a change of the legislative, and so a dissolution of the government.

But this, very importantly, does not ask us to look at the rightness of any particular law or laws, much more generally, it asks us to distinguish between on the one hand, the dissolution of government, and on the other the dissolution of civil society:[20]

> HE that will, with any clearness, speak of the dissolution of government, ought in the first place to distinguish between the dissolution of the society and the dissolution of the government. That which makes the community, and brings men out of the loose state of Nature into one politic society, is the agreement which every one has with the rest to incorporate and act as one body, and so be one distinct commonwealth.

---

19 Peter Laslett (ed.) *Locke's Second Treatise on Government: An Essay Concerning the True Original, Extent and End of Civil Government* [1690] (Cambridge: Cambridge University Press, 1960) Chapter XIX: 'Of the Dissolution of Government' paras 214–217, pp. 408–410.

20 Ibid. para 211, p. 406.

Wholesale dissolution of government and the commonwealth is, of course, possible:[21]

> ... conquerors' swords often cut up governments by the roots, and mangle societies to pieces, separating the subdued or scattered multitude from the protection of and dependence on that society which ought to have preserved them from violence. The world is too well instructed in, and too forward to allow of this way of dissolving of governments, to need any more to be said of it ....

But Locke is not talking about disobedience to one or another 'law', but always to the wholesale abuse of legislative power directed against the fundamental aims of the commonwealth: property and peace, and the ultimate right of a population united under a mutual covenant, to re-establish, if necessary, a *new* legislature to those ends:[22]

> ... revolutions happen not upon every little mismanagement in public affairs. Great mistakes in the ruling part, many wrong and inconvenient laws, and all the slips of human frailty will be borne by the people without mutiny or murmur. But if a long train of abuses, prevarications, and artifices, all tending the same way, make the design visible to the people, and they cannot but feel what they lie under, and see whither they are going, it is not to be wondered that they should then rouse themselves, and endeavour to put the rule into such hands which may secure to them the ends for which government was at first erected ....

And importantly, he goes on:

> ... and without which, ancient names and specious forms are so far from being better, that *they are much worse than the state of Nature or pure anarchy ....*

There is always, as Hobbes pointed out and as Locke acknowledges, the question of who will decide when enough is enough in this regard:[23] '*Here it is like the common question will be made: Who shall be judge whether the prince or legislative act contrary to their trust*?' Locke says:[24]

> To this I reply, The people shall be judge; for who shall be judge whether his trustee or deputy acts well and according to the trust reposed in him, but he who deputes him and must, by having deputed him, have still a power to discard him when he fails in his trust?

He goes on, unhelpfully:[25]

---

21 Ibid. para 211, p. 407.
22 Ibid. para 225, p. 415.
23 Ibid. para 240.
24 Ibid. para 241.
25 Ibid.

> But, farther, this question, *Who* shall be judge? cannot mean that there is no judge at all. For where there is no judicature on earth to decide controversies amongst men, God in heaven is judge. He alone, it is true, is judge of the right. But every man is judge for himself, as in all other cases so in this, whether another hath put himself into a state of war with him, and whether he should appeal to the supreme judge, as Jephtha did.

We do have, in Locke, one or two horrifying illustrations of a complete breakdown of civil trust: that of Nero embarking upon the systematic murder of the people's representatives and the destruction by fire of the entire metropolis, and similarly psychotic contributions from Caligula,[26] but there are, of course, no shortages of such examples we might offer, historical and hypothetical. Contemporary theorists often make the same point. Hart, in support of his *positivist* credentials, tells us that there is no necessary connection between law and morals, but adds, of course, (in pointing out that there is a significant connection between legal positivism and common sense) that 'some laws are too iniquitous to be obeyed'. With Radbruch and Alexy on the other hand, and in attempting to distance themselves from positivism, we are given real and hypothetical examples of evil abuses of legal authority and told that such abuses are not to be acknowledged as law. This might be interpreted as implying that evil commands should not be obeyed, or it might be taken as demonstrating that the mixture of rational prudence and morality required to establish the concept of sovereign authority in civil society is affronted and contradicted by imprudent and immoral behaviour on the part of the legislator. Hobbes no less than Locke advocates disobedience *in extremis*, but ultimately, do not all classical and contemporary attitudes cohere in the 'absolutist' observation that dissolving one sovereign legislature in a civil society entails, at inordinate cost, re-establishing another.

Eunomics and Civil Society

It is because it is quite obviously the case that Legal Idealism or Natural Law thinking is – in *actual or theoretical terms* – powerless to deliver us from Nero, Caligula or The Nazis once it has delivered us into the sphere of Public Right, that Natural Law must become a theory of democratic institutional design. The role of Natural Law critique in a medieval and feudal context was to set up a template of eternal and necessary precepts of right running parallel to mundane and contingent monarchical power or regional military and political power. In a modern Legal Order we have turned and must continue to embrace the idea of constitutional procedures, democratic process, human rights legislation, and even a forum for the examination of national sovereigns in European Courts. These developments can be reconstructed theoretically as historical-empirical manifestations of political institutional design arising from a continuum of practical reason from its *prudential and organizational* social roots through to the

---

26 Ibid. para 237 p. 423. See also Nathan Tarcov 'The Best Fence Against Rebellion' *The Review of Politics* (Vol. 43, No. 2, 1981) pp. 198–217.

logic of morality and on to the broadly Rousseauian and Kantian account of the necessary relationship between legality and democratic politics. This relationship – centrally involving universal obligations to sovereign authority in contexts of diverse interests – is presupposed and must be explained in any coherent conception of civil society. This shows us quite clearly that the focus of a theory of Eunomic development compatible with the legacy of Natural Law or Legal Idealist thinking, is not so much the specific moral *content* of particular laws, but the moral and egalitarian *context* of the institutions that form the environment in which the legal process operates and where legal authority is exercised. This is neither a formalization nor a relativization of the idea of sovereign authority; rather, it is to make the point that because sovereign authority is indispensable to the aspiration to secure justice in a complex and plural society, one must strive to locate it in a maximally legitimate structure of judicial, social, economic and cultural institutions.

The concept of authority in civil society as opposed to natural or anarchical forms of association is linked directly to a consensual willing that is irrevocable in the sense that knowledge of the moral basis of authority, once gleaned through the use of reason, cannot simply be rejected or made optional. A withdrawal or abrogation of obedience to sovereign right is a return not merely to the 'lawless freedom' of a state of nature, but also a denial of the rational evolution of the moral self in that a wilful retreat from the civil sphere cannot be sustained in a set of social relations that sanctions, or assumes the viability of, *unilateral* affirmations of right on the part of individuals, or dispenses with the notion of individual right in its entirety.

Civil Society or 'Civil Society Talk'?

This very general and admittedly classical account cannot, however, be assumed to spring universally to mind when we happen to mention 'civil society' in contemporary debate. Civil Society in classical terms is merely the negation of an equally general and purely theoretical abstraction, that of the 'State of Nature'. Contemporarily, and primarily because of the alleged effects of the phenomenon of 'globalization' and the rise in influence of Multicultural critique, the basic concepts of the notion of civil society have become the focus of much theoretical and empirical suspicion. For reasons arising from a popular mistrust of all things 'official', the terms 'social' and 'civil' in tandem appear to encourage a discourse which celebrates the detachment of 'law' and the business of state, (and, it seems, the decisions of corporate capital),[27] from a sphere of social life configured non-legally, non-politically and non-economically. Thus a sphere of 'pure' civil life

---

27 Among these are historically and geographically localized reasons for these developments and concerns and we must mention the economic and political failures and subsequent upheavals of Eastern Europe and the ethnic restructuring of The Balkans since the early 1990s. and the catastrophic failures of government in parts of Africa. This change of attitude Darrow Schecter presents as a choice between 'sovereign states

is imagined that is seen as authentically human and thus, perhaps, capable of redemption. Our view is that this tendency is philosophically and sociologically impoverished and thus critically deficient. It is a frame of discourse, however, that is undoubtedly becoming hegemonic in contemporary political and social theory and thus some effort to resist this trend must be made here.[28]

Since the early 1990s, worldwide, we have witnessed a great upsurge in the desire to re-examine and 'revitalize' 'civil society'.[29] Much of the theory and language employed in this endeavour has found considerable resonance in the USA. But in contrast to the revolutionary tenets that produced the eighteenth century affirmations of the concept of civil society, much of it has resurfaced in moderately conservative and often unsociological sources in the wake of Robert Putnam's influential elaboration of the idea of 'social capital'.[30] Cohen tells us that a wide range of writers sympathetic to the idea have attempted to establish

---

or political communities' See Darrow Schecter *Sovereign States or Political Communities* (Cambridge: Polity 2003).

28 We discuss and defend the idea of sovereignty as the essential element of civil society in the following chapter in dealing with the conditions under which a genuine pluralism or multiculturalism might be recognized. Ironically, the importance of sovereignty, we argue, increases the more we seek to deepen our commitment to genuine social diversity.

29 See Jean Cohen 'American Civil Society Talk' (Report from the Institute for Philosophy and Public Policy, 1998) later published as 'Trust, Voluntary Association and Workable Democracy: The Contemporary American Discourse of Civil Society' in Mark E. Warren (ed.) *Democracy and Trust* (Cambridge; Cambridge University Press, 2000) pp. 208–248.

30 Cohen refers to writers in fora such as American Prospect and the Project for American Renewal and mentions, *inter alia*, Gabriel A. Almond and Sidney Verba *Civic Culture: Political Attitudes and Democracy in Five Nations* (Princeton, NJ: Princeton University Press, 1963); Robert Putnam *Making Democracy Work* (Princeton, NJ: Princeton University Press, 1993); Robert Putnam 'Bowling Alone: America's Declining Social Capital' *Journal of Democracy* (January 1995); Robert Putnam 'Bowling Alone Revisited' *Responsive Community* (Vol. 5, No. 2, 1995); Robert Putnam, 'The Strange Disappearance of Civic America' *American Prospect* (24, 1996); Antonio Gramsci 'State and Civil Society' in *Selections from Prison Notebooks* (New York: International Publishers, 1971); Alain Touraine *The Voice and The Eye* (New York: Cambridge University Press, 1981); Alberto Melucci 'The Symbolic Challenge of Contemporary Movements' *Social Research* (Vol. 52, No. 4, 1985); Alberto Melucci 'The New Social Movements: A Theoretical Approach' *Social Science Information* (Vol. 19, 1980); Nancy Fraser 'Rethinking the Public Sphere: A Contribution to the Critique of Actually Existing Democracy' in *Habermas and the Public Sphere* Craig Calhoun (ed.) (Cambridge, MA: MIT Press, 1992); John Rawls 'The Idea of Public Reason' in *Political Liberalism* (New York: Columbia University Press, 1993); Margaret Levi 'Social and Unsocial Capital: A Review Essay of Robert Putnam's Making Democracy Work' in *Politics and Society* (Vol. 24, No. 1, 1996); Theda Skocpol 'Unraveling from Above' *American Prospect* (Vol. 6, No. 1, March/April 1996); Albert O. Hirschman *Exit, Voice, and Loyalty: Responses to Decline in Firms, Organizations, and States* (Cambridge, MA: Harvard University Press, 1981, c.1970); Jurgen Habermas *The Theory of Communicative Action* (No. 2, 1981).

the parameters of the debate on 'civic renewal' by first isolating the 'civil' aspect of society from 'the state' and 'the market', and then propounding the values inherent in the residual institutions: family, church, voluntary associations and so on.

This approach strikes a wholesome chord, but leaves the defects and deficits of the formal political process, 'the law', and 'democracy' conceptually untouched, whilst simultaneously naturalizing the plainly unnatural and irreducibly political aspects of the relationship between corporate business interests and government intervention into the market economy. Yet, paradoxically, it is this disenchantment with politics and the market that has inspired the civic revivalists. This present discourse, according to Jean Cohen, is motivated by 'dissatisfaction with the social and cultural effects of modernization':[31]

> Models of social integration, civic engagement, and associational life which were once taken for granted are being strained by new forms of social diversity, by institutional transformation, and by technical, economic, and cultural change.

To underline the themes of detachment from government, politics, and from economic processes, Cohen tells us that:

> Neither the centralized state nor the magic of the marketplace appears to offer effective, liberal, and democratic solutions to the problems of post-industrial societies in an era of globalization. And so, despite its troubles, 'civil society' has become a slogan for the 1990s because it seems to represent an alternative center for political and economic initiatives.

She continues:

> Unfortunately, the idealized, one-dimensional version of the concept that is being revived is hardly up to the task. This version narrowly equates civil society with traditional forms of voluntary association, emphasizing informal modes of socialization that are said to foster civic virtue and the moral 'habits of the heart' necessary to make democracy work. Such a concept is both theoretically impoverished and politically suspect; it blocks efforts even to articulate, much less resolve, the critical problems facing democratic polities in the coming century.

This dissociated discourse, as Cohen points out, is not talking about civil society, but rather, 'civil society talk'.

This tendency to oppose a private world of preoccupations detached at arbitrary points from the state and the economy is, of course, plainly at odds with Marx and his twentieth-century expositors who – for the sake of a scientifically sound approach to the critique of political economy – exhorted us not to compartmentalize these concepts. But it also ignores the invaluable analyses contained in the seventeenth and eighteenth century liberal development of these ideas in what might be referred to as the modern phase of social contract theorizing. What appears to be central to a classical tradition of approaching the

31 See Jean Cohen 'American Civil Society Talk' (op. cit).

understanding of the state and the legitimacy of its coercive capacities through an account of the idea of Civil Society, is the integrity of the public sphere as an arena of critical and transformative individual and institutional interaction. Where a one-sided conception conceives of 'civil society' as a set of perhaps cohesive and mutually supportive institutions of 'social capital' which, in times of change and disorientation merely require strengthening, more comprehensive developments of the notion have emphasized not only this stabilizing function, but, also, '... its role in the formation of values, action-orienting norms, meanings, and identifications'.[32] From this perspective, says Cohen, and notably in the work of Gramsci and Habermas, '... civil society does not only transmit or inculcate established practices or beliefs. It is also a site of social contestation, wherein collective identities, ethical values, and alliances are forged'.[33]

Civil society then, and life within it, is not a natural, informal alternative to politics and economics, it is the active, *built* environment in which political, economic and ethical development can take place, or equally, where this development might be retarded. Activity within this sphere can energize and transform the individual, it can transform the institutions of property, and the institutions of law and state, and by so doing it shows that is thus at once physically and morally *greater* than the state, yet subordinate to it. If there is a paradox here then we must assume that there is a more debilitating one in the pivotal democratic and emancipatory idea of individual freedom residing in the power to legislate to oneself: the idea, that *the People*, however diversely they might be constituted, might, in some sense, be sovereign, and legitimately exercise this sovereignty in pursuit of their own good.

Civil Association and the PGC

In the ideal and initial phase of this argument the notion of individual right is, of course, a form of general or 'basic' right. But in Chapter 1 we expended considerable effort in trying to show, contrary to the arguments of Finnis and other incommensurabilists, that 'basic' right is not to be thought of as a set of obvious and uncontentious rights of unserviceable and contextually inapplicable ambiguity and generality and thus distinct and remote from the rest of our complex ethical experience. Rather, as we illustrated with our discussion of the application of Gewirthian general principles in the bio-ethical philosophy of Shaun Pattinson,[34] the continuum of practical reason not only establishes moral rationality, but shows that a natural hierarchy of goods can structure our most complex deliberations and lead us to the synthesis of new ethical discovery. It follows that practical reason thus developed might inform principle, policy and practice at all levels and in all significant aspects of human association; education, commerce, reproductive technology, and so on. But let us be sensible: an expansive normative conception of law as 'morally legitimate power' stretches as far as the horizons of sociology

32 Ibid.

33 Ibid.

34 Shaun Pattinson *Influencing Traits before Birth* (Aldershot: Ashgate, 2002).

and of ethical conjecture and covers all manner of association, actions, practices and policy. This, of course, presents us with an unwieldy generality. The relevant conceptual matrix becomes more focussed, however, when, as Beyleveld and Brownsword remind us, we look at the infinitely broad canvass of social action and interaction from the point of view of the *enforcement* of norms in the context of the problem of social order – 'abstractly in explaining why the Legal Enterprise ... should exist at all ... and concretely in explaining why the phenomena should take particular forms in particular times and places'.[35]

Various consensual forms of human association pursuing various interests might, of course, be judged in respect of their moral worth and evaluated in terms of the effectiveness or fairness of their internal regulatory structures. But the idea of action and organization geared to *enforcement* presupposes a more problematic constellation of interests and associational relations: Regulation and enforcement in this context leads inevitably to questions of *obligation*, and, obversely to the *validity* of the norms in question.[36] Beyleveld and Brownsword say:

> One way of attempting to explain a particular instance of rule enforcement is to cite the reasons which guide that particular activity. Explanation ... may take the form of specifying the human interests which are served by it. However, if such a form of explanation is to be acceptable then the interests which actually exist, and which could thus actually guide the rule enforcement, must be coherent. The actions (A) of an individual or a group (G) cannot be explained in terms of the interest (I) of G, if only some of I are served by A, whilst A are counter productive in relation to the rest of I. When interest are in conflict, an adequate explanation of A must additionally specify why one set of I was favoured over the rest of I. This cannot be done solely in terms of the interests which were served by what was done.

The value of this approach is that it teaches us to think about the Legal Enterprise in terms of the width, fluidity and constant potential for novelty in addressing the problems of social order. The alternative is to fall back on a clumsy and usually contradictory discourse that constantly seeks affirmation of the existence of a tangible and coherent divide between 'law' and 'society'. That this empirically and conceptually frustrating task is likely to prove ultimately fruitless is illustrated very clearly by Fuller.[37]

He speaks of two principles of association: one of common aims or 'shared commitment', the other of 'legal principle'. This is not intended to be question-begging as to the distinction between 'law' and 'informal association', but rather a refusal to be hamstrung by the defects of the language we inherit in this sphere of inquiry. Fuller uses the term 'legal' irreverently to illuminate something that we might all instantly find empirically familiar, namely the preponderance of law-like or formal rules that govern the relations within an association, perhaps a church

35 Deryck Beyleveld and Roger Brownsword *Law as a Moral Judgment* (London: Sweet and Maxwell, 1986) pp. 145–148.

36 Ibid. p. 145.

37 Lon L. Fuller 'Two Principles of Human Association' in Kenneth I. Winston (ed.) *The Principles of Social Order* (Oxford: Hart Publishing, 2001) p. 90.

or a political party or a literary group. Fuller's first, second and third 'laws' of human association are that, (i) 'in almost all human associations both principles are in some degree present'; (ii) 'in a given case either principle may be tacitly operative or may emerge as an object of explicit and conscious concern'; (iii), 'when an association is first brought into being the principle of shared commitment will tend to be explicit and dominant, even though the association from the outset adopts, or has imposed on it, an internal structure of formal rules'.

There is, he says, a sterility in this formal, rule-based trajectory which undermines the energies of the association to pursue its substantive aspirations; paradoxically, this gives new significance to internal groups within the association who bind together through shared commitment.[38] But Fuller suggests that once the 'legal principle' is dominant it feeds on itself and accelerates: 'the ageing institution commonly displays the symptoms of what may be called creeping legalism'. Finally, he says:[39]

> The conditions of modern institutional life tend strongly to break down the distinction between the law of the political state and the inner law of associations. The result is an expansion of the jurisdiction of the regular courts of law to pass in review decisions of associations. The consequence of this external control through judicial review is to accelerate the tendency I have described as creeping legalism and to convert it into something more like galloping legalism.

A rare creature such as a Llewellynite sociological 'realist' convinced of the Kantian or Gewirthian analysis might begin to explain the position by saying that anthropologically, human association in all circumstances – even small scale and primitive ones, entails a variety of organizational, co-ordinatory and regulatory tasks which might be referred to as 'The Law Jobs'. However, in the particular historical and ethical socio-economic formation properly understood as *Civil Society,* all interaction identifiable under the penumbral notion of the 'The Law Jobs' in respect of the legitimacy of its practical objectives and regulatory rationale, can be said to stem from, or be susceptible to, modification and censure from a sovereign source of authority. Refreshingly, then, although we are by now familiar with sociological jurisprudence that tells us that 'law' can be understood only against a background of 'custom' or 'interaction',[40] in explaining the concept of Civil Society it is more appropriate to point out rather, that custom and interaction can be fully understood only against the background of 'law' – or more precisely, sovereignty.

---

38 Ibid. p. 92.

39 Ibid.

40 It all rather depends, it seems, on what aspect of the legal enterprise one wants to explain. Two fine examples of the flexibility of the thesis are to be found in Roberto M. Unger *Law in Modern Society* (New York: The Free Press, 1977) pp. 54–55; and in Lon L. Fuller's essay 'Human Interaction and the Law' in Kenneth I. Winston (ed.) (op. cit.) p. 233.

Chapter 5

Why 'Pluralism' Fails a Pluralist Society

The problem of explaining and defending a conception of *Eunomic* social order as distinct from some condition of 'natural' anarchy or a pathological state of *Anomia*, is a longstanding and highly developed preoccupation of political philosophy and social theory, although not always under that name. But the problem of accounting for a legitimate and *inclusive* or integrated social order, that is, the problem of conceptualizing and justifying the idea of the legitimacy of law and politics in the modern (or perhaps post-modern), pluralist state, is a project of more recent provenance and presents an exponentially more complex theoretical challenge. Perhaps it is a project that has run its course; for contemporary notions of Pluralism and those mutations of it referred to as Multiculturalism, or more precisely, Cultural Autonomy Theory, demand solutions that go well beyond even the refinements of the ideas of inclusion and integration. Thus optimism about creating and defending the legitimacy of public legal norms, procedures and political processes is difficult to maintain when faced with equally emphatic claims for the 'legitimacy', 'validity' or desirability of each component social grouping, as well as the overall condition of intensely diverse cultural and ethical pluralism that characterize contemporary 'civil society'.

From Universalism to Multiculturalism

The precepts of sovereignty expressed through law, and the correlate notion of obligation, although developed in national contexts, all contain universal implications. This is clear in the classic texts of Enlightenment political theory and appear most famously in Rousseau's treatise on the notion of a Social Contract,[1] a work that inspired the political universalism of Kant.[2] It is the appeal to universalism inherent in notions of political supremacy and legitimacy that makes the borders of sovereignty appear so arbitrary in modern pluralist societies: the 'universe' turns out to be the nation state, and the inclusive universe of 'citizenship', it is often alleged, seems to be the long-term product of a mono-

---

1 Jean-Jaques Rousseau *The Social Contract: or Principles of Political Right* 1762 (translation by G.D.H. Cole).

2 *Idea for a Universal History from a Cosmopolitan Point of View* (1784) (translation by Lewis White-Beck). From *Immanuel Kant, 'On History'* (Indianapolis: Bobbs-Merrill Co., 1963).

cultural attempt to homogenize inconvenient, yet very real, differences. The precepts that celebrated the links between sovereignty, legitimacy and nation reached their ideological zenith in the nineteenth century, but now appear problematic in the context of what we have referred to as the topicalities of global interrelatedness, interdependencies and the 'perforation' of states by various persons, objects and economic and communicative processes.

This multi-faceted 'perforation' and thus the mounting incoherence is especially true of those 'sovereign' states presently responsible for, and subject to, the astonishing acceleration and increase in the political, economic and legal competencies of the European Community. But this fact should not lead us to believe that the idea of the nation state and its self-determination is now redundant or dormant or, for that matter inappropriate as a model for further social, economic and cultural development. Let us bear in mind too that the concept of a European 'federation' of states is far from transparent in either legal or political terms. Yet, we are often told that this condition seems to situate both the theory and actuality of international relations, as well as constitutional law and political culture on a precarious historical cusp of transformation: behind us the 'Westphalian' orthodoxy receding from view, and,on the horizon, what Beck has called 'the second age of modernity' where 'The whole world of national sovereignty is fading away – including 'the container theory of society' on which most of the sociology of the first age of modernity is based ...'.[3]

Equality and Inclusiveness

The idea of reconceptualisng sovereignty and the state entails, of course, reconceptualizing citizenship. Where T.H. Marshall[4] had suggested that the latter entailed the granting of rights by the state in respect of basic civil liberties, the right to participate in political decision making, and the right to a civilized standard of life relative to prevailing social standards, debates in the past two decades have rejected the terms of neutrality as well as the account of the economic and political context on which this vision was based. David Held has re-characterized the idea of citizenship as one not of passive receipt of state beneficence, but of a struggle for membership and participation in the community'.[5] Judith Squires says that with this radicalization of the discourse:[6]

---

3 Ulrich Beck 'The Cosmopolitan Perspective: Sociology of the Second Age of Modernity' *British Journal of Sociology* (Vol. 51, No. 1, 2000) pp. 79–105. See also N. MacCormick *Questioning Sovereignty*. (Oxford: Oxford University Press, 1999).

4 T.H. Marshall *Citizenship and Social Class* (1950) in G. Shafir (ed.) *Citizenship Debates: A Reader* (Minneapolis: University of Minnesota Press, 1998)

5 See David Held *Democracy and the Global Order: From the Modern State to Cosmopolitan Governance* (Cambridge: Polity Press, 1995).

6 Judith Squires *Gender in Political Theory* (London: Polity Press, 1999) p. 167.

> One is able to use citizenship as a means of examining the nature and composition of 'the community' and the terms of inclusion. The nation-state is but one form of community, legal inclusion but one form of membership.

Thus we now arrive at a clear collision between '... formal, universalistic and static' conceptions of citizenship now ranged against 'participatory, embedded and social' conceptions.[7] Of the clutch of issues arising from this critique we might focus on what Squires refers to as the 'universalistic pretensions of citizenship discourse'.[8] Orthodoxly, these pretensions might be exposed by a critique of the *shortfall* of purported universality and inclusion, but the more recent and more forceful objection is that universality as an aspiration, by its very nature, must impose some form of *homogeneity* upon the *demos* or the community, thereby encouraging if not enforcing assimilation into what is abstractly conceived as the political community. Social contract theorists are in the front line here. Rousseau's notion of the General Will is an obvious candidate – for here Squires articulates an indisputable by-product of the process of universalist incorporation[9]:

> The critics of this assimilatory form of universalism argue that the attainment of such unification has always been and always will be, bought at the price of the exclusion of the actual heterogeneity of society, and the public denial of cultural pluralism.

The Multiculturalist dissatisfaction with *assimilatory* conceptions of universality is of great theoretical importance. It challenges the slogans of unity and inclusion and exposes the complaceny of an uncritical acceptance of notions of *integrationist* universality. But as we shall see, this raises fundamental issues about social homogeneity and heterogeneity and about what is genuinely constitutive of a community, and as it turns out, it seems that the writings of Carl Schmitt, have much in common with Multiculturalist critics of 'assimilatory' liberalism.[10] Schmitt says, rather pluralistically:[11]

> In the domain of the political, people do not face each other as abstractions but as politically interested and politically determined persons, as citizens, governors or governed, politically allied or opponents – in any case, therefore, in political categories. In the sphere of the political, one cannot abstract out what is political, leaving only universal human equality.

But where does this revolt against liberal universalism lead us? The apparent contradiction is that of embracing the idea of the inevitability of pluralistic

---

7 Ibid.

8 Ibid.

9 Ibid. p. 171.

10 See for example Iris Marion Young *Inclusion and Democracy* (Oxford: Oxford University Press, 2000); also James Tully *Strange Multiplicity* (Cambridge: Cambridge University Press, 1995).

11 Carl Schmitt *The Crisis of Parliamentary Democracy* (trans. E. Kennedy) (Cambridge, MA: MIT Press, 1985) p. 11.

diversity and its many individual and subcultural manifestations, and yet simultaneously affirming allegiance to the idea of a core of common obligations underpinning a societal universal notion of the Rule of Law. Without the latter, there can be no community. Without the first, community will be illiberal and dictatorial.

The notion of *Eunomic* order will not allow us to conceive of society as a simple struggle for *effective* order through the sheer dominance of one set of interests against another, or all others. Rather, we are required to theorize a form of authority that might serve as the foundation for a set of institutional arrangements that accommodates, and in some way sustains, yet transcends, this plurality. Where the language of obligation in classical accounts of the social contract from Hobbes to Rawls envisaged a unidirectional shift from justifications of systems of customary, sectional allegiances, to justifications of legal rationality within the context of overarching social incorporation, contemporary Multicultural theory reminds us of the need to acknowledge the reverse trajectory. This tendency resists and mistrusts even the benign homogenizing tendencies of 'inclusion' and 'integration' and affirms the importance of diversity and difference of customs and cultures. Ironically and increasingly, however, social theory is being forced to revisit its earlier and more 'mechanistic' insights in acknowledging that the *actual viability* of these arrangements in diversity depends on some form of moral and political *homogeneity*.

Liberalism has often remained undialectical in this regard, relying upon a logically fragile appeal to tolerance and (to counter the uncertainties implicit in its defence of individual self-determination and free markets) a problematic 'majoritarian' and consumerist (rather than a genuinely civil-political and pluralistic) account of the relationship between democracy and generality of the Rule of Law. But the tensions inherent in the attempt to articulate an integrated theory of the state and civil society have seen an attempt within and without the liberal tradition to reverse orthodox liberal priorities. Put simply, this has resulted in an emphasis on community over the individual, and more recently, the influence of suggestions to abandon the commitment to defending Right over the Good. We discussed in Chapter 3 the attempts by philosophers like Michael J. Sandel,[12] Charles Taylor,[13] Alasdair MacIntyre[14] and Michael Walzer[15] to demonstrate the logical, ontological and/or normative primacy of culture and community over Rawlsian conceptions of the individual. Furthermore, we have

---

12 See *Liberalism and the Limits of Justice* (Cambrdige, MA: Cambridge University Press 1998) and *Democracy's Discontent: America in Search of a Public Philosophy* (Cambridge, MA: Belknap Press, 1998).

13 See *Sources of the Self: The Making of the Modern Identity* (Cambridge, MA: Harvard University Press, 1989).

14 See *After Virtue: A Study in Moral Theory* (London: Duckworth, 1985).

15 See *Spheres of Justice: A Defense of Pluralism and Equality* (New York: Basic Books, 1984) and *Politics and Passion: Toward a More Egalitarian Liberalism* (New Haven, CT: Yale University Press, 2006).

more recently seen the publication, notably by Alan Brudner[16] and Martin Loughlin[17] of influential texts in Constitutional Theory and the theory of Public Law that present comprehensive re-examinations of the fragility of the convenient liberal model of the state and its relationship to the individual and democracy. But whilst Rawlsian Liberalism and various brands of Communitarianism have been pluralistic in the sense of acknowledging the great diversity of beliefs and values and the need to acknowledge the equality of differences based on the incommensurability of values, these concessions to pluralism have been arguments about how we should express the legitimate basis of the sovereign state, not an attack on the idea of a unified sovereign state itself.

The post-inclusive, post-universalist attack on the notion of sovereignty has intensified in equal proportion to the enthusiasm which now attends the celebration and promulgation of a now radicalized notion of pluralism. There is plausible logic to the focus of the new critique: legally, sovereignty suggests finality and supremacy; it is the ultimate expression of hierarchy, generality and homogeneity. Sovereignty has also been synonymous with national and territorial isolation and, save for recent exceptions, the idea of a state's right to self-determination. By contrast, 'Pluralism' in its Multiculturalist form points to open-endedness; to the non-hierarchical and incommensurable co-existences of cultures, associations, values, viewpoints and, ideally, to diversity and heterogeneity in political input and, crucially, in political and legal *output*. That is, a plurality of parallel legalities are envisaged as operating simultaneously over diverse communities living and interacting with each other in what hitherto was the same social and geographical 'container'. The monoliths of sovereignty thus appear moribund in the wake of the rise of the globalized, pluralized, 'polyarchies' of difference that are alleged to constitute the New Modernity. But the *old* 'modern' account of state sovereignty and civil society and the *new* 'modern' account of it do share some irreducibly 'modern' attributes and ideas: first, modernity essentially means 'post-traditional', and the 'old' modernity and the 'new' modernity are products of revolution against 'traditional' or late-feudal society and authority structures. Secondly, 'old moderns' and 'new moderns' rely ambivalently, ambiguously, but indispensably upon the weapons used to destroy tradition: critique, the principle of equality, autonomous freedom and the priority of subjective right. The nexus of the old and new, of sovereignty and post sovereignty, lies, we will argue, in these concepts.

Our aim in this chapter will be to outline some of the claims and sources of the critique of sovereignty and highlight their shortcomings. We shall also look at the diverse history of pluralism: for we must bear in mind that 'pluralism' has featured as an argument *for* sovereignty in the form of tolerationism in, for example, Locke and Bodin, yet *against it* in the comparatively recent yet dramatic transmutations of its sociological content from Duguit to the English Pluralists, or later in the mouth of Weber, or Carl Schmitt and his recent rehabilitators. More recently still

16 Alan Brudner *Constitutional Goods* (Oxford: Oxford University Press, 2004).

17 Martin Loughlin *The Idea of Public Law* (Oxford: Oxford University Press, 2004).

we can note that from the 1950s the idea was immensely influential as an antidote to sociological Marxism offering a pluralistic model of democracy shaped and refined by the Political Science of the 1960s and 1970s. Contemporarily, in the form of Multiculturalism it becomes the target of Brian Barry's ire in his analysis of *Culture and Equality.*[18] It is probably in this latter guise that we find the most uncompromising clash with the 'old' conceptual models of modernity based on the ideas of the nation state's claims to political and legal sovereignty and the legitimacy attached to the notion of the generality of the Rule of Law. In sifting through these pluralisms and focusing on some of the currently 'strong' and relevant claims of Multiculturalism and the so-called 'Politics of Difference'[19] we intend to revisit what we have referred to above as the nexus between the 'old' and the 'new' modernity in the hope of showing how the 'new' pluralist critique is energized by the 'old' orthodoxies of anti-tradition – in short, the fundamental claims of Enlightenment Rationalism. Rather than abandoning the concept of sovereignty we might, instead, make a more plausible case for the view that it should be seen as *the normative supremacy of a public infrastructure of justice appropriate to the ideal of a genuinely pluralist society.*

A Brief History of Pluralism

In opposition to the impression that one might form from the vast amount of literature on globalization and Multiculturalism, these phenomena are not entirely novel. The existence of society as a pluralistic entity, that is, consisting of a number of significantly different groups is hardly new, nor is the political and legal attempt to handle and control this social condition. Drucker tells us:[20]

> The last pluralist society in the West existed during the early and high Middle Ages. The Roman Empire tried, quite successfully, to create a unitary state in which Roman law and the Roman legions created political uniformity throughout the empire while cultural diversity was preserved. But after the collapse of the Roman Empire, this unity splintered completely. In its stead arose a congeries of autonomous and semi-autonomous institutions: political, religious, economic, craft oriented, and so on. There was the medieval university, autonomous and a law unto itself. But there were also the free cities, the multi-nationals of the medieval economy. There were the craft guilds, and there were the all but autonomous major orders and great abbeys of the Church…There were any number of landowners, from small squires to great dukes, each all but independent. Next to them were autonomous bishoprics, paying at best lip service to both the pope in Rome and the local prince. At its height, medieval pluralism

18 Brian Barry *Culture and Equality* (Cambridge, MA: Harvard University Press, 2001).

19 This term, which has become a catchword for Multiculturalism was first introduced by Iris M. Young in her *Justice and the Politics of Difference* (Princeton, NJ: Princeton University Press, 1990).

20 Peter F. Drucker 'The New Pluralism' *Leader to Leader* (No. 14, Fall, 1999) available at http://www.pfdf.org/leaderbooks/l21/fall99/new-pluralism.html.

> in western and northern Europe alone must have been embodied by several thousands of such autonomous institutions, ranging from small squires to great landowners, and from small craft guilds and equally small, local universities to transnational religious orders. Each of these pluralist institutions was concerned only with its own welfare and, above all, with its own aggrandizement. Not one of them was concerned with the community beyond its walls.

Pluralism as a political doctrine and as a factual social condition can thus be traced back at least to the politics of the early and high middle-ages.[21] But we need not look earlier than the beginning of the twentieth century in France to find the influential pluralist doctrines of Leon Duguit[22] shaping the constitutional and administrative theory of the Republic and, almost simultaneously, these same themes were taken up by the 'English Pluralists', Laski, Figgis and Cole.[23]

The background for pluralism then, as now, was a reaction to the growing domination of a burgeoning administrative and bureaucratic state apparatus. By reaffirming the rights, and re-emphasizing the importance of, the voluntary associations that constituted civil society, Duguit's aim was to re-examine and rebalance the relationship between state and society. This concern is a basic dilemma of modernity expressed in the simple view that a society of any complexity must acknowledge both the need for a centralized system of government endowed with a *supreme* capacity to make law for that society, and the need for private initiative and institutional creativity as a means to economic, cultural and political flourishing and development. Liberal theories have suggested (unconvincingly) that societies governed by the Iron Fist of authoritarian government tend to fail because of an inability to stimulate the productiveness of human life in all its aspects. On the other hand, societies fragment under the lack of leadership because power accrues to factions that, on attaining a critical mass, break free from state-control and set their own normative agenda. This process gives rise to crises of legitimacy, a call for new government and, in the worst cases, civil war. The issue, rather predictably, appears as theorizing some notion of *balance* between the state and civil society.[24] All of this, including the implicit endorsement of pluralist diversity in a 'well-balanced' society, is not new, but is to be found at the heart of classical political theory as a familiar *concept* of the proper form and function of state sovereignty.

---

21 See Peter F. Drucker's article 'The New Pluralism' in *Leader to Leader* (ibid.) 18–23.

22 Léon Duguit (1859–1928) published *Les transformations du droit public* in 1913, a critique of state sovereignty, arguing for a new understanding of Public Law.

23 See generally, Paul Q Hirst (ed.) *The Pluralist Theory of The State: Selected writings of G.D.H. Cole, J.N. Figgis, and H.J. Laski* (London: Routledge, 1989).

24 See Chapter 4 *supra* pp. 132–135 for a detailed discussion (following Jean Cohen) of the pitfalls of this rather convenient 'civil society talk'.

Pluralism at the Beginning of the Twentieth Century

The English Pluralists, inspired by Duguit, argued in favour of the social channelling of more autonomy to voluntary associations and a corresponding weakening of the power of the state to interfere with their affairs and decision making.[25] For these writers, the fragmented and differentiated character of society meant that the classical notion of national sovereignty which accorded absolute power to the agencies of the state (embodied in either the concept of the supreme political and legal assembly and/or in the physical person of the monarch) should be replaced by a genuinely modern account of legitimate governance. The relationship between ruler and ruled could not adequately be portrayed as a relationship between the King in Parliament and the individual citizen mediated by a broad and conveniently tacit understanding of what constituted the *salus populi.*[26] But whilst agreeing about the central issue, The English Pluralists differed in their approach to theorizing and articulating alternative models and strategies aimed at the solution to this problem. Thus we find diverse and nuanced lines of argument in relation to the general critique of traditional national sovereignty from pluralist writers of the period.

First and foremost the Pluralists argued that sovereignty (the state) should be viewed functionally rather than geographically: sovereignty should be seen to belong to society rather than to the state. By this was meant that the concept of sovereignty understood as the supreme authority of a law-making power in a state, the subjects of which were a people of a geographically limited territory, should be replaced with a concept of sovereignty understood as the network of self-governing functional associations in society. Laski's *The Foundations of Sovereignty and Other Essays* provides an illustration of what this idea implies.[27]

> The real way, surely, in which to organize the interests of producers is by making out a delineation of industry and confiding the care of its problems to those most concerned with them. Anyone can see that the railways are as real as Lancashire; and exactly as the specifically local problems of Lancashire are dealt with by it, so could the specifically functional problems of the railways be dealt with by a governing body of its own.

---

25 John Neville Figgis (1866–1919) was a historian, political philosopher and monk. Educated at Brighton College, he was a student of Lord Acton at Cambridge, and editor of much of Acton's work. Harold Joseph Laski (Manchester, June 30, 1893–March 24, 1950 in London) was an English political theorist, economist, author, and lecturer, and served as the 1945–1946 chairman of the Labour Party. George Douglas Howard Cole (September 25, 1889–January 14, 1959) was an English political theorist, economist and historian. He was a long-time member of the Fabian Society and a principal proponent of Guild Socialist ideas.

26 *Salus populi suprema lex esto* [the welfare of the people is to be the highest law].

27 Harold Laski *The Foundations of Sovereignty and Other Essays* (New York: Harcourt, Brace and Company, 1921) p. 70.

This is sensible stuff; but it is, however, obvious that the interests of those who run the railways might easily come into conflict with other interests in society. We are not talking simply about organized interests such as worker's unions interested in safe working conditions, or land-owners' 'interests' in not having freight trains running through their back-gardens, but also *unorganized* and perhaps unarticulated interests such as the general interest in a clean environment or perhaps some aesthetic or conservationist ideal of the proper division between urban and countryside activity and planning. A plethora of functionally autonomous sovereign units (understood simplistically, that is, in a non-integrated fashion) would produce, potentially, a form of cumulative chaos. If functional self-management is to cater for general social functionality it must be in some sense federated and integrated in order to respond to overarching common problems. In the same way that the geographical shires have federated into England, so the various functional units of the state must federate with a view to orchestrating efforts and directions of each functional association. It seems, then, uncontentious to suggest that this points to the need for a co-ordinating focus of decision-making power. We might not want to refer to this as *sovereign* power, or conceptualize it in its traditional form, but there is an obvious and very significant loose-end to the theory of functional autonomy waiting to be tied up here. Why, then, did the English Pluralists persist with the argument for the shift from geographical to functional sovereignty? The answer is to be found not in simple models of co-ordinated activity, but in the issues of legitimacy. The political basis of pluralism is a dissatisfaction with the account of the nexus between centralized authority and the actual and potential diversity of 'the will' of 'the people'. In Duguit's *Transformations du droit public* (1913), we find a quotation from a speech by the Frenchman Royer Collard[28] made in the French parliament in 1831. Collard (in Laski's translation) says:[29]

> …the majority of individuals…the majority of wills, cannot be sovereign. If they are sovereign let us frankly admit that the sovereignty of the people is only the sovereignty of force, the most absolute form of absolute power. But societies are not merely numerical collections of men and wills. They are not merely made up of numbers. They have a bond stronger than that; they have the privileged right of humanity, and the legitimate interests born of that right. … The will of one, the will of some, the will of all is only force less or more in its strength. We deny that any obedience, any respect is due to their wills merely because they are wills.

This quote, although intended as a critique of parliamentary sovereignty, simultaneously affirms the need for a reconsideration of sovereignty in a more abstract sense. Like Duguit, the English Pluralists were concerned with the political (perhaps, more precisely, the *democratic*) impoverishment of the individual in the

---

28 Pierre Paul Royer-Collard (June 21, 1763–September 2, 1845), French statesman and philosopher. He was the leader of a small political movement who believed that it was possible to reconcile the monarchy with the revolution.

29 Harold Laski *Law in the Modern State* [1919] (London: George Allen and Unwin 1970) p. 16.

face of traditional conceptions of sovereignty. Even after the widening of the franchise and of the constitutional aggrandisement of the English Parliament, central government still appeared as a monolith of absolute authority. It had the mandate of the majority of votes, but that, according to the Pluralists, was far from sufficient to legitimize it. Focusing as always on the increasing plurality of interests, objectives, and life-forms in modern society, the Pluralists believed that the sovereign central power – democratic or not – would always, either support the interests of a faction of society, or support nothing but itself. In this event the state becomes an end itself cut off from society. The Pluralists then, as do those who today propound the priority of cultural autonomy now, located the core problem in the tendency of sovereign institutions and processes to presuppose a homogeneity of interests and life-styles at odds with the real world condition of genuine and significant pluralities. One might not wish to go as far as Paul Hirst and assert that sovereign state power is compatible with democracy only on the assumption that people *are* homogenous, have one interest, and will one thing[30]. But it is certainly a valid and significant objection to the classical account of sovereignty that the regulatory apparatus which springs from a single source cannot, without a great deal of explanation and qualification, hope to 'represent' or mirror the manifold and complex views of the Good that exist in the many groups and individuals in society.[31] Thus we are left with a need to re-examine both sides of the problem: *why* is 'sovereign' power to be regarded as sovereign, and why are vast territories of interests and associations ignored and deprived of any say in the wider affairs of state and society. If pluralism poses these critically indispensable questions then we should all endeavour to be Pluralists.

Here then, in the broad critique levelled by the Pluralists against the English nation state at the beginning of the twentieth century, we find a pattern of arguments similar to, if not identical with, those found in the late twentieth and early twenty-first century in what we will refer to as Cultural Autonomy Theory. At the core of both schools of thought is the idea that, in any plausible account of the legitimacy of the state supposedly grounded in 'representation', sovereignty must be broken down and relativized not only (a) to concede and promote the autonomy required by the functional mechanics of regional and local associations, interests and activities, but also (b) to reject the tendency to assume a condition of homogeneity and rather, actively acknowledge the differences, views and identities of individuals and groups.

Pluralist views are thus common-sensically convincing and attractive if couched in the form of questions about preferences for empowerment, accountability, responsiveness of government, improved communication and so forth. But it is important to assess with some care the extent to which this proposed adaptation of sovereignty to the pluralistic social landscape remains coherent. Let us first note that centralized state power *can* be used to pursue a number of interests simultaneously, and that it may also serve to mediate between opposing interests in society, and to find or create balances. This would amount

30 See Paul Q. Hirst (op. cit.).

31 Ibid. p. 26.

to some form of corporatism, but pluralism in this form contains within it other pathological tendencies. These have been documented dramatically in the now well-known writings of Carl Schmitt.[32]

Carl Schmitt's Analysis of Pluralism

Schmitt saw the growth and fragmentation of sectional interests and the rise of the administrative state as the decline of the *nation* state and the severing of the link between the people (*Volk*) and the government. Writing in the context of the Weimar Republic he saw disparate interest blocs manoeuvring in the world of parliamentary politics, forming larger, pragmatic party alliances and abusing the machinery of political representation to secure power.

What we should note here are the interesting points of agreement and disagreement between Schmitt, and the English Pluralists (and Duguit). All seem to agree, first, that society was then (and is now) more plural than it ever was, and secondly, that the *state* (that is, the English, French and German states at the beginning of the twentieth century) were (and are) incapable of handling this plurality of interests and lifestyles in an acceptably legitimate and genuinely democratic manner. The respective *reasons* for holding this latter view, however, differ fundamentally. For the English Pluralists (and Duguit), the problem was that the state, assuming shared understandings and the belief in basic homogeneity, was still too wedded to the ideology of the nineteenth-century model of legitimacy whereby elected representatives in government and opposition, amenable to rational persuasion, formed a sovereign legislature issuing general laws. Schmitt, of course, would have applauded such a state of affairs, but his work is based on the emphatic account of the passing of this style of regime and the rise of what he regarded as *pluralistic opportunists*.[33]

Schmitt and the Pluralists differed entirely in respect of their political response and perceptions of the political problem. The Pluralists wanted to replace the classic doctrine of sovereignty and its accompanying notion of a centralized state with a monopoly of legislative power with some form of strengthened autonomy for voluntary associations combined, supposedly, with a corporatist state (although, as Hirst points out, they did not agree on what should replace the object of criticism[34]). Schmitt, on the other hand, desperately wanted to *reinforce* national sovereignty by excluding what he saw as the debilitating influence of the

32 These ideas are presented in Schmitt's various works but see particularly Carl Schmitt *The Concept of the Political* G. Schwab (ed.) H. Lomax trans. (University of Chicago Press, Chicago 1996); also, *Der Hüter der Verfassung* (Tubingen, 1931); and *Legalität und Legitimität*' (München, 1932). For important references and analysis see *Canadian Journal of Law and Jurisprudence* (Vol. X, No. 1, January 1997) in its entirety, and particularly Richard Mehring, at pp. 105–107, and Robert Howse, 'From Legitmacy to Dictatorship – and Back again: Leo Strauss's Critique of the Anti-Liberalism of Carl Schmitt' (ibid.) pp. 77–103 (with footnotes and wider references).

33 Dominique Leydet (op. cit.) p. 49.

34 Paul Q. Hirst (op. cit.) p. 27.

great variety of economic and political associations that opportunistically sought representative power. Schmitt's prognosis for pluralism was the rise of a travesty of a constitution based on a mutually perpetuating power-sharing arrangement where groups dived between them the spoils of the state and gained influence and allegiance by distributing largesse to their pet constituencies. This is a disturbing interpretation of what at first appeared to be the benign democratic improvements of a pluralist outlook. Let us pursue Schmitt's ideas in more depth.

Dominique Leydet tells us that Schmitt, from the outset, defined pluralism as 'a situation in which the state has become dependent upon, or subordinate to, the various social and economic associations that make up contemporary industrial societies'.[35] This situation, as the English Pluralists argued, is not self-evidently undesirable. However, in the context of Schmitt's analysis of state and society it is to be understood as the pathological expression of the failure of a complex structure of social and economic institutions. This is important in that Schmitt's analysis of the nature of 'pluralist' society is pivotal to his critique of democracy and legitimacy, for the term as he employs it has a certain ambiguity which requires careful articulation.

Schmitt saw pluralism not as the mere existence of disparate and fragmented interests in society (a sociological conception which is merely a corollary of the very idea of a complex division of labour) but loaded it heavily and perjoratively with a 'welfarist' ideology arising from his conception, of the 'anti-political' 'metaphysics of liberalism' and the very specific features of modern 'corporatist' government. For Schmitt, interest-differentiation *per se* is seen as a developmental and structural instability, and its political expression, pluralism, necessarily descends into a 'welfarist' pathology which precipitates a constitutional degeneration into what he refers to famously as the ethic of *pacta sunt servanda*. This is the situation in which parliamentary groupings effectively hi-jack the state and use its authority and largesse in pursuit of short-term sectional interest. Constitutional 'guarantees' under this arrangement become identical with whatever pragmatic alliances and rules of the political game happen to be agreed between the incumbent interest blocs. This, not surprisingly, he regarded as destructive of the unity and integrity of the *Volk*.

Schmitt's response to this process of disintegration was to argue that the constitution should be urgently protected from the invasion and usurpation of parliament by unruly and anti-democratic forces. In the recurrent parliamentary crises of the Weimar Republic, this meant providing a jurisprudential justification for the interpretation of the crucial Article 48 of the Weimar Constitution as offering an absolutist prerogative to the incumbent chancellor in times of national emergency, and a justification for the view that the parliamentary crisis combined with the social situation at the time in fact constituted an emergency situation. The defence of a prerogative to suspend the normal democratic process is neither uncommon nor illiberal: it operates on the premise that democracy and democratic representation logically cannot extend its freedoms and protections to forces which

35 Dominique Leydet (op. cit.) p. 49 translates and quotes from Schmitt's 'Staatsethik und pluralistischer Staat' (1930) XXXV *Kant-Studien* 28, p. 31.

seek to exploit these privileges to destroy democracy itself – a theory which even today forms part of German constitutional law,[36] and which has recently been accepted by the European Court in the *Refah* judgment.[37]

It is obvious, however, that this is a principle which must be handled with extreme care, and which is bound to cause controversy when applied. As is well known, Schmitt went on to argue that in a situation in which the integral identity of the *Volk* is endangered – what Schmitt called 'the state of exception' – the validity of a decision arises solely from the moral courage of a spiritually gifted leader of the *Volk* to affirm its Will to Power. Such pronouncements are *ipso facto*, for Schmitt, an expression of the democratic will of the people.[38]

This inverted view of democratic representation stems from an interpretation of the ideas of French revolutionary writers and their analysis of the sovereignty of the people as the genuine *pouvoir constituant* unbounded by constitutional principle in their right to assert and defend their identity. This is a contentious reading of what Sieyes meant to convey by the importance of distinguishing between the *constituting* power (the nation) and the constituted power or government (*pouvoir constitué*).[39] However we should note that the logic of *Schmitt's* interpretation of the role of the *pouvoir constituant* in democratic pluralism lies in the idea, contrary to modern critical approaches in constitutional and administrative law, that it is not so much the need to monitor and control the *outputs* of government (that is, laws, policy, delegated authority, and hence, bureaucratic discretionary power), but rather, to 'democratize' the range of *inputs* by *homogenizing* and unifying the 'interests of the people' in an attempt to rescue them from a condition of ideological fragmentation.

For Schmitt's account to make any democratic sense whatsoever, and for it to be assimilated in any way to the theory of representation and the notion of the General Will formulated by Rousseau, Sieyes and later, Kant, it must, of course, be entirely detached from its catastrophic expression in Nazism. If this is possible,

36 That is, Art. 21, 2: Since the Second World War this precept has been developed under the name of *Streitbare Demokratie*.

37 ECHR Judgment of 13 February 2003 in Refah Partisi (The Welfare Party) and Others v. Turkey (Applications Nos. 41340/98, 41342/98, 41343/98 and 41344/98).

38 See invaluable discussions of this in Robert Howse (op. cit.) and in S. Holmes *The Anatomy of Anti-Liberalism* (Chicago: University of Chicago Press, 1993). The idea of 'decisionism' and Hobbesian support for it is developed in Schmitt's *Die Diktatur* (Munich: Duncker and Humboldt, 1928) esp. pp. 21–24. Howse's remarks in this regard are illuminating: he says: 'Schmitt deviates from Machiavelli in a crucial respect – he admires the resolve and honesty of a self confident dictatorship, not domination as such. He seeks therefore, not a combination of the lion and the fox, but rather a *Cesare* with the soul of a Luther. Thus when in *Political Theology*, Schmitt refers to the "exacting moral decision" as the "core of the political idea", this does not refer to the aspiration to ground decisionism in a higher morality, what is morally 'exacting' is the requirement to decide "out of nothingess". Moral exactness means nothing more or less than the courage and honesty to affirm one's own will to power as the only ground of the decision'. See Howse (op. cit.) p. 80.

39 See Martin Louglin *The Idea of Public Law* (op. cit.) pp. 61–69.

and if the Teutonic and ethnic themes of Schmitt's conception of the state can be set aside for theoretical purposes, Schmitt's critique of pluralism raises some important issues and forms a significant counterweight to the arguments of Pluralists past and present.

We have, therefore, two imperfect and antithetical models before us. The English Pluralists seem to presuppose that the human individual will flourish more readily if associations are not only allowed to develop more freely, that is, with less restraints and less state-interference, but more significantly, are recognized as juridical persons in their own right and thus, effectively, influentially integrated into the legislative process. The inner life of associations should be respected for it represents the values and interests of those individuals who participate in them. Integrating the value element and the interest orientation of the association through juridical empowerment seems, therefore to go some way to bringing together the dual concerns of the English Pluralists: first, democratic legitimacy linked to a theory of representation, and secondly, the devolved economic and administrative competences more immediately connected to the idea of functional sovereignty explained above. Schmitt, on the other hand, believed that the autonomous life of associations and their influence in politics had developed so far that *the common interest* had been abandoned in favour of the interests of virulent corporate elites. Rather than promoting integration and human flourishing, 'associationism' was leading to the disintegration of society. And what is worse, according to Schmitt, whilst pluralist *elites* may have benefited from this, the ordinary individual has been betrayed.

Beyond Schmitt and the Pluralists

Behind both approaches lies a conceptual scheme that divides the political elements into three basic and familiar but infinitely ambiguous categories: 'the individual', 'associations' and 'the state'. These are the elements that, in configuration, give rise to the classical questions about what the move from some form of State of Nature (by which we should understand the condition in which individual lives and collective units have not yet gelled or been manoeuvred into an encompassing macro-social unit) to Civil Society (by which we should understand the condition in which public authority is institutionalized as the organiser of the now incorporated units into a commonwealth). From this point, if only ostensibly, the social structure becomes an object susceptible to deliberate design.[40] An account not only of the relationship between the individual and associations, and between associations and the state, but of the roles, rights and entitlements that are assumed to accrue respectively to these elements is thus inevitably required whatever account we might wish offer of the nature of their configuration or of our aspirations to institutional design in this regard. With these three elements

40 For a theoretical analysis of the implications for legal theory of this move from the state of nature to civil society, see H.P. Olsen and S. Toddington *Law In Its Own Right* (Oxford: Hart Publishing, 1999) Chapter 5.

already in place as the terms of reference of a philosophical inquiry we might start from the analysis of the individual and ask fundamental questions about human nature; freedom and structural and historical or cultural determinism; about the existence or not of innate rights, of universal psychological, moral or intellectual traits, and so on. We could proceed to speculation about the location of suitably modelled individuals in associations and ask whether, or to what degree, The state should intervene, support or suppress the *internal* life and dialectical interactions of associations and what are perceived as their members. The answers, of course, would depend on what kind of an association we were talking about, how the public sphere was constructed; what was the internal account of the roles, rights, and relationships between the association and its members, what objective the association purported to pursue, and so on. We must also ask whether membership or participation in the association in question is to be understood as genuinely voluntary for the individual, or whether inclusion and participation (as in the family, 'the state', and, sometimes, religious organizations) is compulsory? How does the relationship between association and individual play out? Does it discriminate against some members? Is it repressive or supportive of the individual? Is it supportive of the state, or is it geared to undermining it?

From the 'top down' we might ask if, in the case of interference or intervention into the activities of an association, the interference by the state is discriminatory? Whose – and what kinds – of interests are protected or undermined by the interference? What would be the consequence of *non*-interference? The point we wish to make here is simply that there are many possible outcomes of inquiry and thus many interpretations of interest-perspectives on which we might base our visions of pluralism or our objections to it. Many of these questions are being asked and responses to them given empirical operation in modern western democracies through the legal process of giving effect to basic rights under the ECHR. Examples concern rights to freedom of association, freedom of religion, freedom of assembly, and so on. An inquiry into the jurisprudence of the court is informative, and we undertake this in Chapter 6 below, but for the moment, let us take the opportunity to look at contemporary pluralist answers to some of these important questions.

From Pluralism to Multiculturalism

While pluralism at the beginning of the twentieth century focused on the role of (the division of) labour and on (the fragmentation of) politics and economics, Multiculturalism at the beginning of the twenty-first century focuses on the differentiation and equality of cultures and particularly ethnic and religious cultures. The basic political problem, however, remains the same and we find today similar oppositions of perspective.[41]

41 For a recent overview of the debate, see Alan Brudner *Constitutional Goods* (op. cit.) Chapter 10 on 'The Liberal Duty to Recognize Cultures'.

Figgis in *The Great Leviathan*[42] argued that associations ought to be recognized as juridical persons in their own right, thereby granting them the right to interact directly with their members and with other persons/associations. Rather than treating associations as a collective of individuals based on an original contract between the members, the association should be recognized as a juridical body with a life of its own, thereby allowing the association to regulate the relationship between itself and its members in accordance with procedural rules of the association. Today, it has long been accepted that associations can be legally constructed with an *external* as well as an internal life of their own. This does not entail that associations are free to do whatever they want. Thus the simple recognition of the capacity of private associations to develop juridical frameworks in their own right does not solve the problem of theorizing the limits of the recognition in terms of the autonomy of the association *vis à vis* the treatment of its members, or of the association in relation to other groups or other, non-associated individuals. Much of the debate about Multiculturalism, however, revolves around this very question.

Should associations such as minority ethnic, cultural or religious groups be allowed to establish legal spheres in which the rules applying to those who are, let us assume, voluntary members of the group, differ from 'the law of the land' – or more precisely, from the general obligations imposed by the state on what are assumed to be its now incorporated associations and individuals. There are several ways to frame this question: For example, to what extent should the state legislature be obliged to ensure that cultural groups in society are protected from forms of negative, and perhaps indirect, discrimination? Let us look at the pluralistic or Multicultural dimensions of the sociological context in which questions like these are posed.

First, we must be cautious about what we mean by 'Multiculturalism'. If we stick with a *descriptive* (as opposed to 'prescriptive' or 'epistemological') pluralism, we can all agree that this refers to a situation in which a society might be divided into a number of different groups, each with its own interests, value-preferences and political agenda. But this is still imprecise, for by what criteria are we to acknowledge, designate or classify groups? To give an answer to this we must qualify what it is that is *plural*. Theoretically, and not implausibly, the phenomena invite constructions of all kinds of pluralities: class or caste pluralism, religious pluralism, moral pluralism, political pluralism, economic pluralism, sexual pluralism, and so on. The various pluralities are today simply lumped under the label of 'Multiculturalism'.[43] It might be worth noting that this form of pluralism, unlike, it seems, all other moral-normative perspectives routinely regarded as 'essentially contested', is apparently accepted as an axiom of modern social and political thought. The regular utterance of 'Today, we live in a multicultural society' is usually issued in justificatory response to objections

42 The article was originally published in 1919 and is reprinted in Paul Q. Hirst (op. cit.).

43 Brian Barry *Culture and Equality* (Harvard: Harvard University Press, 2001) Chapter 1.

to, or unease about, certain cultural practices. The implication seems to be that we should adopt Multiculturalist attitudes to whatever issue is under scrutiny. 'Tolerance' seems to be the master norm in play here; but as we have already noted, it is the scope and limits of tolerance theorized as *part* of an account of the tripartite configuration of 'individual', 'association' and 'the state' in the context of *legitimacy in modernity* that poses the problem. The contemporary reception and application of the idea of Multiculturalism is itself, however, a by-product of the failure to produce a genuinely integrated practical-critical framework of juridico-political concepts in this regard. For as Brian Barry says:[44]

> Many multiculturalists ... maintain that each cultural group [and we must here remember the countless ways that groups may be constituted] within a polity constitutes a source of values for its members, and that the values of different groups are incommensurable. On this view, a society with a single set of rules applying to all its members is bound to be oppressive to cultural minorities, because the rules will simply reflect the culture of the majority. The very possibility of arguing that some rules have more to be said for them than that they articulate majority values is simply dismissed in advance as a piece of sophistry.

Thus despite the self-assurance, Multiculturalism is not a *theoretical* development. It is in a very straightforward sense a concrete fact of social and political life that political and legal theory *seeks to capture, characterize and interpret.* Pluralism is, and always has been, part of the social context in which institutions like law, the family, the economy and so on, operate. Thus the acute *description* of the condition of burgeoning economic and political differentiation of the nineteenth century which pre-occupied Weber[45] was, by the 1920s, condemned as social and political degeneration and constitutional pathology by Schmitt and simultaneously, as noted above, heralded as evolutionary and emancipatory by the English Pluralists. The mere *existence* of a plurality of groups in society thus cannot in itself be an argument for anything. All we can safely say is that complexity and plurality present a set of social circumstances that must be dealt with in some way. The history of the modern state is in many ways the story of the need for some normative singularity – we might say *sovereignty* – constructed in the face of fragmented sources of social, economic and political power.

It is, of course, possible that late or post-modernity presents us with an intensification of the multicultural character of the society in which we live. But even if we are to assume that society is now so fragmented that in some sense there is no society but rather, a number of societies, and that the state, therefore, can no longer cater for the commonweal, the problem remains one of responding adequately to this state of affairs. This still does not suggest that the problem itself

---

44 Ibid. pp. 299–300.

45 See for example Max Weber, *Wirtschaft und Gesellschaft: Grundriß der verstehenden Soziologie* (1922).

has suddenly become transformed into its own solution. There is much, however, to suggest that this *non-sequitur* has become the dominant view.

Thus in the past thirty years Pluralism has been subject to ever more semantic modification. Pluralism today not only refers to the empirical features of cultural, sexual, racial, moral, ideological and economic diversity, but also the inner and ephemeral plurality of the individual identity. But the transformation does not stop here. For the conceptual link to 'equality' in the sense of aspirational egalitarianism is not to be overlooked: the *fact* of the plurality of moral and ideological belief can easily be translated as 'proof' of the groundless subjectivity, incommensurability and thus, it is alleged, the 'equality' of values, and from here to the promotion of regulatory and institutional pluralism in state organs.

At some point, then, pluralism became or becomes something that not only described accurately the individual's social and psychological situation, it most conveniently became a moral and cultural *desideratum* to which it is now widely felt that 'just and fair' individuals and 'the state' on their behalf ought to subscribe. The endorsement of 'Pluralism' now appears to be synonymous with the promotion of Multiculturalism and this in turn means 'diversity' 'difference' 'tolerance' and 'cosmopolitanism', now seen as indispensable components of any aspiration to 'democracy' or 'free' and 'open' as opposed to 'repressive' or 'closed' society. It now possesses multiple and shifting meanings as at once a sociological description-*cum*-organizational theory, and as a political and cultural aspiration of modern, or post-modern, 'civil society'. Not surprisingly, if pluralism is such a good thing, then we should not be surprised to find demands to pluralize all our institutions, including the institutions of law and state, and if they are incapable of pluralization, to abandon or destroy or transcend them. We should, however, now see more clearly the sleight of hand involved in the theoretical reorientation of pluralism from a *description* of our social condition to a *prescription* of how the state ought to be organized *given* this plural condition. But rather than being swept away with the momentum, let us step back for a moment and try to understand the various levels of pluralism.

'Descriptive' and 'Critical' Conceptions of the Pluralist Condition

Pluralism in a *descriptive* sense may simply refer to the assertion that different people hold different values. Description and prescription in the form of the alleged fact/value divide in social scientific discourse raises, as we discussed in Chapter 1, some difficult questions about concept formation. But we might avoid a repetition of that abstruse debate here to make a fairly simple point. Values may be understood as opinions about ethics and politics; about what makes life worth living; how one ought to raise ones children; about what kind of music, food or art is interesting, worthwhile and deserving of praise, and so on. Pluralism in this sense simply means that people differ with regard to preferences. Sociologically, and certainly epistemologically, this is banal and of little use to informed social analysis. We should look for a more significant formulation of the phenomenon, even though we must not underestimate the importance of the fact that for some, the ability to experience Multiculturalism in this sense might be an overriding 'value preference'.

Pursuing the idea methodologically, we could say that pluralism refers to the assertion that people might in some sociologically useful and relevant way be grouped and categorized according to their 'value preferences'. This is a technique that is used by market researchers and political analysts alike. Pluralism in this sense means that people differ from each other systematically in a way that makes it possible to talk about segments or subcultures in society. Examples of the application of this idea is the classification of youth according to their choice in clothes, music and other behaviour patterns or of people into their sexual orientation or again in regard to political preferences Whilst this might be helpful for marketing purposes or the construction of popular opinion polls, it is still less than profound. Pluralism must, if it is to bridge the gap between the mere description of a factual condition and the basis for a normative–practical prescription for institutional and political design, that is, if it is to serve as a premise for further inferences of moral and political significance, mean something more than this. It does, of course, in the sense that connected to this idea of classifying diversity is the assumption that there is not only a desirability and an inevitability, but a validity, or permissibility of the holding of diverse cultural values. Rather than seeing this diversity as the source of danger and conflict, the view is that the existence of many cultures side by side constitutes an enrichment of life, and that value-pluralism (Multiculturalism) should be celebrated and facilitated by giving political and legal autonomy in one form or another to subcultures or groups. If we add to this the recently influential idea that culture is so deeply entrenched in an individual's personality that it cannot be transcended, cultures, and the holding of values that sustain them as discrete and different, therefore, should be respected by according them genuinely effective autonomy. Thus life-enhancing *free* choices *and* structural *determinants* of personality and identity are simultaneously offered as reasons for promoting the autonomy of cultures. But put bluntly, this is to say that cultural autonomy is defended both on the basis that it is good that people have the opportunity to *choose* from a wide variety of cultures ways of life, but also that membership of a culture *determines* our choices about our way of life. Alan Brudner in his recent work, *Constitutional Goods*, touches upon the problem arising from the interaction of these arguments. In a chapter entitled: '*The Liberal Duty to Recognize Cultures*', he offers a synthesis of the two:[46]

> At the egalitarian standpoint cultures are simply life-plan menus from which agents who are complete prior to cultural membership choose their life-orienting values. This picture does violence to the devotee's experience of his culture as something of which he is a vessel and from whose realization through him he derives personal significance. At the standpoint of ethical life, cultures come into view in the way they appeared to Herder and Hegel: as structures of mutual recognition wherein individuals submit to

46 Alan Brudner *Constitutional Goods* (op. cit.) p. 362.

> an ethos for the sake of the personal worth they receive by the virtue of the ethos's reciprocal deference to individual agency for the sake of its existence and vitality.

This account is an attempt to avoid the contradiction contained in the idea that one has the 'right' to *choose* to be part of a personality/identity-shaping culture. We shall return to this 'paradox' presently,[47] but let us for the moment simply observe that if culture determines our personality/identity, then one can not assert the *right* to adhere to this culture. Such a right-claim can make sense only from a standpoint outside the culture, and therefore presupposes *liberation* from the culture which one is claiming the right to adhere to.

This brings us to a third form of descriptive pluralism: the assertion that there exists in society groups that, normatively or morally speaking, differ *fundamentally.* This is to say that certain groups exist in a form of mutual disagreement with respect to values or world-views of the basic aspects of human association and existence. These groups so classified might be referred to as separate cultures within what appears on the surface to be an identifiably discrete society. But unlike the optimistic reception of cultural diversity expressed in the account above, the co-existence of cultures exhibiting fundamental differences is assumed to present a potential for serious conflict. This version of descriptive pluralism, simple in itself, does contain some explanatory value insofar as it also incorporates (reasonable) assumptions: the first is that there is a wider societal imperative (with immense significance to the individual) to avoid or minimize conflict; the second is that the mutually antagonistic values held by the members of the various co-existent groups are *justifiably or validly* held, and that the entitlement to persist in holding them is a legal and political value that should be shared by all groups or cultures in society. Thus with these two assumptions made explicit there is the *appearance* of the metamorphosis of social fact into moral value – an *is* into an identifiable *ought*. Let us examine an example of this.

Paul Hirst, in an article inspired by Figgis[48] argues that, with respect to the role of religions and culture in the modern state, pluralism should be handled by extending the freedom of belief to the freedom of conduct. Cultural heterogeneity has today extended so far, Hirst suggests, that our society can no longer be governed by the principle that the law is the same for all. Instead we should accept that different people may be governed by different rules. Hirst says:[49]

> The only way to contain the conflicts arising from cultural heterogeneity is to extend the principle of pluralism from belief to conduct and to include in it the religious and non-religious. This would be to accept a plurality of rules, to let groups govern themselves side by side in matters of conduct.

There is nothing objectionable about the idea of 'a plurality of rules' in itself, for it may have a number of innocuous interpretations. Thus for example, there

---

47 See the section headed 'The Reflexive Fallacy of Multicultural Critique' *infra* pp. 173–175.

48 Paul Q. Hirst 'J.N. Figgis, Churches and the State' (op. cit.) p. 104.

49 Ibid. p. 116.

may be special rules for people with certain illnesses or manual or ambulatory physical differences, or for students, or for the elderly. Similarly, it is not the case that everyone working for the state does or should be paid the same salary. There are an infinity of examples. What is common to these illustrations of differential treatment is that they have as their purpose either the object of evening out existing differences between individuals, or that of applying the principle that *what is different should be treated differently.*

What Hirst has in mind, however, is more radical than this. What he proposes is that the *individual's* rights and obligations should be determined by their *cultural* (*or religious or group*) identity. This entails (at least in Hirst's own analysis) either the creation of 'special territorial zones where different rules apply' or the setting up of a regulatory system characterized by 'the parallel existence of self-governing communities sharing the same space but applying rules in matters of community concern to their members alone'.[50] Hirst's response to the *fact* of pluralism in society, then, seems to be a perpetuation of the condition rather than an attempt to overcome it. Instead of trying to devise policy instruments dedicated to the purpose of giving equal treatment to all, and thereby attempting to unite a population into a *people*,[51] he promotes the idea of differentiated treatment of citizens according to ... And here we must pause for thought for it is unclear by what criteria Hirst wants to install differential treatment through a plurality of regulatory schemes. He says:[52]

> This means, of course, [*sic*] that people would have to concede the legitimate existence of practices they dislike. Fundamentalist Christians would have to accept the existence of a Gay community with its own rules, including marriage. Feminists would have to accept communities that gave men and women very different rights, like the Mormons. They would not have to submit to such practices themselves, but they would have to swallow their presence in the same society. On some issues, like abortion, this probably would not work, but for most conducts groups would evolve a frosty mutual tolerance.

This gives rise to a host of questions. First, as noted, we must ask by what criteria are we to choose to proceed with the plural classification of groups to be allowed legal autonomy. Hirst mentions Fundamentalist Christians, Gays, Feminists and Mormons as examples. So, religious beliefs, sexual orientation and gender-political beliefs seem to constitute three groups. But what about socialists, environmentalists, human rights activists, people in favour of more rights to disabled people, animal rights activists, and so on? Where do we start and where do we stop?

---

50 Ibid. pp. 116–117.

51 See H.P. Olsen, and S. Toddington ' The Dialectic of Constitutionalism: Coming to Terms with the Autonomy of Law' in *Erkjennelse og Engasjement*: [Cognition and Engagement] *Minneseminar* for David Roland Doublet (1954–2000) (Bergen: *Fagbokforlaget Vigmostad og Bjørke*, 2002) pp. 27–43.

52 Paul Q. Hirst, 'J.N. Figgis, Churches and the State' (op. cit.) p. 117.

Secondly, Hirst mentions that on some issues, his strategy of promoting cultural legal autonomy may not work. He mentions abortion as an example. But why should the right to abortion not be dependent on the person's attachment to a certain group? Are some issues so morally significant that the cultural or group line should be suspended and the individual might be allowed (as are even the much-whipped UK parliamentarians) a 'free vote' on the matter? If this is to be permitted we might make things worse by proposing to relativize all manner of disturbing and sensitive practices. Or we might invert the argument: If abortion should not be allowed to be determined by cultural belonging, then why should, for instance, the equal treatment of men and women be up for grabs?

Thirdly, we might ask where Hirst believes that a disposition to toleration – even a frosty one – might come from? Why should Fundamentalist Christians accept Gay marriage? Why should feminists accept discrimination against women (or the existence of 'very different rights' for men and women as Hirst puts it? Of course, they must 'accept' the existence of these practices if Hirst's programme were to be realized, but why should they act with toleration rather than condemnation? The differential treatment programme proposed by Hirst seems, intuitively, to be counter-productive to fostering the spirit of toleration. By extending freedom of belief to freedom of conduct, cultural groups are allowed to seal themselves off from the surrounding community and to practice what they preach. This might produce as much prejudice and resentment as toleration. And does not this, as noted above, militate against the first of the incorporated assumptions (of conflict management) that appeared to constitute the most sociologically servicable and normatively well-supported conception of pluralism? It is easier for a Christian Fundamentalist to condemn a homosexual if s/he is allowed to perform discrimination on the basis of sexual orientation, for example, when they are employing people as teachers or nurses. 'Parallel governance'[53] would develop parallel social universes and might well destroy the possibility of a common understanding of citizenship and mutual toleration. This could lead to a condition of further fragmentation and, *on the basis of the existence of the condition*, an escalation of proportionately 'justified' claims to even further autonomy, and eventually the complete fragmentation of society.

The solution proposed by Hirst seems precarious and potentially *anomic*. But are we missing something? It should not, after all, come as a surprise to anyone that pluralism (in the sense of the *condition* of ethnic/national/religious/racial/sexual/political and economic diversity) might cause as many social problems as it might enhance one's menu of lifestyle choices. But despite these problems with what we may (with Hirst) call 'parallel governance', some might argue that there is no better response to the fact of pluralism, than to institutionalize the deep-rooted differences among men in a system of governance that allows for differential treatment: Without this measure discrimination will continue and some groups will experience the resentment caused by the brutally homogenizing 'inclusion' of the modern sovereign state process. One might plausibly expect and predict dissatisfaction, frustration, and a general lack of support for the

53 Ibid. p. 116.

state. If discontent becomes widespread it might lead (or possibly has led) to an escalation of conflict and a deep legitimation crisis that might become impossible to solve. If it is the case that society in Western Europe has become so complex and diverse that value pluralism is now a defining attribute of it, politics and the Rule of Law must adapt transformatively to the situation by a commitment to the recognition and empowerment of subcultures. An example of a proposition for such a strategy can be found in Veit Bader's paper *Religious Diversity and Democratic Institutional Pluralism*.[54]

Bader argues that only an associative democracy is efficient as a means of preventing a hidden (or overt) majority bias. He argues that there is a legitimate role for organized religions (presumably on the assumption that religious differences capture the most important of the more loosely defined cultural differences) in the political process: 'That organized religions should be informed, heard and consulted in contested issues and should be a crucial component of democratic participation'.[55]

Broadly in agreement with Hirst,[56] he proposes (with reference to Parekh's *Rethinking Multiculturalism*[57]) that the state should set up advisory religious councils that be given the competence to give opinions 'on all subjects of their interest'.[58] Furthermore, organized religions should be given the opportunity to provide services like education, health care, and care for the elderly. But the institutionalization of pluralism, should not stop here:

> Indeed, even reserved seats for organized religions in legislative committees with a capacity to participate (but not vote) could be discussed and explored.[59]

These propositions imply some form of pluralization of state sovereignty. There is, as noted, nothing new about the idea. Cecile Laborde tells us that the English Pluralists wavered between two contradictory views of the state.[60] The first was that the state should be a functional association put on equal footing with other autonomous groups. The second was that the state should embody the diversity of group claims, along the lines of what would basically be categorized a corporatist state. While the first of these proposals comes close to, or is perhaps identical with, some form of anarchism or anarcho-syndicalism and must perhaps be regarded as somewhat antique, the second proposal is still alive and kicking and emerges clearly in Bader's proposition for institutional(ized) pluralism.

---

54 Veit Bader 'Religious Diversity and Democratic Institutional Pluralism' *Political Theory* (Vol. 31, No. 2, 2003) p. 265.

55 Ibid. p. 265.

56 Bader explicitly refers to Hirst's *Associative Democracy* (Cambridge: Polity,1994) as well as to the above mentioned article 'Figgis, Churches and the State' (op. cit.).

57 Bikhu Parekh *Rethinking Multiculturalism*. (Houndsmill: Macmillan, 2000).

58 Veit Bader (op. cit.) p. 287.

59 Ibid.

60 Cecile Laborde 'The Concept of the State in British and French Political Thought' *Political Studies* (Vol. 48, 2001) p. 540.

Among those authors who seek to further the politics of such cultural autonomy, there is ample disagreement as to the details of what this entails and how it is to be achieved. It would be unfair to lump together these diverse views and present them as arguments for the same case. Nevertheless, there is a significant common trait among them, namely, that granting political and/or legal autonomy to cultural groups (however they may be defined) implies that these groups are either granted or yielded the capacity to create a legal sphere in which they may to some degree actively and practically follow cultural practices even in the face of violation of 'general' legal rules. In other words, membership of a culture will be a central factor in determining the scope of an individual person's legal obligations. An implicit supposition of this view is that the existence of social groups that differ with regard to fundamental values is either unproblematic in the sense that a sharing of common fundamental values is not seen as a condition for social cohesion and justice, or at least so relatively unproblematic, that social conflicts arising from the incompatibility of values can be solved by using adequate regulatory instruments to facilitate the necessary level of social cohesion and justice to satisfy diverse cultural aspirations.

When we feed this into the debate on Multiculturalism this seems to imply that state sovereignty should be divided or apportioned out, so that all cultures have a piece of the cake. But *sovereignty* – in the very obvious sense of singular, normative and authoritative supremacy – is self-evidently unsusceptible to pluralization, and to speak of 'plural' or 'floating' sovereignty is simply a form of word play. It adds little to our understanding to twist the concept of sovereignty to a convenient Multiculturalist fit and assume that we have solved any problems. Rather, if we are committed to pluralism in the sense of the always problematic combination of a democratic *and* rights-based understanding of social diversity and differentiation *in community*, then the pressing question seems to be: 'Does a commitment to this conception of pluralistic social incorporation preclude the orthodox understanding of sovereign authority?' We think it does not. To offer an analysis of the compatibility of sovereignty and pluralism in the modern state we will take as an illustration what has been perhaps in recent years the most contentious confrontation between the state and religious culture: that of the French government's policy of banning of the *hijab* and other religious dress and symbolism in state education.

Multiculturalism and the Case of the *Hijab*

It is a matter of debate among Muslims whether or not the Koran or other religious sources require of Muslim women that they wear a headscarf. Among those who believe that it does there is wide disagreement about the precise detail of the requirement. Thus there exist many different interpretations of what the appropriate headscarf looks like and how it should be worn. Notwithstanding the disagreement, it is a fact that many muslim women wear a headscarf because they consider it to be a religious prescription that ought to be followed; that is, they perceive the wearing of this article of clothing as a religious *duty*. Some Muslim women insist that it is their *right* to wear this headscarf, even in circumstances where they are otherwise not permitted (for non-religious reasons) to dress freely. Examples of this latter would be statutory workplace dress regulations related to health and safety, or where school uniforms are mandatory.

Why is the headscarf an important issue in the context of cultural autonomy theory? One way of seeking an answer to this question is to look at the background for the introduction of the French prohibition on headscarves in public schools (*LOI n° 2004–228 du 15 mars 2004 encadrant, en application du principe de laïcité, le port de signes ou de tenues manifestant une appartenance religieuse dans les écoles, collèges et lycées publics*).[61] The French word *laïcité* means 'secularity' and the law formally sets out to enforce the principle of secularism in public schools by banning not only the religious headscarf, but all religious symbols. The wording of the legislation is as follows:

> Dans les écoles, les collèges et les lycées publics, le port de signes ou tenues par lesquels les élèves manifestent ostensiblement une appartenance religieuse est interdit.

Those who object to the law argue that it violates Articles 9 and 14 of the *European Convention on Human Rights* as well as Article 1 of the 2nd protocol of that convention. Furthermore they argue that the decision to introduce the law indicates a lack of toleration and cultural and religious understanding on behalf of the French government and, by reasonable implication, a large proportion of the French people who are assumed to support the government. It has been suggested that the political and legal strategy to outlaw the *hijab* has the character of a crusade against Islam. On the other hand, many of those who are in favour of the law argue that the headscarf is a symbol of repression of women, and that no public office should endorse such a symbol. Furthermore, public schools (that is, state schools) should be, in principle, religiously neutral spaces free from any forced or traditional religious practices so that pupils might understand that they have a genuine right to freedom of religion. If they do have a genuine right to freedom of religion, then they have it notwithstanding their parents' or their traditional community's views to the contrary. It is also held that the law is necessary to avoid religious and ethnic factionalism supported by dress symbols among children and more generally to prevent the classification of children *qua* students according to religion. Let us ask some straightforward questions in the light of this discussion. First,

(a) *Should the French government (assuming that it grounds its authority on secular, individualist and liberal democratic principles) take steps to ensure that the ethos of its publicly funded educational institutions are tolerationist and secular – as opposed to sectarian, fundamentalist and doctrinally dogmatic?*
From a tolerationist/pluralist perspective, and even in a government coloured by Veit Bader's suggestions for participation and influential input from religious groups and so on, the answer seems to be obvious: '*Yes*'.

---

61 See: http://www.senat.fr/dossierleg/pjl03-209.html.

Secondly, we must ask:

(b) *Should the French government ban religious dress and symbols in public schools?*
From a broadly liberal, pluralist-tolerationist perspective, and ironically, initial intuitions ought to suggest a firm '*No*'. A zealous adherence to '*laïcité*', however, might suggest a resounding and secular, '*Yes*'. But this latter could be interpreted as a determinedly *anti*-religious view as opposed to a genuinely sympathetic and pluralist perspective. The answer, however, lies somewhere in between, in that a *secular*, pluralist government must retain the authority to ban religious symbol and ritual in schools *but not for religious reasons*. Rather, if such a ban is being introduced it should be for reasons of the administration of order, safety and security of teaching and learning environments. Thus, for example, if the *hijab* disturbs the order or introduces an atmosphere of religious intimidation, then, hypotheticaly, and in principle, there might be a good reasons to ban it. But because cultural processes are complex and the discrepancies between effects and intentions in policy implementation can be dramatic and surprising, the decision to introduce such a ban should not be based on an abstract commitment to toleration, nor to promoting symbolically (i.e. by a conspicuous *absence* of symbol) the *ethos* of '*laïcité*', but rather, should be based on a concrete judgment of the necessity of introducing such a ban. There is an infinite amount of possible outcomes of the decision to interfere with religious dress codes on secular pretexts. Some might aid the cause of secularism and toleration, others might militate against it. The state must react to religious symbolism fomenting division and to subcultural attempts to achieve power in this regard, but such a reaction need not be seen as anti-religious in general nor unjustifiably discriminatory against any religious grouping in particular. Rather, such intervention and interference can be seen as *pro-pluralist* and a concomitant of the logic of Multiculturalism.

In his article in *Legal Studies* Mohammad Mazher Idriss criticizes the French decision thus:[62]

> Since the new law targets Muslim schoolgirls who wear *hijab*, who belong to the Maghrebian-Muslim community and who abide by the Quranic norms, the argument that the ban in state schools holds racist connotations may hold some credibility after all. This is because the policy aggressively to apply secular principles confines real human differences (including racial, ethnic and religious beliefs) to the private sphere and this typically French attitude could itself be viewed as 'French secular fundamentalism', since it fails to take into account the various communities and beliefs by which people (and not just Muslim immigrants) structure their lives. The new legislation on secularism demonstrates a level of intolerance towards multiculturalism

---

62 Mohammad Mazher Idriss 'Laïcité and the Banning of the 'Hijab' in France' *Legal Studies* (Vol. 25, No. 2, 2005), p. 260.

because it does not promote integration or acculturation: it simply marginalizes immigrant pupils further by accentuating how different they really are.

This might, however, be a misleading appraisal of the situation. There is no doubt that the law in question is directed at the *hijab* (although the law is framed generally as a ban on ostentatious religious symbols), but the target of the law is the protection of religious freedom – not the ironing out of cultural differences or the marginalization of immigrant pupils. Furthermore, Idriss assumes that the application of *Laïcite* results in a confinement of religious beliefs to the private sphere. However, the *Stasi* report,[63] from which Idriss quotes claims that the purpose of *laïcité* is the exact opposite:[64]

> Dans le cadre laïque, les choix spiritual ou religieux relèvent de la liberté individuelle : cela ne signifie pas pour autant que ces questions soient confinées à l'intimité de la conscience, « privatisées », et que leur soient déniées toute dimension sociale ou capacité d'expression publique. La laïcité distingue la libre expression spirituelle ou religieuse dans l'espace public, légitime et essentielle au débat démocratique, de l'emprise sur celui-ci, qui est illégitime. Les représentats des différentes options spirituelles sont fondés à intervenir à ce titre dans le débat public, comme toute composante de la société.

Thus *laïcité* has nothing to do with the attempt to privatize religion, but everything to do with securing the right to *freedom of religion*; not only as a protection against state imposed religion, but also as a protection against impositions that stem from other individuals or groups. The state, according to the French notion of *laïcité* has an obligation to protect its citizens against *illegitimate* expressions of religion whatever their origin, not to encapsulate religion in the private sphere *tout court*. This means that the state is supposed to assure religious freedom by protecting individuals from all forms of religious pressure, be that physical, psychological or otherwise no matter in which guise such pressure reveals itself. Furthermore, protection against such pressure is all the more needed in the formative years of personhood, i.e. during childhood and youth. Thus the state cannot remain indifferent when faced with attempts to exercise religious pressure, and the state must take appropriate measures to combat such pressure – even when it can only be done through interference with religious practices. It is in this context that the ban on the *hijab* should be understood.

Does this mean that the law does *not* constitute an interference with the religion of those schoolgirls who wishes to wear the *hijab* to school? Certainly not, it *is* an interference, and everyone recognizes this. But, we shall argue, it is a legitimate interference in the sense that it is necessary and proportional, as understood in the jurisprudence of the European Court of Human Rights. This, then, is the

---

63 The report is so called because the commission charged with evaluating the headscarf issue – *Commission de Reflexion Sur L'Application du Principe de Laïcite Dans La Republique* – was led by Bernard Stasi. The report is available at http://lesrapports.ladocumentationfrancaise.fr/BRP/034000725/0000.pdf.

64 Ibid. p. 13.

second issue. Idriss associates the French law with a growing hostility against muslims. He claims that:[65]

> There is now a global suspicion [in France] towards Muslims in general and a consistent element within the debate about Muslims is the assertion that Muslims are all collectively responsible for the fanatical and small-minded cultural practices held by a few. The hijab is portrayed as a symbol of death, especially after events such as the Beslan school hostage siege, and Muslims are simply held 'guilty by association'.

There is no doubt that there is anti-muslim feeling to be found in France, and it is also true that some people have tried to justify the ban on the *hijab* with references to links between Islam and terrorism, but nothing of this nature is to be found in the *Stasi* report. On the contrary, the report clearly states that there are many public areas in which the *hijab* may be worn, and even in comparatively 'public' spaces such as private muslim schools or in the work place, there is no ban on the *hijab*. If the *Commission*, or the French legislators believed that the hijab was a symbol of terror, surely state schools would not have been the only target for a ban. As explained in *Stasi* report, the ban was introduced because the *hijab* was beginning to cause problems in the state schools, and the purpose of the ban was to respond to these problems:[66]

> La commission, après avoir entendu les positions des uns et des autres, estime qu'aujourd'hui la question n'est plus la liberté de conscience, mais l'ordre public. Le contexte a changé en quelque années. Les tensions et les affrontements dans les etablissements autour de questions religieuses sont devenus trop frequents. Les deroulements normal des enseignements ne peut plus être assuré. Des pressions s'exercent sur des jeunes filles mineures, pour les contraindre à porter un signe religieux. L'environment familial et social leur impose parfois des choix qui ne sont pas les leurs. La République ne peut rester sourde au cri de détresse de ces jeunes filles. L'espace scolaire doit rester pour elles un lieu de liberté et d'emancipation.

For some girls, of course, the wearing of the *hijab* is entirely voluntary, and for them the ban *is* an interference with the practice and expression of their religion. But this consequence is not caused by an aggressive application of *laïcité* as Idriss suggests. Rather, according to the rationale of the report in question, it is a consequence of an increasingly aggressive religious environment in which young girls are being exposed to religious pressure not only from parents and other family members, but also from other pupils in and around their school. If one accepts that the state has an obligation to secure freedom *of* (including freedom *from*) religion, then it seems right to interfere in these circumstances. Idriss might be seen, then, to turn the right to freedom of religion upside down when he describes this as *intolerance* towards *multiculturalism*.[67] It is, in fact, the opposite. For the interference is not just concerned with the issue of the *hijab*.

65 Mohammed Idriss (op. cit.) p. 279.
66 Stasi Report (op. cit.) p. 58.
67 Mohammed Idriss (op. cit.) p. 279.

The *Stasi* report points to a number of other issues associated with Islamic intolerance towards the attempt to treat young girls as free and equal pupils within the public school in France. The commission reports of incidents where pupils or their parents refuse to follow certain classes, refuse to countenance certain homework topics, refuse to answer questions put by teachers of a different sex than their own, refuse to take part in gymnastics or swimming classes, and so on. The commission also reports of a growing 'descholarization' among 16-year-old girls. The issue of the *hijab* is merely the tip of the iceberg and, on the findings of the *Stasi* report, seems to represent a balanced attempt to liberate young females from the pressures of a growing Islamic fundamentalism, by creating, an environment in which they can legitimately jettison signs of religious affiliation without fear of repercussions.

The affirmative answer to question (a) 'Should a pluralist state oppose a religiously sectarian system?' does not, however, entail an affirmative answer to question (b) 'Should the French government ban religious dress and symbols in public schools?', and conjoining the two is unhelpful in that they are merely contingently related. Their repeated association increases the obfuscation around the pivotal issue: that of the normative foundations of the ethical defence of toleration in the context of the inescapable factual condition of complex and potentially volatile diversity. Endorsing the answer to (a) *must*, however, be the Multiculturalist/Pluralist position. It would be incoherent to avoid this commitment – even if this is not immediately obvious to the entire body of Multiculturalists.

But the proposition in (b) creates problems either way for the Multiculturalists or Pluralists. To set oneself against it, that is, to oppose the decision to ban religious symbols, on the grounds that an individual has the right to wear or display the article in question, and to give the rights claim a liberal grounding, becomes incoherent if the symbol is assumed (simplistically and implausibly) to be *imposed* upon the wearer against his or her will for reasons which actually represent exercises of authoritarian oppression of group members. A liberal can defend the *right* to wear an article of clothing only on the assumption that the wearer consents to wearing it. If this consent was not forthcoming, the issue for the liberal pluralist would seem to be that of defending the individual's right *not* to wear it. But this means, of course, that the same liberal pluralist must oppose the action of those group members who were responsible for the forced imposition in the first place. This approaches the only coherent position in Multiculturalism and Pluralism: that of endorsing the rights of people to live in communal ways as they see fit as long as they *each* do so consensually and as long as they jointly and severally display a willingness to reciprocate the forbearances shown to them by other individuals and groups. If this is not the case, it seems that the state must use its sovereign powers to liberate certain group 'members' from pressures to conform to various group standards.

The Wider Lesson of the *Hijab*

The prohibition of the headscarf is not a superficial dress regulation or an issue of uniform design, but concerns the role of religious affiliation in the public domain. From the point of view of Multiculturalism (understood in the organizational and policy terms proposed, for example, by Hirst[68]), the best of all possible worlds seem to be one where all religions coexist side by side without any restrictive regulation to impede their exercise. Whilst this is, perhaps, not a bad idea, the imperfect world in which we live forces us to acknowledge that historically and contemporarily some groups use religious affiliation and doctrine as instruments of repression. Examples of such repression ranging over a variety of faiths include the policy of perpetuating inequalities in status between men and women (and from some perspectives of interpretation the muslim headscarf is a symbol of this inequality); the practice of forced marriage or the denial of the right to divorce, and the denial of the right to exit or change religious affiliations and beliefs (on pain of being ostracized from family and community or worse). To assert that these practices are repressive presupposes, of course, the availability of moral criteria appropriate to an understanding of freedom and autonomy and makes no sense unless they are set against a background acceptance of values that acknowledge the importance of individual choice and autonomy. These values are not exclusive to liberal democracies but they certainly coincide with what are broadly understood as the central ideals of liberal-democratic societies. In other words, and for the sake of argument some religious groups subscribe to practices that are not compatible with what are generally perceived as the individual and democratic rights of the members of their group. If these rights of equality, choice, marriage, divorce, freedom of religious belief and so on are held to be more general and fundamental than subcultural religious values, and applicable to all members of a wider society composed of a variety of sub-groups and cultures, it follows in the most rudimentary sense that, whilst it might be possible to celebrate diverse and unrestricted freedom of religion in the abstract, it is neither just nor consistent to endorse or allow the freedom of *any* sub-group to promulgate discriminatory and repressive practices. It seems, then, that the principle of religious (or more generally, cultural) freedom in the collective sense is more problematic than first assumed because of the obvious fact that 'cultural freedom' might sometimes be at odds with the belief in, and institutionalized affirmation and protection of, individual rights.

This becomes even clearer if we bear in mind that this discussion presupposes, accurately, inequalities of power and influence *within* particular groups or cultures. The idea of a culture as an interpretation of the world and a *modus vivendi* appropriate to it must not accede to the naturalistic fallacy that assumes that cultures are objects of a kind that might be discovered, inspected, described, differentiated from one another, and evaluated in terms of properties and attributes in the way that minerals or crustaceans might be. A culture is indeed a way of life: a constellation of beliefs and values and customs, but these ways of

68 Paul Q. Hirst 'J.N. Figgis, Churches and the State' (op. cit.).

relating to self, to others, to the world, and to events are constantly in a contextual flux, and are always susceptible to negotiation and re-negotiation internally and externally. Most importantly, the exposure and presentation of a culture (even a notionally open and minimally stratified community of belief) to the Babel of meaning in modernity comes replete with the distorting potentials of whatever *imprimatur* might emerge from the interests that motivate and sustain that group's *internal* hegemonic processes. Whether these be unself-conscious delusions or forms of denial, knowing strategies of internal manipulation and obfuscation, or external misrepresentations, 'authenticity' – the source of much zealous cultural veneration, protection and special-pleading – is always a *chimera*.

An isolated culture need explain its ways and beliefs only to itself. But even in small-scale isolation there is profound complexity and uncertainty surrounding and mediating the mutual and self-understandings of the moral and political motivations of the group. But a cultural group situated in a society of immense technical, cultural, religious and economic diversity and organicity is indeed a curious and protean phenomenon. Crucially, all such subcultures – and of particular importance for the issue at hand, *religious* subcultures – inevitably take on an attribute that alters dramatically and qualitatively their internal normative dynamics and internal strategies of hegemony as well as their most vital external relations with other subcultures and with the state. That is, a religious culture situated in a modern (as opposed to 'customary' or 'traditional') society can appeal to the overarching and overriding norms of The Rule of Law which enshrine the legal protection of an individualist and *secular* principle of toleration. Thus, ironically, a religious subculture can avail itself of a powerful instrument to preserve, promote and practice collective *traditional* and *religious* ways of life within the otherwise modern indvidualist and secular welfare state.

This being said, it is, of course, incontrovertible that a secular, liberal-democratic state must, broadly speaking, endorse the principle of freedom of belief and of expression and thus of religious belief and expression (but see our reservations in this regard in Chapter 6 *infra*). But this cannot mean that it must seek to endorse and provide political and legal instruments and protections for religious subcultures dedicated to the domination of, and discrimination against, some of their members. On this logic, and if the precarious semiology of the situation might be manipulated simplistically and rather unconvincingly purely for illustration, then the circumstances of the French issue of the *hijab* might be evaluated as follows: *if* the headscarf (or some other appendage) is an outward sign of the oppression of women, and *if* it serves as the symbol of religious tyranny contrary to liberal democratic and secular values; then the prohibition of the headscarf is not a violation of religious freedom, but a step towards the liberation of women from religiously based oppression and inequality. Thus the hypothetically imagined intolerance involved in this case is seen to originate not from those who impose the prohibition, but from those who insist on being allowed to impose restrictions on others.

The comfortable indignation expressed here is, however, easily dissipated by an equally reasonable and likely as accurate interpretation that suggest that the foregoing analysis is simply false, and instead point out that rules on religious dress and differential status between women and men in a religious culture is not a form of oppression but one of mutual respect and reverence for each other as persons and as followers of the faith. *Empirically*, some people, from a wide variety of religious and cultural backgrounds, would affirm this latter view, and some would affirm the former.

The lesson of the *hijab* however, is that there is no way to avoid the problem of sovereignty and no way to avoid the real normative clash between, on the one hand, the idea of legitimate state sovereignty based on 'Enlightenment' liberal democratic values of individual autonomy and anti-tradition and, on the other, the effective abrogation of these principles by way of a conveniently sloppy version of tolerationism that wants to have its cake and eat it.

In short, tolerationism allied to pluralism or Multiculturalism cedes the supremacy of both aspects of its grounding principle to the arbitrary and localized hegemonies of what would, in effect, be cultural sub-states. At some point a less euphemistic formulation must be advanced. For tolerationists opposed to the moral objectivism of ethical rationalism, it must be acknowleged that tolerationism/pluralism/multiculturalism is coherent only on the basis of what has to be a consistent adherence to a *secular* – or perhaps we should say *civic* – understanding of the incommensurability of values, and that this position demands that subcultures that do not share this secular and incommensurabilist world view modify their beliefs and folkways into styles and doctrines that accept the supremacy of democratically institutionalized individual human rights and a Rule of Law modelled in accordance with these basic moral tenets. This would at least go some way to dissipating the complacency and condescending liberality of Multiculturalists and Pluralists unaware of their own claims to normative supremacy. It might also awaken us to the pitfalls of a simplistic analysis of what constitutes a 'culture' or a 'tradition'. The other side of the coin is that members of traditional or religious subcultural groups should not seek to protect and perpetuate illiberal traditions by the invocation of the ethical liberalism that underpins the legal requirement (and the Multiculturalist demand) that citizens tolerate each other.

A strong version of such a cultural autonomy theory would acknowledge that individuals and groups would have or should have the right to live in accordance with whatever values they chose to embrace. A restricted version of it might be expressed as acknowledging autonomy in the sense that an individual or group's rights or legal standing in society should not be affected by their espousal of certain values. This might be referred to as restrictive value pluralism. Why is this a better option? There are two reasons: one is a contingent observation on the inherently conservative and potentially divisive implications of the precarious strategy of awarding rights on the basis of 'frozen' conceptions of group or cultural membership. The other lies in the contradictory logic that surfaces from the unreflexive attempt to state the Multiculturalist case as an attack on traditional sovereignty. Let us consider both of these arguments in moving towards some conclusions for institutional design.

Why Pluralist Theory 'Freezes' Cultures

Puralist theory or Multiculturalism (understood as normative pluralism) and the accompanying degeneration of sovereignty endangers rather than promotes the prospects of a peaceful co-existence of different cultures and religions. What is worse, the Multiculturalist emphasis on *culture* as a regulating factor works as a conservative force in the sense that it freezes the identities of cultural communities as well as the individuals who inhabit them. More specifically, the allocation of different rights to different people depending on their culture (be it religion or whatever) creates unpredictable faction and division in society because the differentiation that is fomented has no publicly defensible, rational foundation other than the blunt assertion of arbitrary difference itself. Culture is not an epistemological or sociological category that can help us to identify or solve problems of social organization. Brian Barry alerts us to the endemic error in Multiculturalist literature to assume that distinctive cultural attributes are the defining feature of all groups. He says:[69]

> This assumption leads to the conclusion that whatever problems a group may face are bound to arise in some way from its distinctive cultural attributes. The consequence of this 'culturalization' of group identities is the systematic neglect of alternative causes of group disadvantage. Thus the members of a group may suffer not because they have distinctive culturally derived goals but because they do poorly in achieving generally shared objectives such as good education, desirable and well paid jobs (or perhaps any job at all), a safe and salubrious neighbourhood in which to live and enough income to enable them to be adequately housed, clothed and fed and to participate in the social, economic and political life of their society.

One's 'culture' may become a repository for an accumulation of frustration over impoverishment, including the impoverishment that follows from not being accepted as an equal part of society despite attempts to integrate, but culture is not necessarily the reason why this impoverishment arises in the first place. The consequences of 'freezing' this condition through 'the politics of difference' is highlighted by Judith Squires remarks on Barry's *Culture and Equality*. She writes:[70]

> I agree that there is something worrying about certain multicultural arguments for group survival, which seem to me to privilege the conservative and traditionalist forces within minority groups at the expense of the more radical and innovative voices within them. Why should one protect a community against cultural revisions or reforms, even radical ones?

Squires refers here to Barry's attack on those who believe that cultures are worth preserving because cultural diversity is a good thing in itself. Our point is that even a moderate Multiculturalism will favour the conservative and

69 Brian Barry (op. cit.) pp. 305–306.

70 Judith Squires 'Symposium on Culture and Equality' *Ethnicities* (Vol. 2, No. 2, 2002) pp. 262–287. Squires' contribution is at pp. 265.

traditionalist forces within cultures that receive special treatment. The reason is simply that special treatment is given to a group (or culture) because it is *special and different*. If it was not, the rationale for giving it such treatment would cease to exist. Hence, there will be a tendency for leaders of the group to freeze the special identity of the group and suppress initiatives that might lean towards mainstream culture.

It is important to be aware of precisely why we oppose the idea that membership of a particular culture or religion should give rise to special status within the regulatory scheme of the liberal state. It is not because we do not think that culture or religion is important. Neither is it because we want to suggest that cultural or religious homogenization should be pursued, or that cultures or religions are somehow intrinsically dangerous – although some, in certain circumstances, become so. The reasons are twofold. The first is that we reject, for epistemological reasons, the idea that fundamental moral claims attach to such sociological entities in the first place; they accrue, for Gewirthian Ethical Rationalists, to agents.[71] The second is that culture and religion – and thus cultural and religious groups – change constantly in very relevant respects. Cultural and religious communities are not cut off from the society in which they exist, they are, on the contrary, constantly forming, and reshaping themselves in the light of the political and legal circumstances that surround them. As Donald Horowitz[72] has explained, even ethnic identity is not static, but changes with the environment.

The fact that a culture is a minority culture, or even a culture on the border of extinction cannot justify any form of protection or special treatment. The only way we can perceive of protection or special treatment is in the form of an individual right to be part of and express a certain culture or religion. Chandran Kukathas expresses this very clearly in his *Are There Any Cultural Rights?*:[73]

> If the condition of the community made no difference to the life of any individual, then the condition of the collective would not matter. None of this implies that there is such a thing as 'the individual' in the abstract [i.e. as culture-free]. Individuals do not exist in the abstract any more than interests do. But interests *matter* only because individuals do ... So groups or communities have no special moral primacy in virtue of some natural priority. They are mutable historical formations – associations of individuals – whose claims are open to ethical evaluation. And any ethical evaluation must, ultimately, consider how actual individuals have been or might be affected, rather than the interests of the group in the abstract.

In other words, and more concretely, if the cultural practices of a given community is considered to be repressive for some members of the community, this repression

71 See our introductory remarks and arguments for the application of Gewirth; for a comprehensive treatment see Deryck Beyleveld *The Dialectical Necessity of Morality* (Chicago: Chicago University Press, 1991) Chapter 2.

72 Donald L. Horowitz *Ethnic Groups in Conflict* (Berkeley: University of California Press, 1985).

73 Chandran Kukathas 'Are There Any Cultural Rights' *Political Theory* (Vol. 20, No. 1, Feb. 1992) pp. 112

is more ethically significant than the general interest of the community in preserving its group identity by upholding these practices. Furthermore we should note that 'cultural rights' may sometimes restrict the opportunity for minorities within a cultural group to affect the cultural identity of their own group. That is to say, that it is not necessarily the case that all members of a cultural community share the same evaluations of the worth of that community. In fact, more often than not, there are groups *within* the group that adopt differing and conflicting interest perspectives relating *to* the group. Minority cultural communities are rarely as homogenous as they are portrayed by the majority culture. Kukathas gives the following example as an illustration:[74]

> ... while aboriginal elites have argued that land rights granted to Aborigines as a people ought to reserve those lands for Aboriginal communities in perpetuity, some individual Aborigines argue that those communities should be free to use the land as an economic asset to be bought and sold.

This is a plain social conflict about the problem of how a society should employ available capital, and shows with simplicity the scope of the misjudgement we might make in this regard. Treating a culture as a homogenous collective entity within society runs the risk of freezing that culture, and thereby making it more difficult to effect social change within that entity, to the detriment of some of the members of the group – and for no good reason.

The Reflexive Fallacy in Multicultural Critique

Fuller has repeatedly emphasized that the legal evolves from the social, but maintains that what is constant in this transition from informal to formal normativity is the idea of a 'Eunomic' Order.[75] Implicit in this idea, and as we discussed at length in Chapters 1 and 2 *supra*, is the quest for 'affirmative freedom', and such freedom is what individuals in various levels of community in association require as fundamental prerequisites for their responsible engagement in the endless interaction of institutional design. Institutional design in turn, is the maintenance of a social structure that allows us the exercise of an engaged and intelligent creative capacity for self-development. In opposition to the stasis and hierarchy of collective-traditional life, modernity sought to promote the value of autonomous critical engagement. The entire political and legal critique of traditional life and its future restructuring is nowhere better expressed and justified than in the work of Rousseau and in Kant, but it is re-affirmed with admirable clarity and contemporary relevance in Fuller's sociological writings on law and *Eunomics*.

---

74 Ibid. pp. 114–115.

75 The article 'Human Interaction and the Law' is particularly illuminating in this regard. See Kenneth I. Winston (ed.) *The Principles of Social Order: Selected Essays of Lon L. Fuller*. (Oxford: Hart Publishing, Revised Edition, 2001).

His suggestion, we might recall, was that that we must assert that to be free is to be enfranchized, involved, and responsible. Freedom is a *means* by which we might come to an awareness of self through engaging in life, and this engagement is about creating and shaping relationships with the world, and with others, and in forging intersubjectively stable and reciprocal recognitions of the value and function of these relations. This, we can say, is what institution building in its most fundamental sense means: creating the conditions under which self-exploration through the exercise of freedom can take place.

This eulogy to autonomy, of course, is the watchword of Enlightenment, and there is no point in hiding one's Rationalist credentials under the bushel of ambiguous endorsements of 'diversity' or 'pluralism'.[76] The Rationalist reading of Fuller's message is that the evolution of formal legal processes from informal ones is driven by human attributes that can be identified as a rational aspiration to autonomous freedom, and that the *essential* aim of the legal enterprise is to provide in social practice some form of protected institutionalization that these aspirations might be realized. Law is the practically reasonable supervision and development of the codified or customary procedures by which the institutional commitment to *affirmative* freedom is regulated and co-ordinated. We might say that guarding this institutional security is, in a very straightforward sense, the job of the sovereign.

If this articulation of the concept of freedom and what it implies is to serve as a starting point for an account of institutional design, then it is a grave error to characterize this conceptual account of the self and the world as simply

---

76 Curtis Bowman provides us with two definitive quotes in this regard: 'It is a grand and beautiful sight to see man emerge somehow from nothing by his own efforts; dissipate, by the light of his reason, the shadows in which nature had enveloped him; rise above himself; soar by means of his mind into the heavenly regions; traverse, like the sun, the vast expanse of the universe with giant steps; and, what is even grander and more difficult, return to himself in order to study man and know his nature, his duties, and his end'. Jean-Jacques Rousseau, *The Basic Political Writings* (trans. Donald Cress) (Indianapolis: Hackett Publishing Company, 1987) p. 3.

And from Kant: 'Enlightenment is man's emergence from his self-imposed immaturity. Immaturity is the inability to use one's understanding without guidance from another. This immaturity is self-imposed when its cause lies not in lack of understanding, but in lack of resolve and courage to use it without guidance from another; Immanuel Kant, 'What is Enlightenment?' in *Perpetual Peace and Other Essays* (trans. Ted Humphrey) (Indianapolis: Hackett Publishing Company, 1983) p. 41.

Bowman says: 'Kant's thought reveals its indebtedness to Rousseau and ... helps to clarify some of its intentions. The point of [Kant's] Critical philosophy is to reformulate and reconstruct in a philosophically precise way Rousseau's reflections on human nature and freedom. Freedom is the ultimate source of value, and thus must be incorporated into our philosophical thinking. Kant's project is, first, to explain the possibility and actuality of transcendental freedom, the absence of natural necessity, in human action; second, to develop an account of autonomy as the source of human value and dignity; and, third, to protect this account from the threat of outside imposition posed by religion'. Curtis Bowman 'Kant and the Project of Enlightenment' available at http://www.phil.upenn.edu/~cubowman/kant.

another 'incommensurable' *nomos* or world view. The confusion is compounded by throwing the form of secular, pluralist liberalism that eventually emerges from it into the melting pot of concepts and theories, predilections and cultural practices that is indeed the *condition* of pluralism. The idea of individual critical freedom and rights (the idea of Enlightenment) that fuels pluralist theory in its drive towards liberation in the form of autonomous, affirmative freedom is, ironically, an idea which attacks the assumed authority of tradition. In showing us that what economically, religiously, sexually, aesthetically, spiritually and morally is portrayed as natural, inevitable and necessary is in fact the product of *social and contingent construction*, cultural autonomy theory is brought, it appears, by its own logic, to defend a thoroughgoing philosophy of contingency and incommensurability. This, however, is not a paradox; it is merely a deficiency of reflexive thinking that allows the liberating spirit of the critique to fall prey to its own naïve dialectic: in failing to defend its own presuppositions it is forced to acknowledge the equal claims to legitimacy of all and any traditions or 'cultural' perspectives.

But let us remember that the critique of tradition must come from a viewpoint that presupposes the concept of a critical sociological and historical consciousness emerging *within* the social structure. In asking whether our consciousness (meaning our significant conscious concerns and self-interpretations including 'reason' itself) is a *product* of our socially located existence, the critic must confront the problem of whether tradition can be recast as ideology and hence as the object of critique. This could also be seen as the key to the classic philosophical question of whether we can or must consider our actions as free or determined. The Cartesian finds the question itself indicative of genuine freedom; others, like Rousseau, see it as the birth of the engaged citizen whose duty it is to search for the criterion of rational interests. But this sloughing off of our 'self-imposed infancy' as Kant would have it, has come to be rendered perversely as, at best, a kind of Rawlsian or Rortyan prioritization of incommensurable choice of identity or of values. At worst it is presented unreflectively as a mere 'secularism' and associated inevitably with the shortcomings of 'positivism', 'scientism', 'Western ethnocentricism' and so on. In short, critical reason becomes simply another religious view *without* the religion, but still, it is alleged, replete with an agenda of hidden interests. It should not be too difficult to see that this is an entirely sterile way of thinking. Instead we should begin our analysis with the clear distinction that this nucleus of our social and critical ontology – a nucleus which *does* support a rational pluralism – is an *epistemological* position, not merely an arbitrarily selected view to be placed on a par with the world-view of one or another religious /traditional or cultural faction.[77] Should we fail to do so, we would, it seems, miss the whole point, not

---

77 We should see this critical conception of Modernity as the basis of the modern theory of *the public sphere* – a sphere of associational life which demands that we reconcile competing views of the private and the public. In fact, is it not clear that *Aufklarung* demands that we reconstruct and reinterpret the public sphere in a way that *institutionalizes* and secures what Loughlin refers to as *the autonomy of the political*. This, as Loughlin says in his *The Idea of Public Law* (Oxford: Oxford University Press, 2004) is not simply the

only of the importance of critical concept formation, but also of the character and status of traditional cultures.

Pluralism and Eunomic Design

We cannot escape the equivocation and ambiguity that surrounds the issue of consent and autonomy in the discussion of group or cultural membership, and of the imprecise notion of the 'rights' of cultures or groups, until we state the principle of pluralist toleration in full acknowledgment of the hierarchical nature of the normative principles of secular and individualist supremacy presupposed by it. And this candid expression of the normative supremacy of secular tolerationism should be repeated and entrenched at every opportunity if only to remind us that it is *not a position of normative neutrality*, and that the substantive rights claims pre-supposed by it cannot be founded upon relativism or incommensurabilism. The tolerationist manifesto should start off something like this:

> *We subscribe to a critique of tradition. We are autonomous individuals capable of judgment, reason and choice. We are not legitimately obliged to accept as truth the dogmas and superstitions of our ancestors or of self-appointed religious, military or political elites. We do not believe that the forms of society and our roles and relationships within it are natural or immutable. We believe in openness and in the equality of persons and in the possibility of change. We believe in the value of the private sphere and in the value of community and in the value of public institutions that make possible individual and communal freedoms. In this regard we believe that predictable social regulation in the form of a Rule of Law is indispensable and everywhere preferable to unpredictable conflict and the arbitrary exercise of disparate powers amongst us.*

But it should *end* something like this:

> *However, we realize that religious beliefs, values and commitments to ways of living are strong and diverse in the human psyche, and we acknowledge that modernity has thrown us together in great plurality. Our proposal, therefore, is that we associate in optimal freedom of religious, political, aesthetic and sexual choice limited only by the supremely secular principles of individual right and personal autonomy.*

---

struggle for the power to subsist, but the struggle for the power to influence institutional development on all levels of cultural belief, a process of individual and group self-creation which constitutes the process of institutional design from a plurality of competing perspectives. But paradoxically, these perspectives – some of which enjoin us to re-embrace 'tradition' – are now seen to be not just *contestable* and ripe for supercession, but, perhaps with greater rational momentum than ever before, *defensible and enduring* as well.

Chapter 6

Obsolescent Freedoms

In this concluding chapter we turn to one of the most pressing tasks of institutional design facing us as we come to terms with the new 'pluralist' condition. In our view, among the most important is the need to support the argument that the right to religious freedom is superfluous in a democratic, pluralist society. There are two reasons for making this case. First, the distinction between, on the one hand, religious, and on the other, secular, political, philosophical, cultural or other beliefs should not be perpetuated in the sense that the former is assumed to attract a superior right or represent a more fundamentally important aspect of freedom. Secondly, even with an understanding of our freedoms that did not make these assumptions, we should consider whether or not our more general provisions for rights and freedoms already extend to what is required to hold and express religious opinion.

Religion and Human Rights

Over the past fifty years human rights have gained increasing importance in the legal systems of Europe This is reflected in the UN Conventions, the EHRC, the EU Treaties and the EU Charter, as well as in a number of other conventions, statutes and EU regulations, which have increasingly (and especially in the last 10 years) proved to contain real and effective legal content. There is an increasing number of court proceedings based on human rights law, and the concept of human rights in relation to interpretation in general now enjoys a prominent position in the legislative process.[1] It is characteristic of this development that many new *types* of rights have been added, whilst old ones remain unchanged. Apart from being guaranteed in various ways in national constitutions throughout Europe, the right to freedom of religion is incorporated in the UN International Covenant on Civil and Political Rights (ICCPR), Articles 18 and 27, and in the European Human Rights Convention, Article 9.[2] In addition, religious freedom

1 For an illustration of the Danish situation, see Report (Betænkning) 1407 on the incorporation of human rights conventions into Danish Law, in particular Chapters 3–5.

2 See ICCPR Articles 2 and 26, and the EHRC Article 14. EU's anti-discrimination legislation also includes prohibitions against discrimination on the ground of religion; see for example, Council Directive 2000/78/EC of 27 November 2000 establishing a general framework for equal treatment in employment and occupation.

is guaranteed in various ways by a general prohibition against discrimination on the ground of religion.[3]

Origins of the Freedom of Religion

The protection of the right to freedom of religion is a significant part of the development of modernity in the sense that it almost defines the demise of absolutism. It has represented an important foundation of the power of the state in its trajectory towards popular-democratic and secularized systems of government. Freedom of religion was first constitutionalized in 1789 as the first amendment[4] to the American Constitution, and, as other European countries were demolishing more or less totalitarian systems of government, freedom of religion was also introduced in Denmark in the constitution of 1849.[5] Freedom of religion as we know it today is thus based on a demolition of the absolutist state's imposed religious compulsion. In his *Constitutional Goods*, Brudner writes:[6]

> The pre-modern constitution was a theocracy that ordered human affairs in accordance with a supernatural end known only through a revelation surpassing rational insight. That end was the pre-modern constitution's conception of the public interest. ... Now, the dissolution of a supernatural end as the public ground of constitutional order entails the privatization of revealed religion – its demotion to the sphere of individual conscience and of civil association – and its consequent pluralization into as many sects as the liberty of conscience and association engender.

After incorporation into national constitutions following these upheavals, the right of religious freedom finds itself incorporated into more recent international human rights conventions. In the updating of national constitutions, the contents of international human rights conventions are now often taken into account, and rights are thus allowed to survive without questioning their justification. The

---

3 *Official Journal of the European Communities* 2000 L 303, p. 16.

4 For a brief account of the background of The First Amendment see: http://www.religioustolerance.org/amend_1.htm.

5 As an example, the right to freedom of religion was introduced in Denmark under the Constitution of 1849. An impression of the conditions originally addressed by the freedom of religion is given by Article 1 of the Danish Succession Act ('Kongeloven') of 1665. It reads as follows (in modern translation and abridged by HPO): 'The best beginning for everything is to begin with God. Our first commandment under this Act is therefore for our descendants, children and children's children in a thousand generations to serve, honour and obey the only right and true God in the manner and fashion revealed by Him in the true and holy Gospel, and our Christian faith and confession as pure and genuine as represented in the Augsburg Confession of A.D.1530, and to keep the inhabitants of this country to that same pure and genuine Christian faith and protect this country from all heretics, zealots and blasphemers'.

6 Alan Brudner *Constitutional Goods* (Oxford: Oxford University Press, 2004) p. 81.

question we raise is whether freedom of religion survives as an anachronism or as a special interest deserving of protection.

The Character of Religion

The manifestation of religious organization in human affairs springs from the belief that there exist supernatural powers and that these powers affect or determine the conditions of human life. Religious belief takes many forms, but monotheism – the belief in a single, omniscient and omnipresent God – provides a common characteristic central to modern European religious culture in Judaism, Islam and Christianity. With these religions comes the central attribute of faith in the form of a determination if not a duty and a virtue to preserve a continuity of belief in the face of uncertainty or confusion. In saying this we are not suggesting that religious belief is a mere life-style preference or consumer choice, and neither do we assume that faith is merely an unquestioning acceptance of dogma. The religious impulse as it is manifest biographically and historically, and religion as it might be ideally conceptualized, undoubtedly is concerned with the attempts to solve existential and emotional questions of fundamental significance.[7] Faith might be seen as a source of the spiritual strength required to face such questions, and Faith and Prayer might be understood as a route to insight or an access to a power to influence one's life by one's own actions or by invoking divine intervention. Under this interpretation, events that some would interpret as coincidence can be characterized as empirical expressions of God's will. In other words, there is no doubt that a religious orientation based on faith fundamentally shapes the perception of reality for the believer.

Individual faith and a frame of orientation to devotion among individuals becomes organized religion when belief is institutionalized. This is typically done through a designation of scripture that authoritatively constitutes the symbolic and ritualistic content and understanding of a faith. There are, of course, considerable variations within and between religions, but institutionalization is a necessary step if several persons are to share a common faith. It is characteristic of most religions that faith is to be made manifest and thus converted into physical action in various ways. This can be achieved though special and occasional ritual but might also extend to the everyday actions of the believer. These active observances might relate to food, clothing, social manners, personal hygiene, the upbringing of children, leisure, sexual activity, and so on. Activity thus imbued with religious significance affirms and enhances the importance of faith in the

---

7 In Denmark, the recommended guidelines from the Advisory Committee on Religious Organizations (2nd rev. edn, January 2002) – a body of independent legal and theological experts set up by the minister of religious affairs – defines religion as '… a specifically formulated belief in man's dependence on a power superior to human beings and the laws of nature, and a belief that provides guidance for man's ethics and morality' (Guidelines, p. 2).

life of the individual by bringing together direct worship through prayer and a wide range of routine activity.

The Right to Freedom of Religion and its Absorption into Other Human Rights

The political and social situation in which we find ourselves at the beginning of the twenty-first century has changed immeasurably since freedom of religion was introduced as a basic right; the rules governing this freedom remain, however, unchanged. It is, therefore, reasonable to suggest that we might re-examine the grounds of traditional acceptance of freedom of religion if only to revitalize our thinking and avoid a complacent stagnation of the jurisprudence relating to the area. We might begin by noting that the right to religious freedom gives rise to conflicts both between different religions, within religions that are ostensibly seen as being the same, and between religion in general and other considerations and interests. Let us examine, then, whether this conflict remains if we analyse religious freedom in terms of indirect protections provided by other fundamental rights, for example, the right to freedom of expression and the right to freedom of assembly and association.

Freedom of Expression

The right to freedom of expression includes the right to receive information and ideas and impart them to others. It protects the spoken and the written word as well as other forms of communication such as images, films, symbols, signs, and gestures. An essential part of the exercise of religion concerns the receiving and imparting of information and ideas. The freedom to choose the information and ideas one wishes to impart and receive, and the freedom actually to so impart and receive them, are necessary conditions for religious action. Examples include access to, or purchase of, religious materials and literature (especially authoritative and sacred texts), the opportunity to listen to the spoken word in religious teaching or respond in discussion. The freedom of expression also covers the right *not* to receive information and ideas, thereby protecting the right *not* to receive *religious* information and ideas. Under the EHRC, Article 10, the freedom of expression also includes the freedom to hold opinions. Therefore, uncontentiously, we may say that the areas covered by the respective freedoms of religion in particular and freedom of expression in general, overlap.[8] Let us consider some examples from the case law.

On 18 February 1999, in *Buscarini* ECHR decided a case about two newly elected members of the San Marino parliament forced to swear by the Holy Gospel when taking office.[9] The members alleged that taking the oath infringed

8 It should be noted n this connection that freedom of religion and freedom of expression are subject to common overall protection under the US Constitution, see the First Amendment.

9 Case of *Buscarini and Others v. San Marino*, Application No. 00024645/94.

their right to freedom of religion, and the Court found in their favour.[10] Claiming an infringement of the right to freedom of religion appears sensible and obvious in the circumstances of the oath, but it would have been equally appropriate to claim an infringement of the freedom of expression. This procedure would have been required had it not been the words '*the holy gospels*', but other words deemed compulsory that an elected member of parliament might not wish to endorse such as, '*to uphold and defend freedom with all my might*'. The fact that elected members of parliament are subject to the compulsory endorsement of lurid formulations as a condition of maintaining a seat must be seen as a restriction of the freedom of expression. This raises the question of whether the restriction complies with the conditions of Article 10(2). The issue in *Buscarini* was whether the conditions of Article 9(2) had been met.[11] The Court could have dismissed the defence of the necessity of the oath just as summarily by referring to the freedom of expression, including the freedom to hold opinions under Article 10. It is, of course, manifestly self-contradictory that membership of parliament, the very purpose of which is to represent a diversity of views and opinions in society, should be conditional upon a prior declaration of allegiance to a specific religion and thereby to a specific set of values.

Similarly, in the case of *Kokkinakis*, it was held that Article 9 had been violated, but again this could have been decided just as coherently and appropriately under Article 10.[12] Kokkinakis, a Greek citizen and a member of the church of Jehovah's Witnesses had engaged in proselytism by calling on persons in their homes and presenting arguments to them in favour of his religious convictions with a view to convincing these persons of the truth and justice of the interpretation of the Christian scriptures defended by Jehovah's Witnesses. A Greek court held Kokkinakis liable for violating a law against proselytic activities. In the course of its decision, the ECHR emphasized that it is necessary to distinguish between 'bearing Christian witness' and 'improper proselytism'. The former is held to be a form of expression regarded as a normal social practice (also applicable to non-Christian denominations), the latter is a deformed version of such a practice characterized by:[13]

---

10 The oath of allegiance ran as follows: 'I, ..., swear on the Holy Gospels ever to be faithful to and obey the Constitution of the Republic, to uphold and defend freedom with all my might, ever to observe the Laws and Decrees, whether ancient, modern or yet to be enacted or issued and to nominate and vote for as candidates to the Judiciary and other Public Office only those whom I consider apt, loyal and fit to serve the Republic, without allowing myself to be swayed by any feelings of hatred or love or by any other consideration' (para. 8).

The two members took the oath in writing, but left out the words 'the Holy Gospels'. Subsequently, they were threatened with forfeiture of their seats in parliament. They then they took the oath in its entirety and in that connection brought the case before ECHR.

11 See paras 36–40. About the conditions for restrictions, see section VI.

12 *Kokkinakis v. Greece*, Application No. 14307/88.

13 Para. 48.

> … activities offering material or social advantages with a view to gaining new members for a church or exerting improper pressure on people in distress or in need; it may even entail the use of violence or brainwashing; more generally, it is not compatible with respect for the freedom of thought, conscience and religion of others.

The Greek authorities had not made this distinction in the case, however, nor had they specified the way in which Kokkinakis had been using 'improper means' in connection with his proselytic activities. On those grounds the ECHR found (para. 49) that the restriction could not be considered 'necessary in a democratic society'.

The point here is that Kokkinakis would have been just as well protected wthout the existence of Article 9. For the freedom to attempt to convince others of one's views (religious or otherwise) may be said to follow from the right to freedom of expression in Article 10 ('imparting information and ideas'), and since the decision as to whether or not the restriction can be considered 'necessary in a democratic society' must be expected to be the same whether the case is argued on the basis of Article 9 or Article 10.[14]

Freedom of Religion and Freedom of Association and Assembly

The right to freedom of association includes the freedom to create and carry on associations for any purpose whatsoever in order to act in organized community with others. The freedom of association further includes the right *not* to be a member of an association. The right to freedom of assembly includes the freedom to meet with others in private or in public. Just as is the case for the freedom of expression and for the freedom of religion, the right to freedom of association and assembly may be restricted on certain conditions.

An important part of the freedom of religion consists, of course, in the individual sharing his religion with others in an institutionalized context. In most cases, the establishment of a religious organization enabling believers to act in community in internal as well as external dealings is an essential goal of religion and, at the same time, necessary for the very existence of a religion. The freedom of assembly and association ensures that groups of persons who share the same religion can meet to observe religious rituals in community, and that they may form and carry on associations for the purpose of observing and disseminating their religion. The freedom of assembly and of association further ensures that persons who do not support the goals of an association may opt out of it, or even establish a new association. There are thus positive and negative aspects of the scope and purpose of the right to freedoms of assembly and association. The case of *Metroplitan Church of Bessarabia* offers a good illustration:[15]

---

14 See further discussion of the implications of Article 9 in conjunction with Article 14 *infra* pp. 184, 191–192.

15 *Metropolitan Church of Bessarabia and others vs. Moldova*, Application No. 00045701/99. The judgment was delivered on 13 December 2001.

Despite repeated applications to the Moldovan state, the Metropolitan Church of Bessarabia failed to obtain recognition as a religious organization. As a result, the church was prevented from acting as such. The judgment reads:[16]

> In particular, its priests may not conduct divine service, its members may not meet to practise their religion and, not having legal personality, it is not entitled to judicial protection of its assets.

All three prohibitions arising from the failure to obtain recognition of the church could have been protected by the right to freedom of assembly and association (possibly coupled with the right to freedom of expression and, for the third and last consequence, the right to a fair trial) as well as by the right to freedom of religion. The judgment goes on to state, on a positive note, that Article 9 should be interpreted in the light of Article 11. The court stated:[17]

> Moreover, since religious communities traditionally exist in the form of organised structures, Article 9 must be interpreted in the light of Article 11 of the Convention, which safeguards associative life against unjustified State interference. Seen in that perspective, the right of believers to freedom of religion, which includes the right to manifest one's religion in community with others, encompasses the expectation that believers will be allowed to associate freely, without arbitrary State intervention. Indeed, the autonomous existence of religious communities is indispensable for pluralism in a democratic society and is thus an issue at the very heart of the protection which Article 9 affords (see *Hasan and Chaush*, cited above, § 62). In addition, one of the means of exercising the right to manifest one's religion, especially for a religious community, in its collective dimension, is the possibility of ensuring judicial protection of the community, its members and its assets, so that Article 9 must be seen not only in the light of Article 11, but also in the light of Article 6.[18]

Thus there seem to be no aspects of the refusal of recognition that could not have been dealt with under other provisions of the EHRC.

In *Manousakis*,[19] similarly, a group of Jehovah's Witnesses had applied in vain for permission to conduct church services and carry on other ceremonies from premises they had taken on lease. The group was not given permission by way of a definite answer, but nevertheless began conducting church services. Subsequently, they were accused of having:[20]

> ... established and operated a place of worship for religious meetings and ceremonies of followers of another denomination, and in particular, of the Jehovas [sic] Witnesses' denomination without authorisation from the recognised ecclesiastical authorities and

16 Ibid. para 10.

17 Ibid. para. 118.

18 Moreover, we might note by way of example that the freedom of Association and Assembly in Denmark is protected under sections 78 and 79 of the Constitution which address respectively the censorship of assemblies and associations.

19 *Manoussakis vs. Greece*, Application No. 18748/91.

20 Ibid. para 12.

> the Minister of Education and Religious Affairs, such authorisation being required for the construction and operation of a church of any faith.

At first instance the defendants were acquitted, but were later fined. They then brought the case before the ECHR which, in the course of its decision, stated that the Greek appellate court:[21]

> ... relied expressly on the lack of authorisation from the Minister of Education and Religious Affairs. The latter, in response to five requests made by the applicants between 25 October 1983 and 10 December 1984, replied that he was examining their file. To date [1996], as far as the Court is aware, the applicants have not received an express decision. Moreover, at the hearing a representative of the Government himself described the Minister's conduct as unfair and attributed it to the difficulty that the latter might have had in giving legally valid reasons for an express decision refusing the authorisation or to his fear that he might provide the applicants with grounds for appealing to the Supreme Administrative Court to challenge the express administrative decision.

On those grounds the Court concluded that the restriction did not meet the conditions of Article 9(2), and that it was therefore in violation of Article 9.

Yet again, it seems obvious that one would have expected the same outcome if the case had been argued on the basis of Article 11. This provision must be considered to cover the right to establish religious associations and to assemble with a view to observing religious rituals.

Freedom of Religion and the Prohibition against Discrimination on the Ground of Religion

An overlap with the freedom of religion under Article 9 is also to be found in Article 14, which prohibits discrimination on any ground.[22] Thus, Article 14 provides protection against discrimination on the ground of religious conviction with any one of the other provisions of the Convention. In some circumstances, such a prohibition against discrimination provides the citizens with the same

---

21 Ibid. para 51.

22 Even if the provision by its tenor only prohibits discrimination in the enjoyment of the rights and freedoms generally recognized under the Convention, it is common knowledge that in practice, ECHR has extended this scope of protection to cover the full scope of the Convention. This implies that the prohibition against discrimination applies whenever a case impinges on a subject falling within the *ambit* of the Convention (cf. the use of the expression 'falls within the ambit' in ECHR 126 *Inze* para 36). As the prohibition also covers both direct and indirect discrimination and is thereby aimed at promoting substantive as well as procedural equality, – see also P. van Dijk and G.J.H. van Hoof *Theory and Practice of the European Convention on Human Rights* (Amsterdam: Kluwer, 1998) p. 719 – the scope of protection has today been considerably extended in relation to the wording of the provision. Protocol no. 12 to the convention contains a general prohibition on discrimination, but this protocol is not (yet) in force.

protection as the right to freedom of religion. Here, the case of *Leyla Sahin*[23] supports this contention:

Sahin had been banned from Istanbul University because she refused to remove an article of religious dress – a headscarf. The Turkish courts found the ban to be in compliance with current law and did not, therefore, overrule the decision of the University. The case was brought before the ECHR. Sahin invoked Articles 8, 9, 10 and 14, and Article 2 of Protocol 1. The Court initially took account of Article 9 and, following a thorough analysis of the case, came to the conclusion that there was no violation of Article 9. With regard to Article 2 of Protocol No. 1 the Court went on to state:[24]

> The applicant alleged that the ban on wearing the Islamic headscarf in higher-education institutions had infringed her right under Article 2 of Protocol no. 1 to the Convention. She also said that it obliged students to choose between religion and education and discriminated between believers and non-believers. That, in her view, constituted an unjustified interference with her rights guaranteed by Article 14 of the Convention, taken together with Article 9. Lastly she complained of a violation of Articles 8 and 10 of the Convention. The Court finds that no separate question arises under the other provisions relied on by the applicant, as the relevant circumstances are the same as those examined in relation to Article 9, in respect of which the Court has found no violation.

Even if Article 14 was not cited with Article 2 of Protocol No. 1, but with Article 9, it is obvious that the outcome would have been the same.

It appears then, that at least in a number of cases concerned with core aspects of religious freedom (the right to assemble and associate with others in relation to religious convictions and ceremonies, the right to express one's religious conviction, and the right not to have certain religious opinions and ideas imposed) there seems to be an unnecessary amount of double protection. Double protection similarly may exist in respect of a number of other fundamental rights provisions, for example, in Articles 6, 8 and 12 of the EHRC.

Against this background it does not seem unreasonable to conclude thus far that, on a number of points, the part of the right to freedom of religion that concerns the right to manifest one's religious belief through church service, teaching and prayers is superfluous. At any rate, the right to freedom of expression, association and assembly provides such ample protection that only the right to manifest one's religion through observance of religious rituals seems to have an independent significance. Even by reference to this part of Article 9 there will be an almost unavoidable overlap with other provisions (for example, Article 8). Let us look, then, at the justification for securing independent protection at a fundamental level for rights covering the observance of religious rituals.

---

23 *Leyla Sahin v. Turkey*, Application No. 44774/98.

24 Ibid. para 116.

Rituals and Rights

Freedom of religion, at least on some points, is undoubtedly protected under the other rights provided for by the EHRC. The examples noted above serve as guidelines for the way in which other cases about the right to freedom of religion might be analysed. The question we address in this section about rituals is whether the freedom of religion, where it is not covered by or included in other rights, is an interest deserving of protection. What kinds of activities do we have in mind?[25]

One of the most common examples of the invocation of the freedom of religion is associated with the wish to wear specific items of clothing. These cases are similar in that what is here claimed as a right may be inferred from the right to freedom of religion on the basis that the item of clothing in question is an integral part of the claimant's observance of his or her religion. Familiar examples are of Muslim women wishing to wear scarves, veils and/or loose-fitting garments; male Sikhs wishing to wear turbans; male Jews wishing to wear skull-caps. We could also mention the claims of male Rastafarians to keep their dreadlocks, and the wishes of male Jews to wear curled hair in front of their ears. The right to a religiously motivated tattoo also falls within this category.

Some cases involve the question of a right of exemption from the duty to adhere to a particular workplace dress code established by a private employer as part of the employee's duties. Examples include work in department stores, airline companies and supermarkets, so that the right is being invoked as an employee's right to exemption from the contractual relationship without sanction. Other cases involve a right of exemption from statutory security or safety requirements, or requirements relating to personal hygiene. Here examples relate to work on building sites, riding a motorbike, and with work related to food preparation and production. Cases might also involve the question of a right of exemption from the duty to wear a full uniform, as in public service (for example, as a police officer) or military service.

A second type of case concerns freedom of religion as a ground for non-compliance with statutory or contractual obligations at specified times. These cases concern certain days that are designated by the person's religion as days of rest, days of fast, days of prayer, days of celebration and the like, and the precedence given to the religious obligations associated with such days over the person's *civil* obligations. Christians consider Sundays, and in particular the

25 The following examples have been found in ECHR case law and in the international literature in the area: Rex J. Ahdar *Law and Religion* (Aldershot: Ashgate, 2000); Rex J. Ahdar and Ian Leigh *Religious Freedom in the Liberal State* (Oxford: Oxford University Press, 2005); Sebastian Poulter *Ethnicity, Law and Human Rights: The English Experience* (Oxford: Oxford University Press, 1999); Carolyn Evans *Freedom of Religion under the European Convention on Human Rights* (Oxford: Oxford University Press, ECHR Series, 2001); Malcolm D. Evans *Religious Liberty and International Law in Europe* (Cambridge: Cambridge University Press, 1997); P. van Dijk and G.J.H. van Hoof *Theory and Practice of the European Convention on Human Rights* (Amsterdam: Kluwer, 1998); Brian Barry *Culture and Equality* (Cambridge, MA: Harvard University Press, 2002).

days around the celebration of the birth of Jesus as holidays. Some Christians also consider Saturdays as holidays. Both Christians and Muslims fast for some days of the year. Some cases involve the question of a right of exemption from a contractual duty to work on certain days, for example, Sundays. Other cases may involve a right to receive full welfare benefits from the state despite the fact that the person is not, technically speaking, 'available for work' on certain holidays. A case may also involve a right of exemption from special types of assignment or from warnings or orders on the ground of incapacity of performing certain assignments due to physical impairment in connection with a fast.

A third type concerns religious rules about food and stimulants. These may involve a religious ban on eating or drinking certain things; either a total ban or restrictions relating to times of consumption. Cases in point include restrictions on eating and drinking during the daytime in certain periods, and general bans on eating certain kinds of meat. Secondly, these cases may involve treatment of food in a certain way as prescribed by religion. Examples include the rule that animals be slaughtered in specified ways, or that certain kinds of foods should not be mixed, for example, that milk products must be stored and consumed separately from other food. Under some religious rules the consumption of certain stimulants might be required. A case in point is the imbibing of symbolic equivalents of sacred flesh and blood, or perhaps hallucinogenic substances.

Some cases have involved the question of a right of exemption from the rules on cruelty to animals or on standards of hygiene on the basis that the preparatory treatment of some foodstuffs are subject to religious prescriptions, and that these prescriptions are integral to religious belief. Hence the exemptions relate to the right to freedom of religion. The main example here concerns the slaughtering of animals. Finally, there are cases where a religious ban on certain types of food is used as an argument for a right to receive special treatment in public institutions, for example, in connection with hospital treatment, service of custodial sentences, meals prepared on site for children in kindergartens, and so on.

We should mention that a number of cases motivated by religion involve the handling of the dead; polygamy, arms possession, and duties of secrecy. Cases involving the handling of the dead may arise in connection with religious proscriptions specifying that deceased persons should not be buried until a certain period has elapsed after death, or that the deceased are to lie in open coffins during the burial ceremony. Examples of exemptions relating to polygamy have involved men wishing to have more than one wife acknowledged as lawful for the purposes of obtaining welfare benefits on their behalf. Cases about arms possession arise out of the fact that religious rituals may involve the use of weapons (typically special knives and sabres), and that persons belonging to religions that observe such rituals claim exemption from prohibitions against carrying weapons. Cases involving a duty of secrecy may concern priests who, in the course of confidential conversations with members of their congregations, or in confession, learn of criminal acts and who claim that the duty of confidentiality owed under their religion be acknowledged by the authorities.

The Right to Observe Religious Rituals

These various examples of the invocation of the freedom of religion do not account for all actual or possible instances, but they do provide an adequate illustration of the range of issues in question. If these can be subsumed under wider, secular protections we must consider why we might continue to insist on discrete and special religious provisions. Where the freedom of expression protects *all* types of opinions and ideas, the freedom of religion specifically protects *religious* opinions and ideas. Where the freedom of *assembly* protects *all* types of assemblies, freedom of religion specifically protects *religious* assemblies. Why should religious opinions and ideas enjoy a distinct (and thus seemingly privileged) status compared to other opinions and actions?[26] For one might reasonably observe that the various religions should be regarded as sub-cultures, and that there is no reason to protect and prioritize the importance of the activities of religious sub-cultures over artistic, sporting, literary, scientific, musical or political sub-cultures. Moreover, why privilege these *latter* orthodoxly recognized 'cultural' activities? Of the infinite range of activities engaged in by individuals and groups, why is one type, or a select number of types, of activity deemed more worthy of protection than another?

A possible answer (and to an orthodoxly religious person perhaps an obvious one) is that religious convictions are, in relation to the concerns of humanity, more significant and comprehensive than other diversions or activities. Religious convictions embrace all aspects of human life from beginning to end, whereas other cultural forms of expression touch only limited aspects of it. The fact, therefore, that religion is so fundamental and essential to human life means that it should enjoy a privileged position with regard to human rights protection. But this attribution of fundamental importance is not a universal view of religion, it is a religious view of the universe. Some are of the view that religion is an ideological opiate. Others, whilst not denigrating the concerns of religion, feel that it is not rationally possible to deal with issues of transcendence in any rational way and, moreover, that the attempt to do so on the part of individuals (and certainly at an institutional level) can be harmful. Thus the claim for attributing special significance to religions must be articulated carefully if we are to avoid the tautology that 'religion is special and fundamental because religious people believe it to be special and fundamental'.

There is, however, a reflex to this secular objection. For one can coherently observe that faith plays a vital part in the lives of a large section of the population, and that faith in some sense – even in the logically unwarranted declarations of the atheist – is an indispensable element of human striving and association. It is, one might say, through *faith in a general philosophical sense* that human beings develop their scientific as well as their moral and ethical views of the world. Since not all people share the *same* philosophy or faith, however, the general democratic process must be particularly sensitive to the issue of the protection

26 For a similar analysis of this issue, see Steven H. Shiffrin 'The Pluralistic Foundations of the Religion Clauses' *Cornell Law Review* (Vol. 90, 2004) pp. 9ff.

of what is broadly understood as faith, and thus broadly understood as 'religion' in this regard. Against this background it may be argued that opinions and ideas and actions reflecting a person's 'religious' conviction requires special protection over other convictions.

In the protection of religious freedom under Article 9 of the EHRC, this point of view seems to have been accepted. However, probably because it is not possible to define what constitutes a religious conviction clearly, the protection has been extended so that religious ideas and other fundamental philosophies of life are accorded equal treatment. Thus in practice the freedom of religion includes more than what is normally accepted as 'religious' convictions. Van Dijk and van Hoof write that the words 'religion or belief':[27]

> ... not only cover the traditional religions and (non-religious) beliefs, but also all kinds of minority views. For instance pacifism, and probably also communism is regarded as a 'belief' falling within the ambit of article 9. Even veganism (strict vegetarianism) may fall within the scope of the article.

Freedom of religion, it seems, is really a freedom of philosophy of life, covering religious as well as secular philosophies.[28] The important dividing line that governs the availability of legal protection is not, then, between religious and non-religious convctions, but between convictions that are part of a total philosophy of life and convictions that are not.[29] But rather than clarifying the justifcation for the special protection of freedom of religion this analysis serves to create further confusion; for now we must ask when does a conviction require special protection due to its very nature? For it requires little inventiveness to present a specific conviction as part of a total philosophy of life and thereby characterize it as an element of the freedom of religion. The interesting thing here, of course, is that this acknowledgment implies that actions expressing a 'total philosophy' will be immune from statutory regulation unless the conditions of Article 9(2) are satisfied. To illustrate the point it might be worth saying a few words about the case that most authors in the field consider as the leading case.

In the Commission's decision of October 12, 1978 in the *Arrowsmith* case[30] it was held that a woman who held pacifist beliefs (she was described as 'undisputedly a convinced pacifist' para. 68) was not protected under Article 9 from punishment as a result of an unlawful distribution of pacifist leaflets. The legal ground for Ms Arrowsmith's conviction was the Incitement to Disaffection Act 1934, which made it illegal to encourage soldiers to desert. The Commission examined the case both in the light of Articles 5, 9, 10 and 14 (which gives further support to the

---

27 Van Dijk and van Hoof (op. cit.) p. 548.

28 A more or less similar situation is seen in the interpretation of ICCPR.

29 Basically, such an interpretation is not compatible with the freedom of religion under section 67 of the Danish Constitution which is explicitly aimed at the right to '*worship God*'. An extensive interpretation of section 67, bringing the content in line with ECHR case law cannot be excluded, however.

30 Application 7050/75, D&R no. 19, p. 5.

theory advanced earlier that other rights might absorb the legitimate protection of religious beliefs and activities) and decided that there had not been a violation of any of the rights in question. With regard to Article 9, the central argument of the Commission – aimed at establishing that there had not been a breach of the convention – was that the distribution of leaflets did not express *the pacifist beliefs* of Ms Arrowsmith. This required the commission to perform some subtle interpretive activity on the text of the convention in question:[31]

> The Commission considers that the term 'practice' as employed in Article 9.1. does not cover each act which is motivated or influenced by a religion or a belief.
>
> It is true that public declarations proclaiming generally the idea of pacifism and urging the acceptance of a commitment to non-violence may be considered as a normal and recognised manifestation of pacifist belief. However, when the actions of individuals do not actually express the belief concerned, they cannot be considered to be as such protected by Article 9.1 even when they are motivated or influenced by it.

It was on this background, that Ms Arrowsmith's distribution of leaflets could not be seen to be protected under Article 9. This part of the decision has attracted some critical comments. Thus, for example, Carolyn Evans says:[32]

> It seems very peculiar that to suggest that a pacifist who spends her time appealing to soldiers to refuse to participate in the use of armed force could be seen to be practising her belief less than someone who outlined the pacifist ideals to the world at large.

But this is a misdirected criticism. First, the distributed leaflets could not properly be labelled pacifist leaflets since they did not recommend total abstinence from violent means, but only abstinence from violent means being used in the *wrong* way.[33] But judgments about what constitute right or wrong uses of violence quite obviously involve an interpretation of events through the prism of political values. The Commission were therefore right to say that 'the leaflets did not express pacifist views'.[34]

Secondly, the distinction between appealing to soldiers and appealing to the world at large makes perfect sense in this context. It is precisely because of the political nature of the distributed leaflets that it may be seen as a further argument against protection that the leaflets were distributed to soldiers shortly to be posted to Northern Ireland rather than to the public in general. To this, it should be added that even if the leaflets distributed by Ms Arrowsmith had been purely

31 Ibid. p. 71.

32 Evans *Freedom of Religion under the European Convention on Human Rights* (op. cit.) p. 113.

33 See para. 72 of the decision where the quote from the leaflet – particularly the part which says '... I'd be willing to fight for a cause I can believe in. But what is happening in Ireland is all wrong' – makes it quite clear that Ms Arrowsmith, although she might have been a pacifist, was not, on the evidence of this particular leaflet, engaged in an expression of pacifist beliefs.

34 Para. 75.

pacifist in nature, the general distinction made by the Court between actions which express belief and actions which are motivated by belief, are entirely relevant and necessary even though, admittedly, it is not always clear whether a performed action belongs to one or the other category. However, the distinction serves to ensure that the right to freedom of religion cannot be exploited to argue that every possible derivation or interpretation of general 'religious' prescription deserves protection under Article 9. According to this interpretation of the *Arrowsmith* decision, actions which are based on derivations of beliefs, should not be offered protection. This seem to fit with subsequent practice of the commission which has stressed that only those actions whose performance are *necessary* for the practice of the belief in question are protected under Article 9.[35] In *C v. UK*, Application No. 10358/83, published in D&R 37 at p. 142, this was expressed, by saying that the protection of rituals is extended only to acts which are 'intimately linked' to the belief in question. This means that protection can be afforded only to 'acts of worship or devotion which are aspects of the practice of a religion or a belief in a generally recognised form'. This view is confirmed in recent ECHR case law. Thus in *Pretty v. UK* the Court said:[36]

> The Court does not doubt the firmness of the applicant's views concerning assisted suicide but would observe that not all opinions or convictions constitute beliefs in the sense protected by Article 9 § 1 of the Convention. Her claims do not involve a form of manifestation of a religion or belief, through worship, teaching, practice or observance as described in the second sentence of the first paragraph. As found by the Commission, the term 'practice' as employed in article 9 § 1 does not cover each act which is motivated or influenced by a religion or belief …. [here follows a reference to *Arrowsmith*][37]

It may of course be very difficult to draw the relevant lines in these complex matters, but as a general principle it must be assumed that only actions of an *inherently* religious nature are covered. Thus church services and actual religious rituals would be covered, whereas religious prescriptions concerning matters which are not directly connected to a religious ceremony would not. ECHR case law is not entirely clear in this area, however. A special form of ritual slaughter of animals was, for example, held to be covered by Article 9 in *Cha'are Shalom Ve Tsedek.*[38]

We learn from the decision that the applicant association was originally formed in 1986 as a breakaway from the *Association Consistoriale Israélite de*

35 See Evans *Religious Liberty and International Law in Europe* (op. cit.) p. 307ff.

36 *Pretty* (Application No. 2346/02), decided on April 29, 2002. Para 82.

37 It should be noted that in its reasoning, ECHR here seems to be taking account of two arguments at the same time, without any possibility of separation, that is: (1) that the belief in the right to have one's life ended at one's own option (assisted suicide) is not a religion in the sense protected by Article 9; and (2) that not every act arising out of a religious conviction is protected under Article 9.

38 *Cha'are Shalom ve Tsedek v. France* (Application No. 27417/95) decided on June 27, 2000.

Paris (*ACIP*). One of its aims was to revive a stricter interpretation of the laws of *Kashrut* – of which the purging of blood from animals to be eaten is central. Religious bodies practising ritual slaughter are exempt under domestic French Law from prohibitions requiring prior stunning of animals, yet are required to appoint and supervise skilled slaughterers. Although the *ACIP* is such a body, and for many years had supervised this ritual technique and levied a tax for so doing, the applicants argued that the process was not rigorous enough in respect of the inspection of respiratory organs, and had sought over the years separate authorisation. This had been persistently denied domestically. Thus, before the ECHR, they invoked Article 9 of the Convention taken alone, and in conjunction with Article 14.

The French Government accepted that the slaughter rituals in question formed part of the practice of Judaism and as such were covered by protections afforded by Article 9. But the religious proscriptions in question did not require *personal* participation in process of slaughter. Refusal to grant authority, therefore, to *Cha'are Shalom Ve Tsedek* violated *the practice* of religion only in so far as it made it impossible for adherents to obey dietary instructions. Arguing (convincingly) that the *ACIP* method of slaughter was, in fact, identical to the applicant's understanding of *Kashrut*, and that thus approved meat was readily available, this was not the case. The ECHR agreed with this precise point and found that Article 9 'cannot extend to the right to take part in person in the performance of ritual slaughter', and that even if the refusal *had* been considered an interference, it would have pursued 'a legitimate aim, namely protection of public health and public order, in so far as organisation by the State of the exercise of worship is conducive to religious harmony and tolerance'.[39]

This seems reasonable, but Evans is, nevertheless, right to say that the ECHR case law is not entirely consistent: The *Arrowsmith* test itself raises some difficult questions about how the Court might determine precisely where the line should be drawn between actions that, on the one hand, 'express directly'/'are necessary for'/'are intimately linked with' a certain belief, and actions which, on the other, are 'merely motivated by'/'contingent in relation to'/'only remotely connected to' that belief. This ambiguity is the source of real difficulties and can but raise doubt about the prospect for proper protection of religious beliefs. Evans – in attempting to create more room for religiously motivated action says:[40]

> ... it is important not to lose sight of the fact that general legislation may impose serious restrictions on religion or belief, particularly the religion or belief of relatively small and powerless groups. Such groups cannot necessarily rely on the democratic processes to see to their needs.

---

39 Finding similarly no violation of Article 14, the court stated that the refusal to authorise 'pursued a legitimate aim, and that there was "a reasonable relationship of proportionality between the means employed and the aim sought to be realised"'. See paras 78–84.

40 Evans *Freedom of Religion under the European Convention on Human Rights* (op. cit.) p. 198

But this remark is not sophisticated enough to capture the essence of the point we are concerned with, for Evans quite clearly does not distinguish between belief/religion and actions, which are seen as expressions of, or are motivated by, religion. Most people might agree that it would, in most cases (but not in all) be wrong to 'impose serious restrictions on religion or belief'. This sanctity of the so-called *forum internum* is in many ways beyond contention (although brainwashing, deprogramming of people who are believed to be brainwashed and so on does pose some real and relevant problems). The real heat, as the Arrowsmith case shows, is generated by religiously motivated *action*. It is the right to be exempt from general legislation for religious reasons that is the focus of issue here, and it is this right the Arrowsmith decision is trying to accommodate by drawing distinctions between various forms of relationship between belief and action.

Let us push the logic behind the Arrowsmith decision a bit further. That is, given that general legislation always imposes restrictions on action, why should we attach special importance to the fact that such restrictions may sometimes apply to actions which are motivated by religious beliefs? In the concluding chapter of her study Evans expresses the view that the current case law of the ECHR does not give adequate protection to religious freedom and that the ECHR does not deal respectfully with the most deeply held beliefs of many applicants. She calls for religions and beliefs to be treated with more respect, and for an acknowledgement that states have interfered in important aspects of religious practices on more occasions than appear in the existing case law.[41] The call is for more and better protection for religiously motivated actions (rituals). But again, we must ask, 'Why do religious beliefs deserve special protection in the first place?'

Freedom of Religion: Conviction and Action

We could say, very generally, that democracy should espouse the idea that individuals are free to hold convictions about anything subject to the limitations that follow from a regard for other people's rights. This is not meant to be a profound contribution to political theory, it is simply a statement of the perfectly reasonable philosophy that people should be allowed to do what they like unless there is a good reason to prevent them doing so.This leads us to the not so simple issue of the content and scope of rights, but we can say, uncontentiously, that among those rights, and as a democratic minimum in any understanding of a pluralist polity, are those of individuals and groups to hold and express opinions in public or in private, alone or in community with others. However, the right to *act* in accordance with one's convictions does not follow from this freedom of expression and opinion. Democratic decision-making procedures safeguarding rights apply to *all* citizens. If certain beliefs and convictions entail actions not permitted under existing law, these actions are prohibited. Individuals thus curtailed in the *realization in action* of their beliefs are free to seek a change of the legal rules by recognized democratic means. But the conviction that *God*

41 Ibid. p. 208.

demands a particular action be performed in relation to a particular belief is not, by itself, sufficient to render a prohibited action permissible. One should, however, be permitted to challenge in some respects the validity of the interpretation and application of the prohibition in a court of law, and, regardless of the success of this challenge, in principle be allowed to attempt to persuade others to support the case for future procedures and measures designed to review the prohibition of the action in question.

Would we want to argue, however, that religious or 'total philosophy' convictions should enjoy a privileged priority and exemption from the general rules governing the relationship between belief and permitted actions? Let us briefly consider a few examples: should persons be exempt from compulsory observance of speed limits if they are genuinely convinced that, in some or most situations, enhancement rather than impairment of traffic safety will be achieved if higher than permitted speeds are achieved? Or should persons who are convinced that it is God's will that they wear a specific type of hat be exempt from wearing a crash helmet when riding a motorbike?[42] Might persons be exempted from the rules governing cruelty to animals on the basis of their belief that the production of the cheapest possible food is the central aspect of the creation of a good life for humans? Should persons who believe that God has ordered them to slaughter animals in a certain way be exempted from the same rules?

The question arises as to why putative deviations from general standards based on religion should be accepted, whilst putative deviations based on non-religious reasons should not be accepted. What is the particular quality in *religious* conviction that may justify a claim for special protection of certain types of action? Why is reference to *faith* in *divine* prescription assumed to be overridingly convincing? Why are actions motivated by religion not treated on equal terms with, for example, politically motivated actions?[43]

42 It is not a valid argument to say that, the former situation is likely to cause danger to persons other than the motorist who is exceeding the speed limit whereas the latter situation is likely to cause danger only to the motorcyclist himself. For in the example it is included as a reason that it may be argued that exceeding the speed limit enhances traffic safety. In addition, in the motorcyclist example, it may be argued that any further injury sustained by the motorcyclist due to his failure to wear a crash-helmet, might, in the case of an accident, affect the person causing the accident in the form of increased guilt and emotional trauma. If the motorcyclist dies due to a crash it may, in the worst-case scenario, involve criminal liability for involuntary manslaughter – a situation which would not arise if a helmet had enabled the motorcyclist to survive.

43 The specialist literature (noted below) concerning the right to freedom of religion does not appear to give any clear answers to the question of why religious convictions or actions based on religion are to be afforded special protection. See Evans *Freedom of Religion Under the European Convention on Human Rights* (op. cit.) for a review of the most common arguments.

Arguing Against the Special Status of Religious Belief

We have up to this point advanced the idea that freedom of expression and association might subsume religious freedoms, and that the latter in a multicultural polity are obsolescent. We have also hinted at reasons why religion might deserve special protection. But this issue deserves particular attention. It has formed the subject matter of some important and specialized European and American literature[44] and of necessity we can look only at a small part of it. We do not include *religious* arguments for the right to religious freedom.[45] This, however, as we shall explain, is not to beg the question against religion.

Our argument throughout has been that if it is possible to adopt a coherent multicultural or genuinely pluralist position on diversity of values and beliefs, then sectarianism or partisanship in fundamental matters is logically precluded from the start. This is not to say that the ideas of a particular group might not contingently coincide with the self-perception of interests of all other groups, or contingently meet with their disapproval. In fact, a *rational* analysis of institutional design and policy might meet with disapproval from various quarters. Removing the special protection of the freedom of religion would undoubtedly provide a splendid example here.

A universally acceptable and defensible pluralist perspective must be articulated, and this cannot be achieved merely by stating one's 'neutrality' or indifference. Genuinely pluralist tolerationism, as we have presented it on the basis of agent rights and duties, is not, we must repeat, a normatively neutral perspective. It is a substantive ethical position offering a logically necessary defence of basic human rights and the values of autonomy and individuality over the many manifestations of 'culture' or 'faith' that seek to deny those rights. It says straightforwardly that diversity is inevitable, permissible and perhaps desirable, but that this is not *carte blanche* for groups to institutionalize inequality or oppression in the name of tradition, faith or culture, or, on the same basis, to exempt themselves from the general legal requirements imposed by systems of civil or criminal regulation.

---

44 The literature includes: Ahdar *Law and Religion* (op. cit.); Barry *Culture and Equality* (op. cit.); Alan Brudner *Constitutional Goods* (op. cit.); Evans *Freedom of Religion Under the European Convention on Human Rights* (op. cit.); Evans *Religious Liberty and International Law in Europe* (op. cit.); Aileen McHarg, 'Reconciling Human Rights and the Public Interest: Conceptual problems and Doctrinal Uncertainty in the Jurisprudence of the European Court of Human Rights *The Modern Law Review* (1999) p. 671ff.; Poulter *Ethnicity, Law and Human Rights: The English Experience* (op. cit.); Frances Rayday 'Culture, Religion and Gender' *International Journal of Constitutional Law* (2003) p. 63ff.; Jens Elo Rytter *Den Europæiske Menneskerettighedskonvention* (Copenhagen: Thomson, 2003); van Dijk and van Hoof, *Theory and Practice of the European Convention on Human Rights* (op. cit.); Shiffrin 'The Pluralistic Foundations of the Religion Clauses' (op. cit.) pp. 9ff. See also footnote 25 p. 186 *supra*.

45 For a review of Christian arguments for religious freedom, see Ahdar and Leigh *Religious Freedom in the Liberal State* (op. cit.) Chapter 1.

This being said, the particular issue of whether, in the context of social diversity, we should acknowledge special protections for religious freedoms, becomes, logically, a secular matter. We do not deny the possibility of a rational theology, but 'faith' arguments of established religions by their very nature attach fundamentally to revelatory texts – *not reason,* and can therefore be considered valid only from *within* a particular religion. Acceptance of the authority or truth of the revelatory texts in question is in fact a *definition* of membership. Thus some Muslims may not accept 'arguments' based on the New Testament simply because they are based on the New Testament. Some Christians may not be disposed to acknowledge 'arguments' based on facts contained in the the The Koran for the same 'reasons'. There are, of course, endless doctrinal divisions *within* the religions, so that, for instance, one group of Muslims may be convinced that The Koran prescribes in fact a right to religious freedom or a dispensation to consume certain foods or liquids, whereas another group of Muslims may be convinced that that is not the case. In short, 'religious' argument based on assumed textual authority, however scrupulous the logic in relation to the textual premises they adduce, is simply unpersuasive to those who do not believe in the authenticity of the textual premises. If religious freedom is an interest that deserves special protection, the reasons given for a special right to freedom of religion must not be conditional upon certain beliefs, for if that is the case, reason will, so to speak, be censured by faith[46]. Thus we can but turn our attention to the possibility of a *non*-religious justification for supporting a special right to freedom of religion.

46 Alan Gewirth, in his *Reason and Morality* (Chicago: Chicago University Press, 1978) explains why belief cannot function as a condition for accepting reason:

> It is indeed the case that there have also been historical demands that reason itself in turn pass various justificatory tests set by religious faith, aesthetic rapture, and so forth. But the very scrutiny to determine whether these tests are passed must itself make use of reason. For example, salient powers of reason must be used in order to check whether the products of logical and empirical rationality are consistent with propositions upheld on the basis of faith, or whether the use of reason is compatible with the experiencing of aesthetic feelings, and the like. *Thus any attack on reason or any claim to supersede it by some other human power or criterion must rely on reason to justify its claims.* (p. 23, our emphasis)

While there may be said to be a difference between questioning the conditions under which a belief is held and overruling those conditions (Gewirth's argument focuses on the latter case) there is enough similarity, to use his argument in the present case. Had the belief in question been a justified one, based for instance on lack of evidence for something (perhaps combined with a pressing need to supply reasons based on whatever indices might be available), then the two cases would have been different. But when the belief in question is of a religious nature, and when the argument is not of a theological nature, but, as here, of a politico-legal nature, then the use of belief-conditions will invalidate the argument.

Evans: Toleration and Peace

Carolyn Evans in theorizing the freedom of religion under the ECHR, examines a number of arguments that may support the special status religion has been given in human rights law. Under the heading 'Instrumental Arguments', she discusses three that we might examine briefly. The first is what we[47]might call *the tolerance for peace argument*.[48] This argument says that we ought to be tolerant towards people of other faiths so as to avoid the occurrence of social problems[49]

> Even if some people perceive that the best society of all is one where all people accept the same, true religion (or no religion at all), they might understand that religious diversity is a fact of life that must be accommodated. Thus they might wish to avert the suffering that religious intolerance and persecution brings, recognizing that it causes social problems without necessarily bringing a religiously cohesive society any closer.

There is, of course, history to support this argument, but it is not entirely convincing. There are three points we might make.

First, and most importantly, the argument does not seem to make any distinction between tolerance and special treatment. While we can agree with the general recommendation that one ought to be tolerant vis-à-vis other religions and that one ought to refrain from the persecution and harassment of those who do not share one's own beliefs, this does not necessarily amount to an acceptance of the principle that religious beliefs should, therefore, receive special constitutional protection. Other beliefs, convictions, and forms of life might well be entitled to the same tolerant respect as religious beliefs. Furthermore, one might argue that attributes and dispositions that are not the result of belief, but of nature, should at least in some cases receive even more protection against intolerance. Thus perhaps race, nationality, ethnicity and sex, should be better protected than religious beliefs because these things cannot be amended, whereas beliefs can and often do change and adapt to new circumstances.[50]

Secondly, as Evans points out, the 'tolerance for peace' argument treats religious tolerance as a means to an end, the end being social harmony. To the extent that such harmony can be achieved *without* showing religious tolerance, the right to freedom of religion is superfluous.

---

47 For an analysis of what tolerance requires, see Joseph Raz, *The Morality of Freedom* (Oxford: Clarendon, 2004) pp. 401–402.

48 See also Ahdar and Leigh (op. cit.) pp. 52–54 (civic peace).

49 Such a desired purpose might for example be religious homogeneity in society, which in turn – perhaps paradoxically – might be seen as a presupposition for social peace. See Evans *Freedom of Religion under the European Convention on Human Rights* (op. cit.) p. 23.

50 Here it might well be worth mentioning that religious belief is also being used as justification for other forms of discrimination. One common example of this is the Catholic Church's refusal to countenance women priests or for their adoption agencies to consider homosexuals.

Thirdly, religion is not the only, and perhaps not even the most significant, source of social disorder. Poverty, political differencess, ethnic and cultural diversities can be as destabilizing as religion. This is not an argument against the idea of religious tolerance, but it does weaken the case for suggesting that religion should be singled out for special protection.

Evans: The Historical Argument

The second of Evans' points we might label 'the historical argument'. This tack is more empirical than normative. Evans explains:[51]

> This argument can be construed, so as to claim that there is nothing particularly important about Freedom of Religion as such except for the fact that historically religion has been used as a basis to justify persecution and repression.

The argument amounts to saying that in order to prevent these past events from being repeated, religious belief ought to be expressly protected. Whilst it is true that past injustices have ostensibly[52] been based on religious belief we should be extremely cautious about policy proposals in this regard. Two things might be worth noting. Some of the religious persecutions that have occurred in the past have indeed, as Evans says, had the character of horrors. However, it is not evident that a protection of religious freedom in an international treaty nor in a national constitution, would have had the effect of preventing them. The political and social forces in play during some of these past events were so powerful that laws, whether international, constitutional or otherwise, would not have assuaged them. Neither will they be able to do so in the future if such forces should be released again. Law has its limits, and whilst it would be wonderful to legislate all horrors out of existence, this is hardly a sensible way to look at the role of law. But there is a more serious defect of reasoning here.

The argument seems to be that not simply religion, but all and any form of belief responsible for creating horrific consequences should be afforded special legal protection. A group's or individual's belief in their racial superiority would, therefore, seem to be qualify for special and reverential protection. Fortunatlely, these kind of beliefs receive precisely the opposite treatment. On this logic, religion would not be singled out for protection, it would be outlawed. Persecution and intolerance may take many forms and have many motives. Thus, if anything, the historical events of religious persecution, should not lead us to protect *religious* beliefs, specifically and distinctly, but should rather prompt us to protect individuals and groups from *persecution generally* whatever its roots.

---

51 Evans *Freedom of Religion under the European Convention on Human Rights* (op. cit.) pp. 24–25.

52 We must note, of course, that religious and political authority were not clearly separated in the past, and that what might have appeared as religious persecution could well have had other, non-religious motives.

Evans: The 'Autonomy and Pluralism' Argument

Evans presents the above as a fundamentally liberal theory which argues that:[53]

> ... Freedom of Religion or belief is an essential and independent component of treating human beings as autonomous persons deserving of dignity and respect. If society so treats people it will commit itself to at least a weak notion of value pluralism, which will allow for a choice between a variety of religious beliefs, practices, and communities to exist and to be given some protection in that society. Thus respect for individual autonomy will also promote the notion of tolerance and pluralism in a society.

This is a straightforward and widely accepted view of what liberalism entails: Autonomy implies the right to decide for oneself, and this, of course, is the very core of the democratic idea of liberalism. Symptomatic of all theories of liberalism, however, is the failure to specify the limits of individual freedom. The sentiment of freedom autonomy and equality is not so much a problem at the level of general principle; Kant, for example, comes pretty close to agreement: *one's freedom extends only so far as it does not infringe on any other citizen's right to exercise his/her freedom.* But the particular application of this principle in deciding how far is far enough, and what is to count as an infringement, certainly does present problems. The answers to these questions are a matter of great political complexity and contention. We have suggested a Gewirthian approach to working towards a specification of the the Kantian equality principle *via* the natural hierarchy of goods found in the 'additive', 'maintenance' and 'subtractive' aspects of agency. There remains, however, plenty of room for disagreement even among Gewirthians. The point is that the *autonomy* argument *per se* bring nothing to the party in deciding whether this or that *type* of belief ought to be specially protected beyond the general provisions for expression and association.

Even if respect for individual autonomy is accepted as a foundation for constitutional law, it does not back up a special protection for religious (or philosophical) beliefs. Evans quotes two attempts to theorize the role of religion within a liberal context. First, Rawls, who says that '... equal liberty of conscience is the only principle that the persons in the original position cannot fail to acknowledge. They cannot take chances with their liberty by permitting the dominant religious or moral doctrine to persecute or suppress others if it wishes'.[54] But, the method of the original position notwithstanding, this does not provide the justification we are seeking. Religious and moral doctrines are here arbitrarily singled out. There are many other areas in which a person in the original position would not want to compromise his or her autonomy: political freedom, freedom in personal matters such as sexual preferences, freedom to choose your partner, whether to become a parent, freedom of artistic expression

53 Evans *Freedom of Religion under the European Convention on Human Rights* (op. cit.) p. 29.

54 Ibid. p. 31; John Rawls (op. cit.) p. 207.

and so on. There seems to be no good reason to single out religious and moral belief in this regard. Evans quotes McDougal, Lasswell and Chen:[55]

> One of the most distinctive acts available to man as a rational being is the continual redefinition of the self in relation to others and to the cosmos. Thus, each individual must be free to search for the basic postulates in a perspective that will unify the experiences of life.

Whether it is true or not that such a 'continual redefinition' is most distinctive to man, and whether or not one accepts the move from *is* to *ought* in this argument, it nevertheless amounts to no more than an argument in favour of a general freedom to soul-search. We have no quarrel with this, but once again, it does not support the special treatment contained in the right to freedom of religion.[56]

Ahdar and Leigh: Liberal Justifications for Special Protection

Ahdar and Leigh offer several liberal arguments for the special status of the freedom of religion. The first we shall call *the checks and balance argument*. They suggest that the gulf between the all-powerful state and the isolated individual needs to be filled by mediating institutions and that religious bodies have a role to play in this regard. They say:[57]

> ... religion may serve a pro-democratic role in that religious bodies may check the totalitarian tendencies of the large, expanding modern state. In *The Culture of Disbelief*, Carter, drawing upon Alexis de Tocqueville's nineteenth-century critique of American society, argued [that] religions, at their best, can serve a valuable role as 'independent mediating institutions' operating as 'bulwark[s] against government tyranny'.

Ahdar and Leigh, again quoting Carter,[58] refer to the faith of believers, a faith which involves allegiance to something other than, and higher than, the state: by operating with an independent normative standard, religions can have a taming effect on states and thus operate to resist or prevent tyranny. This is an ambitious and impressive argument. The problem with it, however, is that it is ultimately

---

55 Evans *Freedom of Religion under the European Convention on Human Rights* (op. cit.) p. 31; Myres S. McDougal, Harold D. Lasswell and Lung-Chu Chen 'The Right to Religious Freedom and World Public Order: The Emerging Norms of Non-Discrimination' (74 *Michigan Law Review* 1976) p. 873.

56 Evans on the other hand seems to embrace the argument – perhaps because there is no better alternative. See Evans *Freedom of Religion under the European Convention on Human Rights* (op. cit.) pp. 31–32.

57 Ahdar and Leigh (op. cit.) pp. 54–55; with reference to Stephen L. Carter *The Culture of Disbelief: How American Law and Politics Trivializes Religious Devotion*, pp. 36–37.

58 For a similar argument see Veit Bader 'Religious Diversity and Democratic Institutional Pluralism' *Political Theory* (Vol. 31, No. 2, 2003).

a religious argument. To argue that religious bodies can and should operate as a counterbalance to governmental power is to introduce faith-based arguments against secular ones, and this one inevitably fails on both of the two criteria we defended in the introduction to this analysis. Religious bodies will always be religious bodies of a particular faith and creed, and hence the 'bulwark' will consist in particular beliefs that in turn can be validated only from the point of view of those who adhere to the particular religion in question. Those who do not share the belief are hardly likely to perceive this as a *pro-democratic* strategy.

Furthermore, it is not obvious or beyond dispute that religious institutions are the best suited to carry out the mediating function here described. Checks and balances can be carried out through a functional division of power, through a vertical division of power (as between federation and states), through an independent democratic basis for government and parliament (as in presidential systems of government), through protection of parliamentary minorities in parliament (for example by demanding qualified majority in some cases), through resort to referenda on certain important issues, through trade union organizations, trade associations, consumer groups, and so on. However jaundiced our view of these familiar and imperfect institutions may be, it is certainly not clear what advantages in serving democracy religious groups have over political parties or interest groups. Indeed religious bodies may themselves have a political agenda (for example, on abortion issues, access to birth control, sexual equality, freedom of sexual orientation, and the like). Some citizens, of course, believe that religions are themselves tyrannical and authoritative precisely because of their reliance on revelation rather than democratic discourse. It seems then, that religion's role in providing democratic 'checks and balances' is hardly uncontroversial, and if performing this function is the attribute that justifies special status and protection, other, secular, institutions have a much stronger case than religion.

Ahdar and Leigh: The 'Duty vs. Preference' Argument

Using a strategy similar to that found in Evan's' presentation of *the autonomy and pluralism* argument, Ahdar and Leigh introduce what we will call the *duty vs preference* argument. This takes the liberal route of claiming that there ought to be a right to *respect for individual autonomy*, but then singles out *religious* belief for special protection by emphasizing its special character. The sincere believer, they argue, is under a special form of pressure when the demands of the state conflict with the religious norms that form part of their belief. This is because the believer is subject to an external, extra-temporal compulsion, which is 'quite unlike other forms of compulsion'.[59] The special character of religious suffering is due to the character of the religious conviction, which is not a preference or choice, but a duty imposed on the individual by God:[60]

59 Ahdar and Leigh (op. cit.) p. 59.

60 Ibid. p. 62.

> Assimilating religious freedom to a general right to choose risks mis-describing the nature of religious conviction and obscuring the reasons why, historically, religion was accorded special constitutional protection [in America?]. Religion is as much about duty as choice … a central theme of many religions runs contrary to liberal thinking – one has a *duty* to seek the truth, to worship and obey God. Liberalism's broad protection of personal autonomy risk's 'confus[ing] the pursuit of preferences with the performance of duties.

So the problem for the believer is that he does not choose God – God chooses him, and that imposes a duty upon him/her. Thus when there is a conflict between what the state demands and what God demands, there is a conflict of duty, whereas in most other cases, where the autonomy argument applies, state demands simply diminish the opportunity to pursue preferences. What does this argument amount to then? On one interpretation this is simply a religious argument for special treatment of religious convictions, for it presupposes an acceptance of revelation as a duty imposing event. This is unconvincing: not only to non-believers but also to those who do not believe in the religion from which the revelation is said to spring. Thus a claim that one has been chosen by the Christian God is unlikely to be accepted as a true revelation by people who although religious, are not Christians, for example, Muslims or Jews. On another interpretation the argument is not religious, but states that people can in some circumstances feel the pressure of their convictions with such intensity, that state interference in the form of legal requirements are perceived as painful interference with their belief. On this reading of the argument it is not the religious character of the conviction which is decisive, but rather the quality of the perceived conviction and its relationship to the conflicting legal requirement. Thus this is not an argument for special treatment of religions, but rather of philosophies of life which are based on deeply felt beliefs.

The European Court of Human Rights, as noted earlier in this chapter, *has* expanded the concept of religion in this way, and the requirement for receiving protection under Article 9 seems to depend on whether a specific belief/action is seen to be part of a philosophy of life. If a belief/action forms part of a coherent belief system, then the special protection under Article 9 is activated . This form of protection might be perceived as valuable to the preservation of autonomy and pluralism on the same grounds argued earlier by Carolyn Evans. But it is thus also vulnerable to the objections we raised there. The 'preference *vs* duty' contention of Adhar and Leigh differs from Evans's argument, however, in that it raises an additional difficulty, that of whether we can legitimately make the distinction between, on the one hand, philosophies of life and on the other, free-standing value-preferences.

There might be some scope for arguing that philosophies of life should receive special protection, but ultimately the argument for legal protection would have to turn on the special harm that is incurred by restraining the freedom of those who adhere to overall philosophies of life as opposed to the mere narrowing down of opportunities that is incurred by those whose values are not part of an overall belief-system. But it is difficult to see why interference in someone's belief-system should necessarily cause more harm than interference with someone's strongly held values. Thus one might, without being a feminist or subscribing to equal opportunities as a more abstract philosophy, believe strongly in sexual equality and for instance, be committed to wearing gender-neutral clothes in the work-place. One might be just as upset and frustrated by an employer's refusal to endorse this practice as someone who *was* a feminist or a fervent subscriber to the philosophy of equal opportunities.

Steven D. Smith: 'Democratic Civic Virtue'

In his 'The Rise and Fall of Religious Freedom in Constitutional Discourse', Smith presents a number of non-religious arguments for the special right to freedom of religion, and rejects all of them.[61] Some of these are identical to the ones described above, and his arguments for rejection are in some respects similar. One of the arguments he deals with, which we have not mentioned above, we will call the *democratic civic virtue argument*.[62] This argument states that religions are particularly suited to foster the moral character of persons so as to make them good citizens in a democratic society. Thus religion performs the task of inculcating in persons the moral character indispensable to a well-functioning democracy.

If this is true, there will be good reasons to give room for religion to flourish. But, says Smith, the argument rests on an assumption about the role of religion in the formation of the moral character of persons that is not supported. Without this support, there is no argument. Religions might influence personhood, but so do families, schools, friends, and non-religious institutions in which a person might be enrolled.[63] Furthermore, the religious influence can be seen as destructive of democratic civic virtue to the extent that religions are seen to exhibit non-democratic habits and endorse or defend non-democratic institutions.[64] Finally, as Smith points out, if religions are important for fostering the moral character of persons, this speaks as much against the freedom of religion as it speaks in favour of it. Since the fostering of civic virtue can be seen as being of vital interest to the state, it is a matter of high importance to the state to control this process. If religion is important in this process, the state will be well advised to survey, and if needs be, regulate religious affairs in order to protect the moral cohesiveness of society.

Another argument which Smith raises is an extension of the autonomy and pluralism argument we discussed above. It may be called' the check on religious

61 *University of Pensylvania Law Review* (November 1991) pp. 149–240 at 140

62 Smith calls this 'the Civic Virtue Rationale', ibid. pp. 199–202.

63 See also ibid. p. 200.

64 – For example, clerical positions of authority might not be filled on the basis of elections; doctrines might manifest non-democratic ideology: God, after all is more often than not portrayed as an authority that does not invite debate.

tyranny argument'.[65] According to this argument religious diversity in society has the function of securing that a single religion does not encroach on governmental power, and thereby install a particular religious regime as part of the regulatory scheme of the state (the law). But it is not obvious how religious pluralism – even if it exists and even if it is accepted that pluralism should be promoted through a special right to religious freedom – can prevent a particular religion from exercising its influence on government and hence on the regulatory scheme of the state. If the argument is that a special constitutional protection of religions will prevent regulatory schemes from having an effect on other religions, then the argument is viciously circular and can be disregarded. If the argument on the other hand is that religious pluralism is effective in securing the spread of religious affiliations among the people's representatives, it has more going for it. In this case, further support might be adduced by noting that the promotion of religious pluralism would make it less likely that we would see one large majority religion in the community ranged against a number of small minority religions. The spread of religious affiliation, it can be argued, will, if religions are allowed to flourish through special protection, approach the normal distribution curve. If, as we noted in relation to the 'democratic civic virtue' argument, religion is seen to be, in political terms, potentially dangerous, creating religious diversity might be a way of checking these unwelcome tendencies. The whole argument, however, seems to rest on the assumption that religious diversity is somehow more important as a means of combating tyranny than other forms of diversity: social, political, ideological, sexual, ethnic, and so on. It remains, therefore, unconvincing to the extent that it is a psychologically and empirically unsupported assumption that religion per se, and religious pluralism in particular, is a more effective fence against tyranny than other forms of pluralism.

65 Smith (op. cit.) pp. 204–207 simply calls this 'the Pluralism Rationale'.

Epilogue: Equality, Diversity and Limits to Social Freedom

In Chapters 5 and 6, and in more general terms throughout this book, we have argued, in effect, for the *removal*, curtailment or limitation of certain rights to forms of behaviour, let us, in these closing passages, enumerate our objections briefly. In the final chapter we tried to show that a right to religious freedom is both superfluous (in the sense that it can be subsumed and given comprehensive effect under a general right to freedom of expression and assembly), *and* a hierarchical form of special pleading that trades on unsustainable distinctions between forms of belief. In Chapter 5 we argued against a generalized 'Cultural Autonomy Thesis' and straightforwardly challenged some of the central claims of Multiculturalism: The first was the assertion that the logic of sovereignty becomes an anachronism when located in the fully democratized 'Politics of Difference'; the second was the idea that hegemonic interpretations of cultural norms might, perhaps in the name of 'authenticity', 'tradition' or usually religious belief, override individual rights or circumvent the requirements of individual consent. In addition, and in respect of the right to wear religious clothing or symbols, we argued that a legitimate sovereign authority – a state – committed to maintaining egalitarian forms of cultural and religious diversity must itself remain secular (not anti-religious), and must set its face against sectarian power in general but particularly in the maintenance of the institutional public sphere: in education, the criminal justice system, local government and so on. Contingently this might entail the duty to intervene and prohibit or discourage forms of cultural and religious expression. Our example was that of the French government's response to the issue of the *hijab*.

Looked at in a certain way these arguments often appear to seek to diminish the scope of freedom, for instance, by suggesting that groups might be coerced by legal regulation into modifying or abandoning cultural practices or that individuals (and groups) be divested of a special right to affirm and practice a religion. It might also be said that there has been an attempt in this book to justify coercion to this end by employing arguments that simply elevate the authority of idiosyncratic and ephemeral individual choice above the stability, wisdom and ways of the group or the community or of enduring systems of faith. These charges are reasonable and, one would have to concede, pretty accurate. It might be useful, therefore, in summing up the general aims of the book to take a final opportunity to appeal for a sympathetic reading of what at times might have appeared as an inflexible attempt to think through the logic of equality and diversity, or more precisely, equality *in* diversity.

There is something orthodoxly and unfashionably *bourgeois* about arguing, as we do, for a reaffirmation of the notion of a sovereign state based on if not a 'monolithic', then certainly an anti-'Multiculturalist', conception of individual rights. The mood of the times seems much more open to reception of the ideas of a political and cultural *de-centredness* and there is always available the well-rehearsed but often disingenuous antipathy to 'individualism'. But as we tried to explain at some length in Chapter 3 and in conjunction with our detailed explanation of Gewirth in the introduction to the book, *epistemologically* we see no coherent alternative point of departure for the initial synthesis of the concept of rights and duties other than from a model of the individual agent. This is not, however, a sociological, economic or even an ethical endorsement of individualism. In fact, the Gewirthian analysis of agency and the ensuing normative implications are significantly similar to Fuller's 'social practice' model of the understanding of a genuinely sociological concept of freedom – that is, the concept of *affirmative* freedom.

Let us remember that in Chapter 2 we noted that in Fuller's energetic critique of J.S. Mill, and in his endorsement of the *sociological* superiority of James Fitzjames Stephen's account, 'affirmative freedom' is to be understood as '... effective agency, that is, the capacity to realize one's choices in the world ...'. If we reflect upon Fuller's warnings about the '... dangerous ... tendency to take for granted the facilities offered by an organized and functioning society ...', we see immediately that the conditions of the agent's social location is crucial to the presentation of a feasible account of freedom. That is, the issue of what constitutes a functioning organizational form of society cannot be divorced from the agent's own understanding of his or her own attitude to freedom, nor can agents in interaction choose to ignore the relationship between themselves and the freedom of others as mediated by organizational forms. Thus the question of *limits* to 'freedom' are immediately implicit in the very attempt to articulate the concept.

It does not follow necessarily and simply from this, of course, that agents must therefore *accept* limitations on their aspirations 'to realize [their] choices in the world'. Nor, without more being said, must they necessarily accept ethically onerous responsibilities in respect of the design and maintenance of these mediating organizational forms. However, it does follow that *prudentially*, and unavoidably, they will have to worry about these arrangements in most if not all circumstances, because left unattended, organizational form and function inevitably develops in ways which seriously affect an agent's '... *capacity* to realize [his or her] choices in the world'.

What Gewirth offers on a sociological level can quite reasonably be seen as a reiteration and endorsement of these Fullerian observations and concerns; the added value is to be found in the Gewirthian detail discovered when we investigate the prudential dimensions of effective agency not from the seemingly obvious viewpoint of social interaction, but perhaps unexpectedly, from what Communitarians, committed structuralists, or proponents of 'dialogical' discourse would regard as the socially 'disembodied' and entirely private world of the hypothetical agent. Here we find that the logic of agency brings the prospective, purposive agent to the realization that the capacity to realize one's choices in the world depends upon securing access to, and stable disposition over, a set of *categorically basic goods*, namely, a viable quantum of freedom and well-being that makes the successful pursuit of freely chosen purposes feasible. Claims to these goods as rational entitlements are, for a prospective, purposive agent, justifiable because they are logically unavoidable The associative implications of this logically idealized individual judgement stem not from the social dissemination of the plausibility of this observation in the form of political or ethical discourse, but, again and ironically, from a further stage of the internal logic of the ideal and hypothetical agent: the realization that the unavoidable claim to rights to freedom and well-being arise not from the uniqueness or worth of personal aspirations or biographical identity, but from the general property of agency. Thus *the individual* comes to realize the validity of the rights claims of other agents – simply because they are other *agents.* Thus the phenomenology of freedom modelled as agency contains not only the logical authority to claim rights to the wherewithal to pursue one's chosen purposes, but simultaneously and *a priori* – which is not to deny that we might not also experience this *pragmatically* – the recognition of a *limitation* to the range of one's legitimate choices for purpose fulfilment. These limits to one's action, expression, devotion and the like are set by the requirement not to violate the generic rights of other agents.

We can see that the promotion and protection of generic rights as expressed in Gewirth's Principle of Generic Consistency serves as a powerful substantive moral synthesis that strengthens the general Fullerian account of freedom and the evolution of regulatory social form. In Chapter 3, in our interpretation of Fuller's thinking on law and freedom, we maintained that justice appears as 'the mediating *rationale* between law and freedom', and that the substantive *content* of justice could be found in an 'ethical and sociological analysis of what rights and obligations attend the institutionalized *guarantees* of that freedom'. In Gewirthian terms, Justice appears at the level of individual practical reason as an adherence to the Principle of Generic Consistency, in our collective arrangements it is an ethical principle and, in co-ordinatory and regulatory terms, it must also function as a *legal* principle. Let us try in these final passages to give this formulation a little more specificity and precision, and also explain why we have advocated limits to cultural autonomy and the modification of a right to freedom of religion.

That agent rights are 'waivable', and that we might *choose* to associate collectively in a host of institutional forms ('cultures', churches, clubs, and other 'associations') that impose all manner of restrictions and impositions upon us for the sake of a concerted pursuit of various ends, is of course, undeniable. If we maintain the idea that the idea of affirmative freedom leads us to seek the protection of generic rights as a rationally overriding principle of social organization, it might seem problematic that many institutions appear to violate generic rights as a matter of course through penalties and prohibitions. The internal regulatory and administrative 'powers' exercised in voluntary associations, almost paradoxically, appear to interfere with the free reign of generic rights, yet the interference is, of course, licensed by *consensual* judgements about the efficiency and effectiveness of participation *in concert* towards some particular purpose. It is thus individual consent, perhaps involving conditional waivability of certain rights, that conveys legitimacy to the institution's incursion into what, naturally, would appear to be the generic rights of an individual. Perhaps, as the social contract theorists maintain, *the state* similarly imposes its will upon us by our own 'consent', but there is a pretty obvious distinction between institutions with which one might voluntarily engage and disengage, and institutions, such as the criminal law, which offer no such choice. With this distinction in mind it might be useful to remind ourselves of Beyleveld and Brownsword's suggestion that we adopt a general understanding of law as 'morally legitimate power'. If the issue of 'moral legitimacy' is to have any genuine significance in our characterization of the laws it must mean in practical terms that the coercive norms in question ought to be promulgated and obeyed. The property of moral legitimacy, however, is not what distinguishes legal norms from cultural or associative norms, for these latter too can undoubtedly be morally legitimate. But we can be pretty sure – at least theoretically – that the moral legitimacy of cultural or associative norms arises from the plain understanding of the *voluntary* acceptance of them as regulatory, thus their legitimacy derives from consent. One can, of course, as a voluntary member of a club or a church organization *object* internally, and externally to the way in which the organization interprets its own rules and makes decisions, and thus declare that one does *not* consent. The withdrawal of one's consent does not, of course automatically make the aims, regulations and procedures of the organization in question illegitimate, but whatever the substantive outcome of such disagreement, in terms of obligation, one should be able – again theoretically – simply by *choice*, to put oneself entirely beyond the normative force of the association or organization in question. If this appears to be impermissible or impossible then the organization in question either *is* exercising, or is purporting to exercise (perhaps vicariously), sovereign (non-voluntary) powers. The test for this, of course, is for the organization (a group, culture, association or perhaps an individual) to demonstrate that they are exercising *morally legitimate power* over a person or persons that does not derive from, or require, their consent.

Of course, if Multiculturalism or Cultural Autonomy Theory accepts that consensual norms takes priority over cultural norms, and that consensual expressions of culture should affect non-consenting persons only in ways which these latter deem to be unobjectionable, then this is akin to the banality of Mill's 'harm' principle which, divested of its aura of profundity, suggests merely that if there is no good reason to prevent someone from doing something, then we should allow them to do it. If, however, it does not accept the priority of consent in these circumstances, then we have before us something much more sinister than a dissatisfaction with the occasional insensitivities to 'difference' that Universalism, Inclusivity and Equality Before the Laws inevitably entails.

The very notions of voluntariness and consent in the sense of affirmative freedom diversely expressed presuppose a system of institutional protections. The coercive norms that constitute these guarantees and protections are not optional, yet there is no paradox here, they merely affirm the intention to support what is a concomitant of the idea of *valuing* individual autonomy, namely, the authority of consent. There are, of course, potentially as many cultures as there are possible examples of shared expressions of individual autonomy. This is what rationally is to be understood as the inevitability of *diversity* in society, and it is, of course, the only ethically necessary reason (as opposed to the many contingent ones) why 'difference' and 'plurality' should be regarded as intrinsically valuable.

Author Index

Ahbar, Rex J. 186, 195, 197, 200–202
Alexy, Robert 24, 25, 58, 59, 131
Anderson, Elizabeth 22
Aristotle 31, 62, 72, 73, 81, 82, 115
Aquinas, Thomas 7, 31, 36–44, 52, 58, 126

Bader, Veit 161, 163, 200
Barry, Brian 144, 154, 155, 171, 186, 195
Beck, Ulrich 140
Bentham, Jeremy 40, 102, 121
Beyleveld, Deryck 6, 7, 25, 29, 30, 31, 33, 42, 44, 45, 57, 64, 70, 83, 136, 172, 210
Bodin, Jean 143
Bowman, Curtis 174
Boyle, James 60
Brownsword, Roger 25, 29–31, 33, 42, 44, 45, 57, 64, 70, 136, 210
Brudner, Alan 63, 143, 153, 157, 178, 195

Carey, John 103
Cohen, Jean 13, 133, 134, 135, 145
Cole, G.D.H. 3, 4, 88, 101, 139, 145, 146

Dahrendorf, Ralf 103, 104
Dewey, John 11, 12, 26, 51
Dijk, P. van 184, 186, 189, 195
Drucker, Peter F. 144, 145
Duguit, Leon 143, 145–7, 149
Durkheim, Emil 16, 18, 102, 103, 122
Dworkin, Ronald 21

Evans, Carolyn 186, 190, 192–5, 197, 198–200

Figgis, John Neville 145, 146, 154, 159, 161, 168
Finnis, John 10, 30, 31, 36–49, 57, 135
Freud, Sigmund 102
Fromm, Erich 88, 98, 102

Gewirth, Alan 3–11, 13, 33–6, 38–40, 43, 46, 52–6, 64, 65, 70, 81, 83, 84, 85, 101, 120, 135, 137, 172, 196, 199, 208, 209

Habermas, Jürgen 4, 8, 24, 25, 59, 83, 133, 135
Hart, H.L.A 3, 15, 20, 21, 23, 30, 31, 59, 61–4, 67, 70, 80, 97, 100, 122, 131, 136, 152, 173
Hayek, Friedrich 67
Held, David 140
Hirst, Paul Q. 145, 148, 149, 154, 158, 159–61, 168
Hobbes, Thomas 3, 44, 63, 72, 88, 91, 99, 101, 102, 104, 107–11, 120–27, 130, 131, 142, 151
Hoof, G.J.H van 184, 186, 189, 195
Horowitz, Donald L. 172
Howse, Robert 149, 151
Hume, David 26, 35, 88–92, 121, 122, 124, 127

Inkeles, Alex 103

Jung, C.G. 102

Kant, Immanuel 3, 4, 8–10, 13, 34, 44, 93, 99, 102, 109, 111, 114, 120–28, 132, 137, 139, 150, 151, 173–5, 199
Kukathas, Chandran 172, 173

Laborde, Cecile 161
Laski, Harold Joseph 145–7
Leigh, Ian 186, 195, 197, 200–202
Leydet, Dominique 149, 150
Locke, John 3, 7, 44, 72, 89, 99, 100, 101, 124, 129–32, 134
Loughlin, Martin 13, 143, 175
Lukes, Steven 116

MacIntyre, Alasdair 75, 96, 97, 142
Marshall, T.H. 140
Marx, Karl 16, 17, 21, 22, 102, 103, 116, 121, 123, 134, 144
Merton, Robert K. 103
Mill, John Stuart 67, 69, 71, 72, 74–7, 79, 80, 87, 88, 92, 93, 102, 117–19, 121, 208

Newman, Saul 21
Nietzsche, Friedrich 75, 102, 121

Parekh, Bikhu 161
Pattinson, Shaun 52–7, 135
Peirce, C.S. 26
Plamenatz, John 88
Plato 22, 62, 84, 99, 103, 124
Poulter, Sebastian 186, 195
Putnam, Robert 133

Quine, W.V.O. 27

Radbruch, Gustav 10, 131
Rawls, John 4, 40, 93–101, 117, 119, 122, 133, 142, 143, 175, 199
Raz, Joseph 31, 122, 197
Rousseau, Jean-Jacques 3, 4, 44, 72, 88, 89, 99, 100, 102–4, 111, 120, 123, 124, 127, 139, 141, 151, 173–5

Sandel, Michael J. 96, 100, 142
Schmitt, Carl 141, 143, 149–52, 155
Selznick, Philip 11, 12, 24–31, 33–5, 40, 42, 46, 78, 79
Shiffrin, Steven H 188, 195
Simmonds, Nigel E. 63, 72, 73, 81
Smith, Steven D. 102, 204
Stasi, Bernard 165–7
Stephen, James Fitzjames 69, 76, 200, 208
Squires, Judith 140, 141, 171

Taekema, Sanne 11, 25, 26, 31, 33, 35, 47–52
Taylor, Charles 95, 96, 98, 142

Unger, Roberto M. 30, 137

Waldron, Jeremy 124, 126, 128
Walzer, Michael 142
Weber, Max 31, 78, 79, 121, 143, 155
Westerman, Pauline 61–3
Winston, Kenneth I. 20, 22, 61, 67–71, 74–7, 80, 81, 83, 97, 136, 137, 173

Young, Iris Marion 143, 144

Zeno 103

Subject Index

a priori 11, 24, 28–9, 34, 38, 47–52, 57
affirmative freedom 12, 63, 68–71, 80–87, 98–9, 119, 173–5
agency 5–9, 36–40, 52–55, 68–72, 81–4, 88, 93, 99–102, 115, 119, 157, 199
American Realism 20
anomia 103–4, 139
appetites 107, 114–16
architecture 1, 12, 73–7, 80–84
areté 29, 47, 63, 97
authoritarian government 145
authoritative institution 21, 45
authority of law 10, 40–41
authority, institutionalised – *see* institutionalised authority
authority, legal – *see* legal authority
autonomy of law, the 8–11, 26, 43, 159

basic goods 31, 36–9, 41–2, 45–7, 58, 85, 209
basic rights 8, 10–11, 36–39, 43–9, 52, 57, 85, 126, 135, 153, 180
  see also claim rights
belief 2, 15, 18, 74, 96, 117, 122, 135, 141, 149, 156, 158–160, 164–165, 168–170, 175–205

Case Against Freedom, the 12, 20, 67–8, 80
Categorical Imperative 4, 8, 13, 23, 120–26
central case 31, 42
checks and balances 201
Christian 159–60, 178–81, 186–7, 195–6, 203
citizenship 4, 31, 67, 127, 139–41, 160
civil society 2–3, 8–13, 21, 44, 72, 99, 105, 110–13, 123, 129, 131–5, 139, 142–5, 152, 156
claim rights 5–6, 38, 54, 209
  see also basic rights
cognitive interest 9, 17, 28, 31, 78
commonwealth 12, 24, 109, 127–30, 152
communicative action 4, 25, 83, 133
communitarian 69, 87, 93–4, 101, 143
concept formation 21–6, 29–31, 78–9, 105, 156, 175
concept of law 9, 19–20, 29–31, 35, 45, 48, 60, 64, 70, 80, 101
conception of law 3, 13, 31, 37, 41, 65, 135
consent 87–91, 107–9, 116, 127–9, 167, 176, esp. 207, 208
consistency 4, 6–9, 33, 38, 41–2, 60, 84, 109, 114–15, 126, 166–70, 192, 196
container theory of society 140
continuum of practical reason 3, 8, 13, 44, 47, 59, 85, 87, 113, 119, 121, 125–8, 131, 135
correspondence theory of truth 26
Cultural Autonomy Theory 139, 148, 163, 170, 175
cultural rights 172

democracy 13, 26–29, 32–4, 72, 77, 126–8, 133–4, 140–44, 148–51, 156, 161, 193, 201, 204
description 5, 17–19, 71, 88–90, 96, 103, 124, 155–157
determinatio 10, 41–5, 49, 52–3, 58, 126, 140–43, 175
determinism 87, 101, 115, 120, 153
discrimination 154, 160, 169, 177–8, 184, 197, 200

enforcement 45, 63, 136
English Pluralists, the 143, 145–7, 149–52, 155, 161
Enlightenment 7, 9, 13, 103, 131, 139, 144, 174–5
epistemology 11–12, 22, 26–7, 42, 87
Essentialism 26, 29, 102
ethics 4, 8–10, 24–6, 40, 52–4, 82, 93, 97, 156, 179
ethical objectivism 65, 70
ethical rationalism 4, 9–12, 26–8, 31, 35–6, 40, 49, 53, 56, 60, 83, 170
evaluation 17–18, 22, 77, 104–5, 172
equality 43, 69, 73, 76, 82, 94–6, 103, 113, 117, 123, 127–8, 140–44, 153–6, 168–71, 176, 184–6, 195, 199, 201–7

fact/value distinction 18
foundationalism 11, 26–28, 31–5
foundationalist 12, 24, 30, 34, 42, 46, 49–51
freedom, affirmative – *see* affirmative freedom
freedom of assembly 153, 180–83, 188
freedom of association 153, 182–3
freedom of expression 180–85, 188, 193–5

Game Theory 23, 40
general will 4, 141,151
generic goods 38–40, 44–5, 52, 58, 83–5
globalization 132–4, 144
good, conception of 23, 36
good order 1, 15, 18, 23, 62, 70, 81–2
goods, basic – *see* basic goods
goods, intransitivity of 40, 84

hermeneutic 15–18
hierarchy of values 40–42, 49–51
hijab 162–70, 207
homogeneity 98, 141–3, 148–9, 197
human flourishing 81, 152
human interests 1, 17–19, 22, 83, 104–6, 116, 136
human nature 34–5, 72, 76, 81, 88, 99, 103–4, 110, 118–19, 153, 174

ideal type 31–3, 78–9, 90
ideal typical 17, 33, 78, 88, 122
idealism 8, 11, 34, 40, 103, 126–8, 131
incommensurabilism 11–12, 24, 36, 43–4, 58, 65, 176
incommensurability of values 10–11, 24, 35–7, 40, 46–51, 59, 143, 170
incommensurability theory 84, 97
institutional design 1–3, 11–13, 24, 59, 63, 68, 71–3, 75–7, 80–84, 98, 104, 110, 131, 152, 170, 173–7, 195
institutionalization of right 8, 10, 13, 121, 124–6
institutionalized authority 8, 46, 87
instrumental reason 112–15
interpretation 1–3, 10–12, 15–17, 23–4, 44, 56, 59, 95, 107, 110, 122–5, 150–53, 158, 162, 168–9, 175–81, 189–91, 194, 202–3
Islam 163, 166–7, 179, 185

jurisprudence 2–4, 9, 12, 15, 19, 20–21, 28, 36, 60, 63, 70–72, 79, 82, 101, 111, 126, 137, 149–50, 153, 165, 180, 195
justice 1, 4, 10–13, 24–6, 30, 68–70, 73, 81–4, 87, 90, 93–7, 122–4, 132, 142–4, 162, 181, 198
justification 7, 11–13, 18, 21–3, 43, 57, 74–5, 90, 93, 113, 117–19, 142, 150, 178, 185, 196–200

Koran, The 196
see also Qu'uran

labour 16–18, 24, 54, 92–3, 100–102, 146, 150, 153
legal authority 4, 8, 12, 37–46, 56–8, 88, 125, 131–2
legal enterprise, the 25, 30, 81, 104, 136–7, 174
legal idealism 8–9, 33, 40–42, 62, 68, 125–8, 131–2
legal norm 18, 19, 139, 210
legal obligation 13, 47, 99, 108, 113, 122–3, 128, 162
legal order 1, 12, 19, 59, 64, 68–70, 110–11, 131
legal positivism 8–12, 23–6, 37, 43, 63–5, 80, 124–8, 131
legal reason 3, 9–11, 37, 41, 47, 58, 119–22
legal reasoning, transparency of 9–11
legal science 2, 9, 18, 23, 28–9, 45
legal system 1, 2, 30, 50, 58–60, 92, 122–5, 128, 177
legal theory 7–9, 13–15, 18–20, 24–6, 31–3, 47–8, 50, 65, 70, 123, 127, 152, 155
legal validity 8, 11, 60, 127
legality 13, 19–20, 23, 28, 111, 121–8, 132
legitimacy 2, 9, 13, 19–20, 25, 29, 44, 57–8, 83, 88–9, 108, 125, 134–40, 144–5, 147–51, 155, 175
liberty 20–21, 67–76, 87, 92–8, 109, 117–19, 178, 186, 191, 195, 199

market, the 97, 134, 142, 157
Master Ideal 26–8, 31–6, 46, 78–9
means and ends 7, 12, 61, 71–80, 84, 97, 104–5, 111–16
method 4, 12, 16–17, 20–22, 25–9, 42, 56, 72, 78–9, 91–3, 103–5, 114, 199

methodology 7, 11, 15–17, 20, 24–31, 34, 42, 46, 65, 70, 78–9, 88, 157
modernity 13, 63, 103–5, 111, 140, 143–5, 155, 168, 173–6, 178
moral dilemmas 48–52
moral foundation 24, 33–4, 46, 49
moral judgment 2, 17, 21–3, 29–31, 37–9, 51, 57, 64, 79, 117, 136
moral rationality 7–10, 42, 135
moral reason 3, 7–11, 32, 36–7, 40, 44–9, 72, 87, 102, 112, 121–4
morality of aspiration, the 29, 62–3, 72–3, 84
morality of duty, the 28, 63, 72–3
morality of law, the 12, 23–5, 29, 59–65, 73, 80–82
multiculturalism 2, 14, 69, 133, 139, 144, 153–8, 161–71, 205, 210
muslims 16268, 186–187, 196, 203

nation state 44, 111, 139–41, 144, 148–9
national sovereignty 131, 140, 146, 149
natural morality 13, 47, 126
natural rights 3, 13–14, 31, 36–38, 41–2, 45, 64, 100, 107, 124
naturalist 23, 79, 168
Nazism 10, 151
negative freedom 67, 70–72, 80, 83
normative supremacy 108–9, 144, 170, 176
normative theory 26–8, 32–3

objectivity 10, 18, 51, 111, 121
obligations 3, 9, 32, 47, 53, 71, 88–93, 101, 111–14, 118, 125, 128, 132, 142, 154, 159, 162, 186
omnilateral 3–4, 44–7, 124
original position 40, 94–5, 199
other-regarding duties 6–8, 34, 40, 43

parallel governance 14, 160
people, the 109, 127, 129–31, 135, 146–51, 205
personal autonomy 104, 176, 202
petitio principii 6
PGC (Principle of Generic Consistency) 4–7, 9, 13, 33, 38, 44, 52–7, 64, 84, 101, 135
philosophy of life 189, 202–3
Pluralism/pluralist society 2, 13, 97, 117, 133, 139–75, 177 183, 199, 201–5
political theory 13, 20, 88, 103, 139–40, 145, 161, 172, 193, 200
politics 16, 69, 72–3, 81–2, 85, 96–7, 131–5, 139, 142–5, 149, 152–3, 156, 161, 171, 200
politics of difference, the 69, 144, 171
positivist 3, 10, 23, 26, 41–2, 60–65, 68, 81, 111, 121, 124–8, 131
potential agency 53–5
practical rationality 3, 15, 16, 22, 34, 42, 47, 81, 101
Pragmatic 9, 12, 20–21, 24–38, 47, 50–51, 60, 70, 89, 114, 122, 149–50
Pragmatism 2, 11–12, 20, 24–8, 31, 33–6, 40, 46, 65, 126
Pragmatist 11, 26–9, 36, 42–3, 46–52, 56–7, 70, 122
praxis 24, 70, 120
pre-legal 82, 99, 101, 121
preference 43–4, 47–9, 79–81, 84, 94, 97, 111–13, 115–19, 148, 156–7, 179, 200–203
prescription 5, 9, 17, 100, 119, 156–7, 162, 187, 191–4
proceduralism 24–5, 32, 44, 59, 65
property 22, 49, 58, 84, 90–91, 100–102, 107, 130, 135
prudence 2, 7, 36, 40, 43, 90–91, 94, 111–16, 119–28, 131
prudential reason 4, 7, 13, 40, 87, 90, 111–15, 119
psychoanalysis 102
psychology 18, 102, 113
public sphere 92, 133–5, 153, 175, 207
purposive action 5, 40, 84
purposive activity 4–5, 39, 60, 82–3

Qu'uran, The – *see* Koran, The

rationalism 4, 11–12, 26–8, 31, 35–36, 40, 49, 52–3, 56, 60, 83, 144, 170
reflective equilibrium 23
representation 22, 99, 114, 148–52, 169
ritual 164, 179, 182, 184–8, 191–3

salus populi 146
secular 26, 163–4, 169–70, 174–8, 188–9, 196, 201–2
self-evidence 37–8
self-love 90, 102

separation of law and morals 126
separation of powers 128
social contract 3–4, 12, 60, 87–93, 100–101, 107–10, 134, 139–42, 210
social institution 16, 19, 77–81, 103
social norm 18–19, 78, 104
social order 1–3, 15, 18–20, 61–3, 67–8, 80–82, 89, 97, 104, 136, 139, 173
social organization 16–18, 30, 44, 71, 171, 209
social policy 68, 76–7, 80, 103
social power 16, 104
social practice 12, 18, 21–3, 28–30, 34–6, 69, 73, 174, 181
social science 15–18, 24–7, 65, 79, 133
social structure 15–16, 70, 83, 152, 173–5
social theory 2, 10–12, 18–19, 24–6, 40, 70, 78–9, 89, 133, 139, 142
sociological analysis 15, 18, 71, 78
sociological explanation 16
sociological jurisprudence 4, 12, 15, 30, 70, 79, 137
sociological method 17, 78, 105
sovereign 3, 63, 89, 91, 107–11, 116, 125, 131–2, 135–7, 140, 143, 147–9, 160–62, 167, 174
sovereignty 2, 12–13, 92, 101, 107–17, 127–8, 133–52, 155, 161–2, 170
standpoint 22–3, 81, 84, 157–8
state of nature 72, 99–101, 120–26, 129–32, 152
subjective right 63, 143
subjectivity 18, 75, 78, 117, 156

tolerance 100, 142–143, 155–6, 159, 164–6, 169–70, 176–8, 195–9
traditional cultures 173–5
transparency of legal reasoning 9–11
truth 8, 25–7, 33–5, 43, 49, 82, 85, 93, 97, 107, 109–10, 176, 181, 196, 202

unilateral 3–4, 9, 13, 44–7, 121, 124, 132
universal pragmatics 25
universalization 5–9
unjust laws 128
Utilitarianism 23, 40, 74, 92, 117
utility 2, 75, 102, 116–17

validity 3–8, 11–12, 25, 31, 34, 38, 44, 47, 51–3, 60–61, 107–9, 117, 126–7, 136, 139, 151, 157, 194
value judgment 10, 28, 46, 65
value-free / value-laden 17–19, 28–31, 78–9
value-pluralism 157, 161, 170, 199
value-preference 44, 75, 78–80, 84, 97, 114, 154, 157, 202–3
values, incommensurability of – *see* incommensurability of values
veil of ignorance 94, 119

Weimar Republic, The 149, 150
well-being 4–6, 34, 38–9, 46, 72, 84–5, 107, 123

www.ingramcontent.com/pod-product-compliance
Ingram Content Group UK Ltd.
Pitfield, Milton Keynes, MK11 3LW, UK
UKHW011007180926
475701UK00004B/605
9781138266247